SELECTED

JOACHIM DU BELLAY and PIERRE DE RONSARD were the most prominent members of the group known as the Pléiade who led an extraordinary flowering of poetry in sixteenth-century France. Determined to create a vernacular literature worthy of French imperial ambitions, the poets of the Pléiade urged an intense study of Greek and Roman classics which, combined with a generous dose of mythology and a creative adaptation of Petrarchism, produced a body of verse that reflects the vigour and variety of European Renaissance culture. Du Bellay broke new ground with two sonnet sequences that are not concerned with love: the *Regrets* which provides a witty and critical view of papal Rome and *Les Antiquitez de Rome* which broods over the rise and fall of the Roman Empire. Ronsard, in a series of sonnet sequences (to Cassandre, Marie, Astrée, and others), innovates on the Petrarchan tradition with a wider range of situations, a richer imagery, and a more robust sensuality. Though now mostly read as the master of love poetry, he excelled in an astonishing variety of forms and genres: sonnets, elegies, odes, philosophical hymns, pastoral scenes, mythological narratives, political and religious controversy. Du Bellay and Ronsard are major poets of European stature who stand with Rabelais and Montaigne in the pantheon of French Renaissance literature.

ANTHONY MORTIMER is Emeritus Professor at the University of Fribourg, Switzerland, and also taught for many years at the University of Geneva. In addition to his scholarly work on English Renaissance poetry, he has produced a series of verse translations from Italian, French, and German, including Dante (*Vita Nuova*), Cavalcanti (*Complete Poems*), Petrarch (*Canzoniere*), Michelangelo (*Poems and Letters*), *The Song of Roland*, Villon (*The Testament*), Baudelaire (*The Flowers of Evil*), and Angelus Silesius (*Sacred Epigrams*). For Oxford World's Classics he has translated Pirandello, *Three Plays* (2014) and *Italian Renaissance Tales* (2019).

OXFORD WORLD'S CLASSICS

*For over 100 years Oxford World's Classics have brought
readers closer to the world's great literature. Now with over 700
titles—from the 4,000-year-old myths of Mesopotamia to the
twentieth century's greatest novels—the series makes available
lesser-known as well as celebrated writing.*

*The pocket-sized hardbacks of the early years contained
introductions by Virginia Woolf, T. S. Eliot, Graham Greene,
and other literary figures which enriched the experience of reading.
Today the series is recognized for its fine scholarship and
reliability in texts that span world literature, drama and poetry,
religion, philosophy, and politics. Each edition includes perceptive
commentary and essential background information to meet the
changing needs of readers.*

OXFORD WORLD'S CLASSICS

DU BELLAY AND RONSARD

Selected Poems

Translated with an Introduction and Notes by
ANTHONY MORTIMER

OXFORD
UNIVERSITY PRESS

OXFORD
UNIVERSITY PRESS

Great Clarendon Street, Oxford, OX2 6DP,
United Kingdom

Oxford University Press is a department of the University of Oxford.
It furthers the University's objective of excellence in research, scholarship,
and education by publishing worldwide. Oxford is a registered trade mark of
Oxford University Press in the UK and in certain other countries

Published in the United States of America by Oxford University Press
198 Madison Avenue, New York, NY 10016, United States of America

British Library Cataloguing in Publication Data

Data available

Library of Congress Control Number: 2023930588

ISBN 978-0-19-284799-7

Printed and bound in the UK by
Clays Ltd, Elcograf S.p.A.

ACKNOWLEDGEMENTS

FOR practical help and advice I am indebted to Martin Dodsworth, Lukas Erne, John Jackson, Olivier Pot, and Richard Waswo. Less directly but no less effectively Indira Ghose and Neil Forsyth have been hugely supportive in difficult times. In preparing a sixteenth-century text with modernized spelling I have been fortunate to benefit from the generosity and experience of François Roudaut. The librarians of the Bibliothèque universitaire de Genève have earned my gratitude by guiding me through the complexities of the new simplified borrowing procedure.

Simona Cain was my student when I first came to Geneva and has been an unfailing friend and constant counsellor ever since. To her I offer whatever is mine in this book.

CONTENTS

Contents

INTRODUCTION

A New Poetry

THE most useful starting-point for any introduction to the poetry of
Joachim Du Bellay and Pierre de Ronsard is the publication in 1549
of the *Deffence et Illustration de la Langue Françoyse*,[1] a tract written at
least in part as a reply to Thomas Sébillet's *Art Poëtique François*
(1548) which had presented the work of Clément Marot and his
followers (the so-called *marotiques*) as a vital new departure in French
poetry, thus cutting the ground from beneath the feet of those who
were about to make the same claim for themselves. The author is
announced as Du Bellay, but the *Deffence* is generally assumed to
represent the views of a number of young poets known to each other
as the *brigade* but to posterity as the Pléiade. The nucleus of the group
(Ronsard, Du Bellay, Antoine de Baïf) had studied in Paris at the
Collège Coqueret under the inspiring direction of Jean Dorat; others
(Jodelle, Belleau) came from the neighbouring Collège Boncourt,
while Jacques Peletier du Mans, translator of Horace's *Art of Poetry*,
was a powerful early influence. What these sons of the minor aristoc-
racy or wealthy bourgeoisie had in common was a rigorous education
imbued with the spirit of Renaissance humanism—its readiness to
challenge convention, its reverence for the newly available literature
of ancient Greece as well as rediscovered Latin texts, its preference
for Plato and Neoplatonism as opposed to Aristotle and the scholastics,
its wholesale assimilation of pagan mythology. It was a curriculum
that gave them the self-confidence and ambition of a cultural elite.

   The *Deffence* does not present an entirely coherent argument.
There are obvious tensions between the demand for a new poetry and
the recommended subservience to the Graeco-Roman model, between
denunciations of decadence and prophecies of progress, so that we
may indeed agree with Margaret Ferguson's definition of the tract as
'a significant pattern of contradictions'.[2] That said, its three central

---

[1] I agree with Henderson that this should be translated as *Defence and Enrichment*.
[2] Ferguson, 'The Exile's Defense: Du Bellay's *La Deffence et Illustration de la Langue
Françoyse*', *PMLA* 93 (1978), 276.

and closely connected concerns are clear enough: the idea of empire, the problem of the vernacular, and the ideal training and function of the poet. Empire (Du Bellay's term is *monarchie*) was in the air that the Pléiade breathed. France had recovered from the Hundred Years War and was now a major European power challenging the Habsburgs for domination of a politically fragmented Italy. Though Charles V was acknowledged as the Holy Roman Emperor, François I also claimed the inheritance of Rome. An illuminated manuscript of 1519 shows him receiving the sword and caduceus from Julius Caesar while inventive genealogies reinforced the Roman connection by tracing the ancestry of French and English monarchs back to Francus and Brutus, the legendary brothers of Aeneas. Spectacular pageants like the Field of the Cloth of Gold (1520) and new imposing architecture sought to rival the past glories of the Eternal City. François, who died only two years before the publication of the *Deffence*, had been a passionate patron of the arts and this must have encouraged Du Bellay to see *monarchie* as involving not only territorial expansion but also and crucially a cultural hegemony that required a language with the universal extension of Latin and the prestige of Greek:

The time, perhaps, may come—and with France's good fortune I hope it will—when this noble and powerful kingdom shall, in its turn, obtain the reins of empire and when (if it has not been completely buried with François) our French language, which is now beginning to take root, will spring up from the ground and rise to such height and breadth that it will equal the very Greeks and Romans, producing, like them, Homers, Demosthenes, Virgils, and Ciceros, just as France has occasionally produced its own Pericles, Nicias, Alcibiades, Themistocles, Caesar, and Scipio. (p. 202)

France, we are told, has already produced military and political leaders who can stand comparison with the towering figures of Greece and Rome, but the literary achievements, without which no cultural domination is possible, are still lacking. Borrowing extensively from Sperone Speroni's *Dialogo delle lingue* (*Dialogue on Languages*, 1542), Du Bellay argues that although, as things stand, French is not capable of producing great literature, this does not result from any inherent defect in the language, but from the failure of writers to cultivate the language as they should. And it is, of course, significant that he should recycle an Italian text, for Italy with Ariosto and Sannazaro, with Bembo and Boccaccio, and above all with Petrarch, was the only modern nation that had produced a vernacular literature deemed worthy to

stand comparison with the rich heritage of classical antiquity. To fol-
low the Italian example, the literary language of French needed to be
reshaped to meet the demands that would now be placed upon it, and
Du Bellay goes on to indicate how this is to be done. The language
should be flexible enough to accommodate new words that reflect new
situations, but also to revive older ones and place them where they
will lend majesty like the relics of saints in a bejewelled setting.
Figures of speech and a generous sprinkling of mythology will ensure
that the language is remote from the commonplace. Essential to the
whole project is an intense study of the Greek and Roman classics
and an imitation not only of their 'artifice and ornament' but also of
the literary forms in which they excelled. Out go the old French ron-
dels, ballads, and virelays and in come the elegies of Ovid, the odes of
Horace, the satire, the eclogue, and the epic, while the sonnet, thanks
to Petrarch, is the only non-classical form to be recommended.

What strikes the reader as excessive in all this is the near-blanket
dismissal of poets of the previous generation, and especially of
Clément Marot and the *marotiques*, accused of triviality and lack of
learning. To thus denigrate his predecessors hardly strengthens Du
Bellay's argument for the literary capabilities of the vernacular and
when he boasts that he is 'the first among the French who has dared
introduce what is practically a new poetry', it is not surprising that
the *Deffence* provoked a number of outraged rebuttals.

It is not uncommon for literary history to see continuity where
contemporaries saw rupture and such is the case with the rise of the
Pléiade poets who had more in common with Marot than they were
usually prepared to admit. Many of their aims were shared by the
Lyons school of Maurice Scève, Louise Labé, Jacques Peletier, and
Pontus de Tyard, some of whom were associated with both groups.
But even when all this is taken into account it must be admitted that
the achievements of the Pléiade group justified the ambitions so
boldly stated in the *Deffence*; they extended the ambition and scope of
French poetry and with Ronsard's *Amours* and Du Bellay's *Regrets*
provided two of its most enduring monuments.

Petrarchism

Along with Du Bellay's *Deffence* came the simultaneous publication
of a volume of his poems, including *L'Olive*, the first fully-fledged

Petrarchan sonnet sequence in French literature. Rather than an epoch-marking innovation, this should be seen as the culmination of a process that had begun some years earlier. Marot had translated six sonnets from Petrarch's *Canzoniere* in 1539, and in 1544 Maurice Scève produced *Délie* where the poems are *dizains* (ten lines) rather than sonnets, but which otherwise clearly belongs to the genre that the *Canzoniere* had created. It is not easy to account for the extraordinary influence that Petrarch exercised over poetry in the sixteenth century, but one may point to the general prestige of Italy as possessing the most advanced culture in Europe, the home of seminal innovations not only in literature, but also in science, philosophy, political theory, music, and the visual arts. There is also the fact that the *Canzoniere*'s limited subject matter is matched by the narrow range of Petrarch's language—what Gianfranco Contini has called his 'unilinguism' as opposed to the 'plurilinguism' of Dante.[3] This made Petrarch's verse both easily readable for foreigners and, especially after Bembo's recommendation, a welcome example of how a vernacular might achieve something like the stability and permanence of Latin. And there is surely more to it than that. If criticism in thrall to Romantic notions of sincerity once tended to regard the notorious 'Petrarchan conventions' as a stylistic straitjacket from which major poets were bold enough to escape, we are now more ready to see how those conventions enabled rather than hindered some of the century's most characteristic achievements. What the *Canzoniere* provided was a kind of grammar of the emotions, where devices such as antithesis, analogy, paradox, and oxymoron could be used to examine and accommodate a wide variety of tensions, stretching from the amorous and erotic to the philosophical, religious, and political. In the light of this polyvalence, we should perhaps speak of Petrarchisms rather than Petrarchism.

Unlike Scève's *Délie* with its bold baroque anticipations, *L'Olive* is little more than a competent imitation of the Italian Petrarchists who had added a dash of Bembo's Neoplatonism to the original mix (see DB 3[4]). *La nuit m'est courte* ('The day's too long for me', DB 2) is a standard exploitation of Petrarchan antitheses, redeemed only by

---

[3] Contini, 'Preliminari sulla lingua di Petrarca', *Francesco Petrarca, Canzoniere* (Turin: Einaudi, 1964).

[4] For an explanation of the reference style used in this volume for poems of Du Bellay and Ronsard, please see Note on the Texts, pp. xxxiii–xxxiv.

a vigorous last line. A more telling example of what is lacking in *L'Olive* is provided by *C'était la nuit* ('It was the night', DB 1) which is adapted from *Era il giorno* ('It was the day', *Can.* 3). Petrarch recounts his first sight of Laura on Good Friday and, in imitation of Ovid (*Amores* 1. 2. 22), accuses Love of cowardice for attacking him while he was unarmed. By substituting Christmas for Good Friday Du Bellay avoids the shocking juxtaposition of the passion of the lover with the Passion of Christ and thus diminishes the tension between sacred and divine love that animates the *Canzoniere*.

'Contre les Pétrarquistes' ('Against the Petrarchists', DB 70) can be read as an antidote to *L'Olive*, but it would be a mistake to see it as a serious recantation. Nothing prevents an author from parodying his own work; the tone is jocular and the bluff speaker who proclaims that his sole aim is sexual satisfaction (*jouissance*) is no more 'the real Du Bellay' than the idealizing lover of the sonnet sequence. Both are personae and indeed the supposedly anti-Petrarchan speaker gives the game away when he concludes by saying that he is ready to play the Neoplatonic lover if that is what it takes. By the late sixteenth century, the anti-Petrarchan poem was to become part of the Petrarchan repertoire as in Shakespeare's 'My mistress' eyes are nothing like the sun' (*Son.* 130) or Sidney's dismissal of 'poor Petrarch's long deceased woes' (*A&S* 15).

It has become a cliché of modern criticism, but one that bears repetition, that we should not look for autobiographical revelations in a Renaissance sonnet sequence. One need only think of all the time and energy wasted in attempts to establish the identities of the Fair Youth and the Dark Lady in Shakespeare's *Sonnets*. Though the text might, perhaps deliberately, tease the reader into seeking the facts behind the poem, the sequence is not ultimately there to recount an episode in the poet's love life, but rather to convey an imaginative vision of what love is like—a vision that stands or falls by its own autonomous vividness and complexity and not by some supposed sincerity or truth to personal experience. And this is not simply the reaction of a sceptical modern mentality. In 1336, when the *Canzoniere* was just beginning to take shape, Giacomo Colonna could already express his doubts as to the real existence of Laura since all that really aroused the passion of Petrarch was the laurel of poetic achievement.[5]

[5] Petrarch, *Familiarium Rerum Libri* 1. 9.

At the end of the sixteenth century Claude Binet, Ronsard's first biographer, suggested that the inspiration of the *Cassandre* sequence was the lady's name rather than her person.[6] We shall return to this problem in our discussion of Ronsard's *Amours*.

Du Bellay: Les Regrets

In June 1553 Du Bellay arrived in Rome to take up an appointment as secretary and household administrator to his relative, Cardinal Jean Du Bellay, head of a French mission to the Vatican tasked with persuading the pope to take the French side against the Habsburg emperor in the Italian Wars. It must have seemed a golden opportunity—not only the beginning of what might lead to a distinguished diplomatic career, but also a chance to savour the atmosphere of the city that was both the centre of Catholic Christianity and the source of the Latin literature he admired so much. The result of his four-year stay would be, on the one hand, personal frustration and disappointment, and on the other the two sonnet sequences that have assured his place in the canon of French poetry: the *Regrets* and *Les Antiquitez de Rome*, both published in 1558, after his return from Rome.

The *Regrets* is a quite extraordinary achievement. Most of the sonnet sequences that derived from Petrarch's *Canzoniere* were, like Ronsard's *Amours* or Du Bellay's own *Olive*, mainly or entirely concerned with love. Later in the century there would be a wave of sequences with a religious theme like the sonnets of Jean de Sponde. When Du Bellay arrived in Rome, Alessandro Piccolomini (*I cento sonetti*, 1549) had already begun to introduce a more varied subject-matter and the trend was continued by Du Bellay's friend Olivier de Magny (*Les soupirs de Magny*, 1557). Berni and Ariosto had written satires that Du Bellay certainly knew, but not in the condensed form of the sonnet. There was, indeed, no real precedent for a sonnet sequence that excluded love as completely as the *Regrets* and that engaged so closely with a given society in a specific place. What we have is a sequence of 191 sonnets which can be roughly divided into three sections: elegiac, satirical, and encomiastic. The first of these records the poet's disillusion with Rome and his nostalgia for France

---

[6] Binet, *Vie de Ronsard*, ed. Paul Laumonier (Paris: Hachette, 1909), 15.

with frequent echoes of Ovid's *Tristia* and *Ex Ponto*, the ironic difference being that Ovid complains of being exiled *from* Rome while Du Bellay laments his exile *to* Rome. The second section turns outwards to give an unforgiving portrait of Rome and especially the court of the Vatican. By its exposure of civic decay and corruption in high places, it prepares us to look for a counter-example of virtuous authority, and this is provided in the third section where the poet, on his return to France, sings the glory of the court, culminating in the praise of Henri II and especially of the king's sister Marguerite de France. This conclusion may disappoint modern readers who usually have little time for the encomiastic poem, suspected of self-seeking flattery unless there are some obvious aporia or hints of ambiguity. But we must understand that such poems are not primarily intended as lifelike portraits, but rather as representations of an ideal which those in power ought to embody. The poet, by representing such an ideal, helps to bring it into being. Thus we can read the *Regrets* as the account of an ascension from self-doubting exile to an affirmative homecoming.

We begin with sonnets that seem to renounce all the high ambitions outlined in the *Deffence*. The poet has lost the Apollonian *furor poeticus*, the *divine ardeur* that Ficino and the Neoplatonists regarded as the mark of true inspiration, and he has been abandoned by the Muses (DB 8). This, however, does not mean that he himself has abandoned poetry, but rather that, instead of a register rich with the learning and eloquence of antiquity, he will adopt a new style like jottings in a notebook (DB 5); his poems will be a kind of halfway house between poetry and prose, *une prose en rime ou une rime en prose* (DB 6); they will not seek to imitate the Greeks or Horace or Petrarch or even his friend Ronsard (DB 7). Instead of seeking exalted themes, he will be content to find his subjects and to write *à l'aventure* about whatever turns up (DB 5). Stripped of its vast public programme, poetry remains a pleasant labour and a consolation in old age (DB 10). This is the beginning of a reconquest: by descending to a low starting point in the *sermo pedestris*, the poet allows for the development of a personal elegiac poetry which will in turn mutate into the moral vigour of satire and the final rediscovery of a subject worthy of praise.

Seen in this light, the apparent self-denigration should perhaps be read as a kind of *captatio benevolentiae*, a rhetorical device to attract sympathy by denying any competence in rhetoric. That we are not to take it too seriously is already suggested by the reflection that his new manner will not prove as easy to imitate as some might think (DB 6), and the proof is provided by the sophisticated erudition with which the nostalgic exile celebrates the simplicity of his rural home in a sonnet that every French child is expected to learn by heart (DB 15): Ulysses and Jason offer classical analogies and the famous evocation of smoke rising from the village chimneys comes to him from Homer's *Odyssey* via Ovid, Erasmus, and Marot.

That vision of a happy homecoming is, however, one of the rare positive moments in the elegiac section which, at least on the surface, conveys the speaker's boredom, fatigue, indecision, and paralysis (DB 17). The energetic (and much-quoted) patriotic invocation of a France that is *mère des arts, des armes, et des lois* ('Mother of arts, of arms, and of the laws', DB 9) rapidly collapses into the rather embarrassing vision of himself as a lost lamb, *comme un agneau qui sa nourrice appelle*; the fruitless voyage (DB 13, 16) replaces the Golden Fleece of Jason, and the failure to obtain any of the accomplishments that Italy was supposed to provide (DB 16) contrasts with the mature well-stocked wisdom that Ulysses has learned from his wanderings. In this context of a society that, for all its flamboyance, has nothing serious to offer, Du Bellay seems desperate to remind us that he still belongs to an exclusively French intellectual community: all the people to whom the sonnets are addressed (Ronsard, Morel, Bouju, Panjas, Mauny, Doulcin, etc.) are either friends he has left in France or Frenchmen who, like himself, are resident in Italy. The increasing sense of isolation and frustration comes to a head in DB 20 where, given the failure of the French mission, he resolves to share the fate of his patron and kinsman Cardinal Du Bellay; the navigation metaphor culminates in a drowning.

It is one of the strengths of the *Regrets* that its three sections do not have clear boundaries; they feed into each other in a way that prevents us from being suddenly confronted with a new register or a new voice. Thus DB 20 for the first time originates in a specific event and in DB 22 he confesses his interest in hearing the latest gossip, *des nouvelles du Pape, et du bruit de la ville* ('The Pope's affairs and what's the talk in town'). Sporadic sonnets still record personal dissatisfaction, but any feeling of lassitude is overcome by the sheer vigour of the satire. The overall movement is now outward—quite literally so

in DB 26 where the poet first goes to the Vatican with its scarlet prel-
ates, then walks down to the bankers and usurers at the Exchange,
then through the quarter of the prostitutes, *de Vénus la grand' bande
lascive*, to end up amid the desolation of ancient Roman rubble. It is
almost a programme for what follows. The theme of papal corruption
is taken up in the hilarious description of the conclave (DB 27), in the
more or less explicit references to Innocenzo del Monte, the catamite
of Julius III (DB 47), and in the cloacal image of the all-too-brief
reign of Pope Marcellus II (DB 48). The usurious bankers turn up in
DB 29, 41, and 52. As for prostitution and its attendant syphilis, in
the sequence DB 36–41 they become an overriding metaphor for the
poisonous effect that Rome can have on a young Frenchman.

Several sonnets help to frame the Roman experience as the
sequence heads back to France. The dubious Truce of Vaucelles
(DB 51), as a probable defeat for French diplomacy (in fact, it lasted
only seven months), recalls the disgrace of Cardinal Du Bellay (DB 29),
and the homecoming of Ulysses (DB 15) is reimagined in a negative
key (DB 54). On the way home, satirical accounts of stops in the
republics of Venice and Geneva (DB 55, 56) imply the superiority of
the monarchical system to which we now return. The praise of Des
Masures as a reborn Virgil (DB 57) lacking only a Maecenas indicates,
perhaps, the kind of patronage that the speaker expects for himself.
Finally, the Apollonian oracular frenzy, the *divine ardeur* lost in DB 8,
is restored as the *vive étincelle* and *antique chaleur* emanating from
Marguerite de France (DB 59).

For most modern readers the *Regrets* will be memorable above all
for its satire, but we have seen, I hope, that the middle section gains
from a reading that takes account of its place in the whole sequence.
And we would do well to remember the etymology of *satire* from the
Latin *satura*, which Quintilian claimed as a uniquely Latin genre and
which can be roughly translated as a medley, a bringing together
of disparate elements. With its shifting registers—elegiac, satiric,
encomiastic—and its blend of varied motives—personal, poetic, and
patriotic—the *Regrets* is designed to fit that definition.

Du Bellay: Les Antiquitez de Rome

Les Antiquitez de Rome is a sequence of thirty-two sonnets and is followed
by fifteen closely linked sonnets entitled *Le Songe* ('The Dream'),

loosely based on Petrarch's visionary canzone *Standomi un giorno* ('Standing one day'), but substituting an allegorical account of the fall of Rome for the Italian allegory of the death of Laura. The short title of the first sequence *Antiquitez* is misleading if it suggests anything like a topographical interest. The full title reads *Le Premier Livre des Antiquitez de Rome contenant une generale description de sa grandeur et comme une deploration de sa ruine* ('The First Book of the Antiquities of Rome containing a general description of its greatness and some lament for its ruin'). In other words what we are to expect is not a description of monuments but a meditation on Rome's greatness and the reasons for its fall. The ultimate purpose, we are told in the unnumbered introductory sonnet, is to encourage Henri II to reproduce that greatness in France (*De rebâtir en France une telle grandeur*). As with *Les Regrets*, Du Bellay breaks new ground—not this time by descending to the *sermo pedestris* but, on the contrary, by laying claim to an exalted register (*sermo gravis*) in a daring move that evokes Rome's greatness in the one non-Latin genre at his disposition. The distance from the other sequence could hardly be greater and there can be little doubt that Du Bellay expected his readers to take its measure. Where the *Regrets* begins by announcing the flight of the Muses, the loss of inspiration, and the choice of a prosaic manner to suit an everyday subject matter, the *Antiquitez* immediately establishes the poet as *vates*, prophet and priest, performing a sacred rite to conjure up the *antique fureur* of the dead (DB 60). As he implores the abyss to open at the sound of his voice, he assumes heroic status and we recall the visits to the Underworld of Odysseus (*Od.* 11) and Aeneas (*Aen.* 6).

Du Bellay's attitude to ancient Rome is neither simple nor wholly consistent. On the one hand he insists on the totality of the destruction; the ancient ruins are nothing more than a shadow, like a ghostly corpse conjured up by nocturnal magic (DB 62). On the other hand, he insists on the continuing presence of Rome in our historical imagination. Latin poetry has, of course, spread the city's image through the world, but that alone, it seems, is not a sufficient explanation of why ancient Rome still matters. Du Bellay comes up with a remarkable paradox when he argues that what still makes the world marvel at Rome, despite all the natural and man-made bouts of destruction, is the greatness of the nothing they have left behind, *la grandeur du rien, qu'ils t'ont laissé* (DB 64). In other words, we measure the greatness of Rome by the size of the gaping void that its fall has left. The crucial question of how or why that fall came about receives a variety of answers—as a punishment for excessive pride, as the work of ever-destructive time, as the inevitable implosion resulting from an expansion that, after world conquest, has nowhere left to go. After a brief outline of Roman history (DB 65), he toys with the idea of a cyclic process in which Rome, having been founded by shepherds, is finally restored to shepherds in the form of popes. But this, given the anti-papal allegory of *Le Songe* and Du Bellay's personal experience of the papacy's distinctly unpastoral aspects, can only be read as bitter irony. Somewhat more comforting is the harvesting metaphor (DB 67) which, taken a little further, might imply that empires rise and fall within a seasonal pattern; but there is very little in the sequence to support the initial prophecy (*bienheureux présage*) that France will inherit the glory of empire. The fact that there is practically no description of any specific monuments contributes to the feeling that, whatever Du Bellay may have believed, his ancient Rome is an inescapable but amorphous image that can be shaped to fit almost any version of history. *Les Antiquitez* concludes with Du Bellay's boast that he is the first Frenchman to have sung the ancient honour of the Romans, *l'antique honneur du peuple à longue robe* (DB 68). There are no lessons to be learned, but Du Bellay the poet has claimed the inheritance of Virgil.

Ronsard: Les Amours *and the Mythological Imagination*

During his lifetime Ronsard was recognized by his fellow Pléiade members and also by court circles as the greatest poet of his age. Already in 1553, in the second edition of *Le Premier Livre des Amours*, a commentary by the humanist Marc-Antoine Muret could hail him as the prince of French poets, and after a period of relative neglect in the seventeenth and eighteenth centuries, he was once again installed as a major figure by the age of Hugo and Baudelaire. His output and his range are enormous, excelling in practically all the genres open to him—ode, elegy, sonnet, philosophical hymn, pastoral, epithalamia, and celebratory verses for court occasions, political and religious polemic. Even in his only failure, the aborted epic *La Franciade*, there are fine passages that one would not want to lose. And yet, for all but scholars, Ronsard is essentially the poet of love and the *Amours* remains his most readable and successful achievement. Ronsard himself lends some authority to this evaluation. In all the six editions of the *Œuvres* that he edited between 1560 and 1584, whatever modifications he makes to the (non-chronological) order, the *Amours* retain their pride of place at the beginning.

The women who inspired the major sequences have been identified: Cassandre, whom he met when she was about 15, is Cassandre Salviati, daughter of an Italian banker; Astrée is Françoise Babou, marquise d'Estrées, mother of the Gabrielle d'Estrées who will become the mistress of Henri IV; Marie is Marie Dupin, a country girl better known as Marie de Bourgueil, though the poems *Sur la mort de Marie* refer to the untimely death of Marie de Clèves, beloved of the Prince de Condé, later Henri III; finally Hélène, a woman of Ronsard's own age, whom he seems to have courted rather assiduously between 1570 and 1575, is Hélène de Surgères, noblewoman and maid of honour to Catherine de Médicis. These are the bare facts and although they provide us with more biographical information than we shall ever glean from Shakespeare's *Sonnets*, they do not allow us to read *Les Amours* as a sentimental autobiography. That the country girl Marie can be so easily conflated with the noble Marie de Clèves and that the other three have names that offer full scope to the poet's mythological imagination would suggest that Ronsard is finding women who fit his poems rather than the other way round. Looking back at the evolution of the *Amours* through the many editions of the *Œuvres* published during Ronsard's lifetime, we see how often he modifies the text or the order of the poems, even changing the name of the woman as he switches a sonnet from one sequence to the other, and in this context it is also worth noting that he differs from other Renaissance sonneteers in celebrating four or five women as opposed to a chosen one like the Laura of Petrarch, the Délie of Scève, the Olive of Du Bellay, the Stella of Philip Sidney, or the Delia of Samuel Daniel. He obviously needed that plurality in order to accommodate the shifting nature of the passions he wished, as a poet, to represent. At times it would seem that Ronsard associates a given woman with a given stylistic level: Cassandre with the elevated, Marie with the low (R 22, 27), and Hélène with something in between; but there is no absolute consistency; the high style for Cassandre does not exclude the erotic itemization of *Élégie à Janet* (R 21); and what do we make of the famous *Mort de Marie* sonnet *Comme on voit sur la branche*

('As on its stem', R 29)? Is it written for the country girl Marie de Bourgueil or for the noble Marie de Clèves or for some conflation of the two—perhaps a Marie de Clèves in pastoral dress? In the long run, it hardly matters, since most of these women are not allowed a personal existence that could justify us in finding one poem more appropriate than another. Cassandre, the two Maries, and Astrée are essentially blank pages on which Ronsard can write and stylize a whole range of the complex emotions associated with the general topic of love—aesthetic admiration for beauty, sexual desire, tenderness, an acute awareness of transience, melancholy, and, perhaps above all, frustration, for only in dreams is there any physical consummation. And even that frustration is a literary stratagem rather than a biographical event in that it is the necessary pretext for the poetry. Lacking even the skeletal narrative structure of Petrarch's *Canzoniere*, Sidney's *Astrophil and Stella*, or Shakespeare's *Sonnets*, the sequences that make up the *Amours* are not so much love stories as explorations of what love involves.

For a generation whose literary education is no longer based in the Greek and Roman classics, the most salient feature of Ronsard's love poetry (and, perhaps, the greatest obstacle to its appreciation) must be the abundance of mythological reference. Mythology had, of course, been associated with love poetry ever since Petrarch made the Apollo–Daphne myth a recurrent motif in the *Canzoniere* and this may well have influenced Ronsard in his choice of the Apollo–Cassandra story. In both cases it is the divine patron of poetry who is frustrated, thus suggesting paradoxically a poetry that is born of its own defeat. Also inherited from an earlier century were such figures as Love the blind Archer (Cupid) and Actaeon torn to death by his own hounds as a punishment for seeing the naked and chaste Diana. Ronsard, however, goes far beyond this predictable gallery. Taking as a sample only the limited selection of *Cassandre* sonnets included in this volume (a mere 19 out of 229), we find Jupiter, Danaë, Europa, Narcissus, Aurora, Apollo, Venus Anadyomene, Tantalus, Ixion, Tityos, Sisyphus, Adonis, Endymion, Theseus, Heracles, and Alcmene. At a superficial level this is simply a way of establishing credentials. 'And let there be no verse without some vestige of rare and ancient learning', says Du Bellay in the *Deffence* as he recommends 'those ancient fables that are no small adornment of poetry' (p. 202). The sixteenth century may have revered the *furor poeticus*, but it had no place for the untaught genius: the plethora of mythological reference was both a guarantee of profound erudition and the appropriation of a distinguished poetic ancestry. There must also have been an awareness of contemporary mythological painting which casts a magical light over the whole field.

For Ronsard, however, mythology clearly meant a great deal more than that. There is a key passage in the *Abbrégé*: 'For poetry in that first age was no other than allegorical theology employing pleasant and vivid fables to instil into the brains of rough men those secrets which they would have been unable to understand had their truth been revealed too openly' (p. 208). The problem there is the term *theology* which, in the sixteenth century, could only mean Christian theology. We have no way of knowing whether Ronsard gave any serious attention to the syncretism of Pico della Mirandola and the Neoplatonists or whether the phrase is simply a sop to placate the religious authorities. What is certain, however, is that Ronsard sees mythology as offering access to truths that could be conveyed in no other way. Terence Cave has argued that in Ronsard 'the role of myth is the role of poetry itself: it evokes a magical world which is unreal and which nevertheless seems to comprehend truths fundamental to reality'.[7] Perhaps another way of putting this would be to say that mythological imagery and analogy create a distance between the experience of love and its representation. Stripped of its contemporary circumstances of time and place, the experience is re-enacted in a vivid theatre of the passions that illuminates but does not reproduce our own condition.

Another important feature of mythology is that, precisely because it tells stories rather than advancing propositions, it remains open to reinterpretation both by the author of the poem and by the poem's reader. Consider, for example, the famous sonnet *Je voudrais bien richement jaunissant* ('I wish I could grow yellow', R 4). In the octave the speaker imagines himself in the role of Jupiter as the irresistible lover of Danaë and Europa, exercising both soft and hard power, both seduction and rape. Where the union with Danaë is slow (*goutte à goutte*) and her lap (*giron*) is ready to receive the golden shower (painters from Titian onwards portray her reclining naked with her head thrown back in an orgasmic trance), the conquest of Europa by the

---

[7] 'Ronsard's Mythological Universe', in Terence Cave (ed.), *Ronsard the Poet* (London: Methuen, 1973), 207.

white bull is a demonstration of sudden phallic force, after which the evocation of Narcissus comes as a surprise. Thomas Greene has spoken of an attempt to go beyond the limits of the self, of 'a plunge into otherness'.[8] But surely if the woman is like a fountain that reflects the speaker's own image, then surely his plunge into the water is essentially self-regarding and sterile. Thus the sestet undermines the octave by providing a negative contrast with the procreative vigour of Jupiter. We need not ask whether Ronsard himself could have envisaged such a reading; the point is that the mythological imagination makes such readings possible.

The two books of sonnets for Hélène were published in 1578 when Ronsard was already 53. Though the idiom remains largely Petrarchan and the mythological imagination is given plenty of scope by the lady's name (R 39), there is an added presence of precise details of person, time, and place that mark a significant departure from the stylized and relatively timeless settings of the *Cassandre*, *Marie*, and *Astrée* sequences. The speaker is now identified as Ronsard (R 43 and 45), and the lady is twice given her patronymic (Surgères). We see Hélène against the background of court life, in dazzling form at a ball (R 44), ensconced in her high tower at the Louvre (R 46), and looking out over Montmartre to the countryside while she trots out conventional pieties as to the superiority of rural solitude over court life (R 37); she strolls with the poet in the gardens and announces her fashionable preference for melancholy verse (R 36). There is an underlying and recurrent struggle for dominance. The chaste Hélène offends the poet by giving him permission to seek another woman (R 34) which is precisely what he threatens to do almost immediately afterwards (R 35). There are repeated hints that Hélène has been corrupted by courtly company and is excessively proud of her noble status (R 34, 35, 36, 46); and though Ronsard seems to accept her authority when he boasts of having been chosen as her poet (R 45), he takes the upper hand when he contrasts her future decrepitude with his own literary immortality (R 43) in a poem that is, perhaps, more vindictive than many of its admirers would want to admit.

Before leaving Ronsard's love poetry, we should note his proficiency in explicitly erotic exercises, where the sophistication of Ovid's

[8] Greene, *The Light in Troy: Imitation and Discovery in the Renaissance* (New Haven: Yale University Press, 1982), 210.

Art of Love meets the specifically French tradition of the *Blasons du corps féminin*. Two of these pieces (R 12, 21) are, rather surprisingly, inserted into the *Cassandre* sequence where they would seem to contrast with the dominant Petrarchism of the sonnets. But Ronsard, however much he may exploit the Petrarchan mode, does not buy into the spiritual and idealizing aspects of the Petrarchan ethos; physical desire is rarely far below the surface.

Ronsard's World

Once we move away from the familiar territory of the *Amours*, we face a production so vast and so varied as to render even a summary description out of the question. Readers new to Ronsard may, however, be helped by some comment on the most vital aspects of his mindset as revealed in the *Hymnes* and the 'Remonstrance'.

The two hymns included here present Ronsard's vision of the cosmos ('Hymne du Ciel' / 'Hymn to the Sky') and of man's place in it ('Hymne des Étoiles' / 'Hymn to the Stars'). The cosmos remains essentially as Ptolemy, building on an Aristotelian base, had mapped it in the first century—finite, spherical, and with the earth at its centre. Surrounding the earth are crystal spheres, first those of the seven planets—the moon, Mercury, Venus, the sun, Mars, Jupiter and Saturn—then that of the fixed stars. To these, Christian theory added the sphere of the Prime Mover (*primum mobile*) which moves the other stars, and finally, stretching out to infinity, the realm of the Empyrean which is the dwelling-place of God, His angels, and His elect.

To the traditional picture, however, Ronsard added some of the new fashionable ideas that the humanists and Neoplatonists had derived from a variety of ancient sources, including Stoicism, Epicureanism, and Hermeticism. In the Christianized Ptolemaic system there was a rigid division between the extra-lunar realm where all is peace and perfection and the sublunar world which is ever subject to mutability and decay. In the Neoplatonist scheme there is a new emphasis on the correspondences and interplay between microcosm and macrocosm—that is, between each individual human creature and the overall pattern of creation. The kind of interaction that this presupposes is reinforced by the vaguely heretical notion of some mystical force known as the *Anima Mundi* (World Soul) or, to use

Ronsard's term, *l'Esprit de l'Éternel*), whose breath gave the Prime
Mover its circular motion and whose influence pervades the
universe, maintaining the fragile balance between its contrasting
powers and preserving it from a descent into chaos. An excursion
in the 'Remonstrance' (R 63) associates the *Anima Mundi* with
the sun:

> Great Sun, I say, who as the seasons pass,
> With his twelve houses marks them out for us;
> Whose powers revealed pervade the universe,
> Who with a single glance makes clouds disperse;
> World-soul and spirit, flaming up on high,
> In one sole day traversing all the Sky,
> Constant yet still in motion, his great round
> Sees in the world below his only bound;
> Restless in rest, idle yet cannot stay,
> Nature's firstborn and father of the day.

Ronsard wards off possible objections by reminding us that this is the
paganism he would have embraced had he not been granted the truth
of Jesus Christ, but the fact is that his preference for a Neoplatonic
Anima Mundi over the Aristotelian Unmoved Mover is an instinctive
aesthetic option for movement over stasis to which his whole output—
sonnets, songs, elegies, odes, hymns—bears witness. Unlike Spenser
who, in the *Cantos of Mutabilitie*, deplores the constant flux of the
world, Ronsard is happy to entertain the prospect of an endlessly
shape-changing process. Even as he laments the destruction of his
beloved forest of Gastine, he finds comfort in the vision of a future
where land and sea, mountain and plain, have changed places because
'Matter endures, and form will fade away' (R 60). It is not surprising
that his poetry embraces a broad range of natural phenomena
observed with such animation that, even when used as metaphor, they
assume an autonomous energy. He sees the life vibrating in nerves
and muscles (R 21) or emerging from the supposedly dead trunks of
trees (R 62); he notes the lily washed by spring rain (R 26), the grasses
in a cold winter that bristle like hair (R 17), the triangular formation
of cranes in flight (R 44), the sudden illumination of lightning in
a cloudy night (R 30), the ever-shifting shade in the forest of Gastine
(R 60). Streams and rivers figure prominently, flowing in patterned
ripples towards the sea (R 47), melting from mountain snow and
descending to the valley (R 26), or meandering through lush meadows

(R 54). The life of man is imaged as a fragment of ice bobbing from
side to side on the rough surface of a torrent (R 62). Despite Ronsard's
affection for his native Vendôme, there is little topographical about all
this. The recurrent elements that compose his natural world—wind
and water, woods and fields—remain generic. But that does not
stop them from possessing an extraordinary dynamism—evidence of
a fascination with motion that Ronsard shares with some of the most
powerful figures in Renaissance art and thought.[9]

The 'Hymn to the Stars' initially shares the sense of wonder that
governs the 'Hymn to the Sky', but that vision is challenged by the
crucial question of whether the influence of the stars is so great that
man has no power to forge his own destiny. Ronsard cannot bring
himself to share the dour determinism of his source in Marullus and
builds in a get-out clause for saints and sages. But the list in stanzas
8–11 of injustices and tragic destinies, including a reference to the
death of Admiral Coligny, casts a gloom over the whole poem and
brings the reader down from the stars to the earthbound strife-ridden
society of contemporary France.

The religious wars that tore France apart in the second half of the
sixteenth century forced poets and intellectuals to take sides. Marot
leaned towards the Reform; Du Bartas and D'Aubigny were fervent
Protestants; Jean de Sponde began life as a Protestant and later con-
verted to Catholicism. That Ronsard chose the Catholic and royal
side may seem natural in that by 1562 (the date of *Discours des Misères
de ce temps*) he already held a court position as King's Almoner
(*Aumônier ordinaire du roi*) roughly equivalent to Poet Laureate. But
there can be no doubt that his heart and mind were committed to the
struggle against what he saw as an attack on the traditional values of
France as embodied in the monarchy and the Church. In an age when
the tone of religious controversy was anything but polite, he proved
a formidable debater, paying little attention to doctrinal problems but
condemning subversive attitudes and their negative results—the
attack on traditional learning and the way the Reformers had divided
the French Church to the detriment of national unity. Occasionally
he risks giving arms to the enemy. The lengthy and tender evocation
of the pagan gods, from which we have quoted the passage on the sun,

[9] See Michel Jeanneret, *Perpetual Motion: Transforming Shapes in the Renaissance from
Da Vinci to Montaigne* (Baltimore: Johns Hopkins University Press, 2001).

seems suspiciously disproportionate in a poem that is supposed to support the one true Christian Church, and the argument that it is illogical to deny transubstantiation when one accepts such extraordinary biblical miracles as Balaam's ass surely diminishes the status of the Eucharist. Ronsard's religious thought is rarely Christological and he shows little interest in the drama of redemption. But if there is a vein of scepticism in Ronsard, it is not unlike that of his great contemporary Montaigne whose loyalty to the Catholic Church reflects at least in part his feeling that there are areas of thought where unaided human reason will not take us very far.

If, in the end, Ronsard was not prepared to follow Marot, Bèze, and Du Bartas on the road to Geneva, it was because the whole ethos of the Reformation—its rejection of tradition in favour of a supposed original purity, its democratizing appeal to the unlearned, its distrust of ceremony, its preference for plain speaking over rhetoric—was fundamentally uncongenial to the kind of poetry he felt most happy to write.

English Reception

The English reception of Du Bellay and Ronsard should ideally be seen as an episode in the larger story of French influence on English poetry from Thomas Wyatt's debt to Marot in the 1520s to Joshua Sylvester's widely read and much-quoted translation of Du Bartas (1598 and 1604). The relation between Du Bellay and Spenser is the most obvious example of a direct influence and is all the more important in that it begins in 1569 with Spenser's first published work, his contributions at the age of 17 to Jan van der Noot's *Theatre for Worldlings* which included eleven sonnets translated from *Le Songe* ('The Dream'), the visionary anti-papal sequence that Du Bellay appended to *Les Antiquitez*. These reappear in a revised form (rhyme replacing blank verse) as *The Visions of Bellay* in *Complaints* (1591), a volume which also contains, among other things, a complete version of the thirty-two sonnets of *Les Antiquitez* entitled *The Ruines of Rome*. A concluding 'Envoy' confirms the French poet's status as an innovator by praising 'Bellay, first garland of free Poesie | That France brought forth'. There is good reason to think that the whole of Spenser's career was influenced if not determined by this early engagement with Du Bellay. Both *Les Antiquitez* and *Le Songe* contribute to his growing obsession with mutability and the way in which it impinges on the national idea of empire. If the Roman Empire fell not because of any specific fault but because the rise and fall of empires is the law of history, then what will be the destiny of Gloriana's realm? It is no accident that *The Faerie Queene* stops short with the 'Cantos of Mutabilitie'.

Spenser is the exception. Half-a-dozen other English poets make sporadic use of Du Bellay (*L'Olive* more often than *Les Regrets*), but only Arthur Gorges and Samuel Daniel offer anything like a creative engagement. In the field of criticism it seems highly probable that Mulcaster (Spenser's teacher at the Merchant Taylors' School), Puttenham, Samuel Daniel, and Philip Sidney had all read the *Deffence*. But Du Bellay's name is rarely mentioned either in poetry or in prose, and he seems to have been more privately appreciated than publicly acclaimed.

With Ronsard the situation is very different. There is no lack of hyperbolic praise; a random selection from Prescott's survey[10] gives us 'Prince of Poets', 'the flourishing Ronsard', 'the honour of his native soil', 'the ornament of France', 'the famous Poet Ronsard', and 'Great Paragon, of Poets richest Pearl'. What may seem surprising, given Ronsard's reputation as a love poet, is that the only substantial trans-lation of his work should be Thomas Jeney's *A discourse of the present troubles in France* (1568) which is a version of *Discours des misères de ce temps*. But Ronsard was an apologist for official French policy, and Jeney (who later reverted to Catholicism) must have felt that his voice was worth hearing. The *Discours* avoids engagement with doctrinal questions while pleading for compromise and unity. Only in the conclusion does Ronsard threaten the Huguenots with terrible conse-quences if they continue their stubborn resistance. Jeney omits this passage, thus turning the *Discours* into a relatively eirenic text that might recommend itself to Queen Elizabeth—a hope soon extin-guished by the Rising in the North (1569) and the St Bartholomew's Day Massacre (1572). In the years that followed, Ronsard's reputa-tion stood high with the group around Gabriel Harvey, Spenser, and Sidney, but translation was never more than sporadic. Arthur Gorges produced a sensitive version of the famous *Je voudrais bien richement*

[10] Anne Lake Prescott, *French Poets and the English Renaissance* (New Haven: Yale University Press, 1978).

jaunissant (R 4), as did Thomas Lodge whose *Phillis* contains at least half-a-dozen sonnets with a source in the *Amours*; but by the end of the century Ronsard's love poems were losing ground to the smooth Petrarchism of Philippe Desportes while his cosmic visions were being eclipsed by the more obviously Christian world-picture of Du Bartas. All told, the influence of Ronsard on English poetry is not to be traced in translation or direct borrowing, but in something more diffuse—in the lyric grace of Herrick, Lovelace, or Waller, and also in the more robust sensuality of certain poems by Donne, Marvell, or Carew. Though 'Go, lovely rose' and 'To his Coy Mistress' are very different poems, the voice of Ronsard can be heard in both.

This Translation

The translator of Du Bellay and/or Ronsard is faced with three major problems: diction, metrics, and rhyme. Of these the first is by far the most important, for the choice of diction reflects the answers given to questions that must be asked before one even begins to translate. What kind of audience does the translation hope to reach? How much prior knowledge can one reasonably expect readers to possess? What appropriations, adaptations, and mediations are involved in the attempt to transfer a poetic experience from one language to another and from one age to another? John Dryden famously announced that he had endeavoured 'to make Virgil speak such English as he himself would have spoken, if he had been born in England, and in this present age';[11] but this begs too many questions. There are experiences and attitudes so firmly linked to a given period that we no longer have a lexicon for their adequate expression. To remain only in the area of love poetry, the erotic poems of Catullus may go down very well in the idiom of our sexually permissive society, but what are we to do with Dante's allegorizing of Beatrice or the social distinctions of courtly love or the elevations of Neoplatonism? The translator is left to navigate between the Scylla of inappropriate and misleading contemporary speech and the Charybdis of archaism and pastiche. In the case of Du Bellay and Ronsard the problem of diction is rendered more acute by the fact that both poets have such a broad stylistic range. The

---

[11] *Works of John Dryden*, v. *Poems, 1697* (Berkeley and Los Angeles: University of California Press, 1988), 330.

diction of the *Regrets* is very different from that of the *Antiquitez* and the sonnets of Ronsard's *Cassandre* poems exploit a Petrarchan register that has little in common with his erotic elegies or with the 'Remonstrance'. My translation opts for a fairly neutral but flexible modern diction. There is, of course, a danger of flatness and also, inevitably when a single translator deals with two poets in a single volume, a tendency to make them sound more alike than in fact they are. The reader will judge how far I have managed to avoid these pitfalls.

French poetry of the sixteenth century relies for the most part on two distinct metres: the decasyllable and the twelve-syllable alexandrine. Thus Du Bellay uses the alexandrine throughout the *Regrets* but alternates decasyllabic and alexandrine sonnets in the *Antiquitez*, while Ronsard opts for the decasyllable in the *Cassandre* sequence but turns to the alexandrine for *Hélène*. The period does, in fact, see the gradual establishment of the alexandrine as the dominant metre of French verse, occupying a position similar to that of the iambic pentameter in English. Unfortunately, the English hexameter, which is the nearest thing we have to the alexandrine, usually sounds so awkward (and so foreign) that Sidney, in one of his attempts at the metre, felt forced to admit that 'others' feet still seemed but strangers in my way' (*A&S* 1). I have translated both French metres with the familiar iambic pentameter, but not without an uneasy awareness that a significant distinction has been effaced.

Finally, we come to the vexed question of rhyme. Rhymed translation has had a bad press and it is not hard to see why. There are too many verse translations where the quest for rhyme has led to a riot of awkward syntax, improbable vocabulary, periphrasis, and paraphrase. Yet rhyme was a vital weapon in the poetic armoury of the Pléiade and without it we end up by turning a sonnet into fourteen lines of blank verse. As I first argued twenty years ago, it is not some external ornament that is lost, but the whole sense of formal constraint and containment that the rhyme scheme creates. I have, therefore, chosen a compromise solution which is to consider all varieties of slant rhymes, assonantal and consonantal echoes, as acceptable rhymes. This, I hope, conveys a sense of the original rhyme scheme without making rhyme the idol to which all other considerations must be sacrificed. An added justification for this practice may be sought in the fact that rhyming in French, being relatively easy, does not have the same emphatic ring as rhyme in English.

The selection is a compromise between what I would have liked to translate and what has proved amenable to translation. For Du Bellay the emphasis on the *Regrets* and the *Antiquitez* was inevitable, though I could not resist the satirical verve of 'Contre les Pétrarquistes'. For Ronsard the choice was more difficult, given his virtuosity in a wide variety of forms and genres. I have tried to achieve a balance between his love sonnets and the odes, elegies, and hymns but have found no room for the longer poems, with the one exception of an extract from the 'Remonstrance' to demonstrate his skill in public religious controversy.

NOTE ON THE TEXTS

THE standard text for Du Bellay has long been the *Œuvres poétiques*, ed. Henri Chamard, 6 vols (Paris: STFM, 1908–31), but this is gradually being superseded by a new *Œuvres complètes*, ed. Olivier Millet (Paris: Garnier, 2003–). Volume I (2003) includes the *Deffence et Illustration* and Volume IV/1: *1557–1558* (2020) contains *Les Regrets* and *Divers Jeux Rustiques*, but not *Les Antiquitez*.

All serious students of Ronsard are indebted to the monumental *Œuvres complètes*, ed. Paul Laumonier, completed by Raymond Lebègue and Isidore Silver, for the *Société des textes français modernes*, 20 vols (Paris: Didier, 1914–75). Less unwieldy is the new Pléiade *Œuvres complètes*, ed. Jean Céard, Daniel Ménager, and Michel Simonin, 2 vols (Paris: Gallimard, 1993–4) which is based on the sixth edition of the poems (1584), the last published in the poet's lifetime. Ronsard's use of the terms 'Elegy' and 'Hymn' to define sections of the volume may mislead modern readers. 'Elegy' here points to form rather than content and, following classical example, can be used of any poem that has a couplet form: Ronsard's elegies tend to be explicitly erotic. 'Hymn' is not reserved for sacred songs, but can indicate any meditation on a subject of cosmological, religious, or philosophical importance, as in Spenser's *Fowre Hymnes* (1596).

Spelling has been modernized except where to do so would have radically altered the pronunciation of a word or disturbed rhyme or rhythm. Out of deference to tradition, the original spelling has been retained for certain titles (*Les Antiquitez de Rome, La Deffence et Illustration de la Langue Françoyse, Abbregé*). In both French and English texts I have preserved the somewhat erratic capitalization of nouns to indicate title, personification, or emphasis. The Ronsard poems do not follow the chronological order of composition, but follow the sequence imposed by Ronsard himself in the 1584 edition. Chronology would, in any case, be problematic since Ronsard was an inveterate reviser and many of his poems exist in several versions. Rather than making my own choice among the various versions on offer, I have preferred to let Ronsard have the last word.

In the Introduction and Notes the initials DB and R are used to indicate the author concerned. In the text the bracketed number is that given to the poem in the relevant sequence or series. In this context I have followed DB's own significant use of Arabic numerals for *Regrets* and Roman numerals for *Antiquitez*.

SELECT BIBLIOGRAPHY

In keeping with the policy of Oxford World's Classics, this bibliography is restricted to works in English. I would, however, like to name some francophone scholars who have proved particularly useful: Yvonne Bellenger, Guy Demerson, André Gendre, Olivier Pot, Marcel Raymond, François Roudaut, François Rouget, and Jean Vignes. For recent developments in the field the most comprehensive coverage is provided by *L'Année ronsardienne* published annually by Gallimard since 2019.

Criticism

Castor, Grahame, *Pléiade Poetics: A Study in Sixteenth-Century Thought and Terminology* (Cambridge: Cambridge University Press, 1964).

Cave, Terence (ed.), *Ronsard the Poet* (London: Methuen, 1973).

Coleman, Dorothy G., *The Chaste Muse* (Leiden: Brill, 1980).

Ford, Philip, *Ronsard's Hymnes: A Literary and Iconographical Study* (Tempe: Arizona Center for Medieval and Renaissance Studies, 1997).

Goul, Pauline, and Usher, Phillip John (eds), *Early Modern Écologies: Beyond English Ecocriticism* (Amsterdam: Amsterdam University Press, 2020).

Greene, Thomas M., *The Light in Troy: Imitation and Discovery in the Renaissance* (New Haven: Yale University Press, 1982).

Hui, Andrew, *The Poetics of Ruins in Renaissance Literature* (New York: Fordham University Press, 2016).

Jeanneret, Michel, *Perpetual Motion: Transforming Shapes in the Renaissance from Da Vinci to Montaigne* (Baltimore: Johns Hopkins University Press, 2001).

Katz, R. A., *The Ordered Text: The Sonnet Sequences of Du Bellay* (New York: Peter Lang, 1985).

Keller, Marcus, *Figurations of France: Literary Nation-Building in Times of Crisis (1550–1650)* (Newark: University of Delaware Press, 2011).

Kenny, Neil, *An Introduction to Sixteenth-Century French Thought: Other Times, Other Places* (London: Duckworth, 2008).

McGowan, Margaret, *Ideal Forms in the Age of Ronsard* (Berkeley and Los Angeles: University of California Press, 1985).

McGowan, Margaret, *The Vision of Rome in Late Renaissance France* (New Haven: Yale University Press, 2000).

Prescott, Anne Lake, *French Poets and the English Renaissance* (New Haven: Yale University Press, 1978).

Quainton, Malcolm, *Ronsard's Ordered Chaos: Visions of Flux and Stability in the Poetry of Pierre de Ronsard* (Manchester: Manchester University Press, 1980).

Russell, Nicolas, *Transformations of Memory and Forgetting in Sixteenth-Century France* (Newark: University of Delaware Press, 2011).

Silver, Isidore, *Three Ronsard Studies* (Droz: Geneva, 1978).

Sorsby, Karen, *Representations of the Body in French Renaissance Poetry* (New York: Peter Lang, 1999).

Stone, Donald, *Ronsard's Sonnet Cycles: A Study in Tone and Vision* (New Haven: Yale University Press, 1966).

Sturm-Maddox, Sara, *Ronsard, Petrarch and the* Amours (Gainesville: University Press of Florida, 1999).

Tucker, George Hugo, *The Poet's Odyssey: Joachim Du Bellay and the* Antiquitez de Rome (Oxford: Clarendon Press, 1990).

Wilson, D. B., *Ronsard, Poet of Nature* (Manchester: Manchester University Press, 1961).

Yandell, Cathy, *Carpe Corpus: Time and Gender in Early Modern France* (Newark: University of Delaware Press, 2000).

Translations

Du Bellay, Joachim, *The Regrets*, trans. C. H. Sisson (Manchester: Carcanet, 1984).

Du Bellay, Joachim, *'The Regrets,'* with *'The Antiquities of Rome,' Three Latin Elegies, and 'The Defense and Enrichment of the French Language'*, trans. Richard Helgerson (Philadelphia: University of Pennsylvania Press, 2006).

Ronsard, Pierre de, *Cassandra*, trans. Clive Lawrence (Manchester: Carcanet, 2015).

Ronsard, Pierre de, *The Labyrinth of Love: Selected Sonnets and Other Poems*, trans. and introd. Henry Weinfield (Anderson, SC: Parlor Press, 2021).

Ronsard, Pierre de, *Selected Poems*, trans. and introd. Malcolm Quainton and Elizabeth Vinestock (London: Penguin, 2002).

Shapiro, Norman R. (trans.), *Lyrics of the French Renaissance: Marot, Du Bellay, Ronsard*, introd. Hope Glidden (New Haven: Yale University Press, 2002).

Spenser, Edmund, *The Visions of Bellay* and *The Ruines of Rome* (1591), in *The Shorter Poems of Edmund Spenser*, ed. William A. Oram et al. (New Haven: Yale University Press, 1989).

Source Material

For Petrarch, *Canzoniere*, see the prose translation by Robert Durling in *Petrarch's Lyric Poems* (Cambridge, MA: Harvard University Press, 1976); verse translation by Anthony Mortimer (London: Penguin, 2002).

For the following classical texts, there are plain prose translations in the Loeb Classical Library and more ambitious ones in Oxford World's Classics: Ovid, *Metamorphoses* and *Amores*; Virgil, *Eclogues* and *Aeneid*; Horace, *Odes*; poems by Catullus and Propertius; Homer, *Odyssey*; Theocritus, *Idylls*.

Further Reading in Oxford World's Classics

Alighieri, D., *The Divine Comedy*, trans. C. H. Sisson, ed. David H. Higgins.

Alighieri, D., *Vita Nuova*, trans. and ed. Mark Musa.

Ariosto, L., *Orlando Furioso*, trans. Guido Waldman.

Boccaccio, G., *The Decameron*, trans. Guido Waldman, ed. Jonathan Usher.

Italian Renaissance Tales, trans. and ed. Anthony Mortimer.

Shakespeare, *The Complete Sonnets and Poems*, ed. Colin Burrow.

Sidney, Sir Philip, *The Major Poems, including* Astrophil and Stella, ed. Katherine Duncan-Jones.

The Song of Roland and Other Poems of Charlemagne, trans. and ed. Simon Gaunt and Karen Pratt.

CHRONOLOGY

1522   Birth of Joachim Du Bellay at Liré in Anjou.

1524   Birth of Pierre de Ronsard at the manor of La Possonière in the Vendômois.

1525   François I defeated by imperial forces of Charles V at Pavia.

1525–30   Tyndale's English Bible.

1528   Castiglione, *Book of the Courtier*.

1530   Bembo, *Rime*; Sannazaro, *Rime*.

1532   Machiavelli, *The Prince*; Ariosto, *Orlando Furioso*; Rabelais, *Pantagruel*.

1534   Rabelais, *Gargantua*.

1535   Olivetan, Bible in French.

1536   R is page to Dauphin François and then to Charles, Duke of Orléans. Calvin, *Institutio Christianae Religionis*.

1537   R is part of retinue accompanying Madeleine de France to Scotland for her marriage to James VI.

1540   R attached to household of Lazare de Baïf, father of Pléiade poet Jean-Antoine de Baïf. Illness leaves him partially deaf and ends hopes of a military career.

1543   R receives tonsure which commits him to celibacy but qualifies him to receive ecclesiastical benefits. Meets poet Jacques Peletier who encourages him to study ancient literature.

1544   Scève, *Délie*. R begins study under Jean Dorat who will later become master of the Collège Coqueret in Paris. R's colleagues at the Collège will include DB and Baïf.

1545   R meets Cassandre Salviati, daughter of Italian banker.

1545–6   DB studies law at Poitiers; first meetings with Peletier and R.

1546   Rabelais, *Tiers livre*.

1547   Death of François I, accession of Henri II. R and DB publish first poems in *Œuvres poétiques* of Peletier.

1548   Sébillet, *Art poétique français*.

1549   In answer to Sébillet, DB publishes *La Deffence et Illustration de la langue françoyse*, outlining the ideals of the Pléiade. Also publishes *Recueil de poésie* and *L'Olive*, a fifty-sonnet sequence of Petrarchan and Neoplatonist inspiration. Tyard, *Erreurs amoureuses*; Bèze, *Abraham sacrifiant*.

1550 R publishes first four books of *Odes* and *Bocage* and is criticized by court poet Mellin de Saint-Gelais.

1551 DB inherits family estate and is embroiled in succession dispute with powerful Constable de Montmorency. Friendship with dramatist Etienne de Jodelle and poets Pontus de Tyard and Rémy Belleau. Publishes *Complainte de Didon* and translation of *Aeneid*, Book 4.

1552 R, *Les Amours* (Cassandre) and fifth book of Odes. Baïf, *Les Amours de Méline*; Rabelais, *Quart livre*.

1553 R, second edition of *Amours* with commentary by Marc-Antoine Muret. First performance of Jodelle's *Cléopatre captive*.

1553–7 DB in Rome as head of household for his cousin Cardinal Jean Du Bellay whose mission is to persuade the pope to support France against Spain in the Italian Wars. Meets Tyard and Scève on his passage through Lyons. Friendship with poets Olivier de Magny and Rémy Belleau. DB writes the sonnet sequences that will assure his fame, *Les Regrets* and *Les Antiquitez de Rome*; also Latin *Poemata*.

1555 R *Continuation des Amours* and *Hymnes*. Alexandrine replaces decasyllabic metre. Baif, *L'Amour de Francine*; Louise Labé, *Œuvres*. Death of Pope Julius III, short pontificate of Marcellus II, election of Paul VI, fall from favour of Cardinal Du Bellay.

1556 *R* continues *Les Amours* (Marie), publishes second book of *Hymnes*. Belleau translates Anacreon's *Odes*. Short-lived Truce of Vaucelles between Spanish and French forces. Abdication of Emperor Charles V.

1557 French defeat at Saint Quentin. DB returns to France via Venice, Geneva, and Lyons, now a rich man but seriously deaf. *Tottel's Miscellany* contains Petrarchan poems by Wyatt and Surrey and translations from Clément Marot.

1558 DB publishes *Les Regrets*, *Les Antiquitez de Rome*, *Divers jeux rustiques*, *Poemata*. R appointed court poet (Almoner to the King) by Henri II.

1559 Death of Henri II. DB writes poems on state affairs and royal occasions. Peace of Cateau-Cambrésis puts an end to French ambitions in Italy.

1560 R publishes first collected *Œuvres*. Death of François II, succeeded by ten-year-old Charles IX; regency of Catherine de Medici. Death of DB in Paris. English Protestant exiles publish Geneva Bible.

1562 R takes Catholic side in Wars of Religion, *Discours des misères de ce temps*.

1563 R increasingly involved in religious polemic, *Remonstrance au peuple de France*.

Foxe, *Acts and Monuments* ('Foxe's Book of Martyrs').

1565 Rémy Belleau, *La Bergerie*.

1567 Second edition of R, *Œuvres*. New outbreak of religious strife.

1569 Jan van der Noot's *Theatre for Worldlings* includes Edmund Spenser's translation of DB's *Songe*.

1570 Roger Ascham, *The Scholemaster*.

1571 Third edition of R, *Œuvres*.

1572 R, first four books of unfinished epic *La Franciade*. Fourth edition of R, *Œuvres*. St Bartholomew's Day Massacre of Huguenots in Paris.

1573 Philippe Desportes, *Premières Œuvres*.

1574 Death of Charles IX, accession of Henri III, end of royal favour for R.

1575 Tasso, *Gerusalemme Liberata*.

1577 Agrippa d'Aubigné begins Protestant epic, *Les Tragiques*.

1578 R seldom present at court; fifth edition of his *Œuvres* includes *Sur la mort de Marie* and *Sonnets pour Hélène*. Guillaume Du Bartas, *La Semaine*.

1579 Sidney writes *Defence of Poetry*; Spenser, *The Shepheardes Calendar*.

1580 Montaigne, books 1 and 2 of *Essais*.

1581 Sidney works on *Arcadia*.

1582 Sidney writes *Astrophil and Stella*.

1584 Sixth edition of R, *Œuvres*, now divided into seven sections. Du Bartas, *La Seconde Semaine*.

1585 Death of Ronsard at priory of Saint-Cosme near Tours.

1587 Seventh edition of R, *Œuvres*; biography of R by Claude Binet.

SELECTED POEMS

Joachim Du Bellay

L'Olive

1 (5)

C'était la nuit* que la divinité
   Du plus haut ciel en terre se rendit
   Quand dessus moi Amour son arc tendit
   Et me fit serf de sa grand' déité.
Ni le saint lieu de telle cruauté,   5
   Ni le temps même assez me défendit :
   Le coup au cœur par les yeux descendit
   Trop attentifs à cette grand' beauté.
Je pensais bien que l'archer eût visé
   À tous les deux, et qu'un même lien   10
   Nous dût ensemble également conjoindre.
Mais comme aveugle, enfant, mal avisé,
   Vous a laissée (hélas) qui étiez bien
   La plus grand' proie, et a choisi la moindre.

2 (26)

La nuit m'est courte, et le jour trop me dure,
   Je fuis l'amour, et le suis à la trace,
   Cruel me suis, et requiers votre grâce,
   Je prends plaisir au tourment que j'endure.
Je vois mon bien, et mon mal je procure,*   5
   Désir m'enflamme, et crainte me rend glace,
   Je veux courir, et jamais ne déplace,
   L'obscur m'est clair, et la lumière obscure.
Vôtre je suis et ne puis être mien,
   Mon corps est libre, et d'un étroit lien   10
   Je sens mon cœur en prison retenu.
Obtenir veux, et ne puis requérir,
   Ainsi me blesse, et ne me veut guérir
   Ce vieil enfant, aveugle archer, et nu.

3 (113)

Si notre vie est moins qu'une journée
   En l'éternel, si l'an qui fait le tour
   Chasse nos jours sans espoir de retour,

The Olive

1 (5)

It was the night when the divinity
    Descended from high heaven to earth below
    When Love came over me and bent his bow,
    Enslaving me to his grand deity.
The holy place barred not such cruelty,   5
    Nor did the time protect me from the blow
    That entered through my ravished eyes to go
    And strike my heart, transfixed with that great beauty.
I truly thought the archer would take aim
    At both of us, and that the very same   10
    Sharp wound he makes would bind us close together;
But that blind boy, careless as children are,
    Left you untouched, alas, although you were
    The greater prey, and chose to shoot the lesser.

2 (26)

The day's too long for me, the night is short,
    I flee from love and follow in his trace;
    Self-punishing, I come to you for grace,
    And I enjoy the torments that I sought.
I see my good, yet ill is what I court;   5
    Though passion burns, fear turns me into ice;
    I long to flee, yet will I not change place;
    The light is dark to me and darkness light.
Since I am yours, I must not be my own;
    My body's free, yet I'm condemned to groan   10
    Under a chain that keeps my heart in jail.
I cannot ask for what I long to gain;
    Thus he who gave the wound won't heal the pain:
    This agèd child, blind archer, naked fool.

3 (113)

If our whole life be less than one short day
    In time eternal, if each turning year
    Takes in its course the days that come no more,

Si périssable est toute chose née,
Que songes-tu, mon âme emprisonnée ? 5
  Pourquoi te plaît l'obscur de notre jour,
  Si pour voler en un plus clair séjour
  Tu as au dos l'aile bien empannée ?
Là, est le bien que tout esprit désire,
  Là, le repos où tout le monde aspire, 10
  Là, est l'amour, là le plaisir encore.
Là, ô mon âme, au plus haut ciel guidée,
  Tu y pourras reconnaître l'Idée*
  De la beauté qu'en ce monde j'adore.

Les Regrets

4 A SON LIVRE

Mon Livre (et je ne suis sur ton aise envieux)*
  Tu t'en iras sans moi voir la cour de mon Prince.
  Hé chétif que je suis, combien en gré je prinsse,
  Qu'un heur pareil au tien fût permis à mes yeux !
Là si quelqu'un vers toi se montre gracieux, 5
  Souhaite-lui qu'il vive heureux en sa province :
  Mais si quelque malin obliquement te pince,
  Souhaite-lui tes pleurs, et mon mal ennuyeux.
Souhaite-lui encor qu'il fasse un long voyage,
  Et bien qu'il ait de vue éloigné son ménage, 10
  Que son cœur, où qu'il voise, y soit toujours présent :
Souhaite qu'il vieillisse en longue servitude,
  Qu'il n'éprouve à la fin que toute ingratitude,
  Et qu'on mange son bien pendant qu'il est absent.

5 (1)

Je ne veux point fouiller au sein de la nature,
  Je ne veux point chercher l'esprit de l'univers,
  Je ne veux point sonder les abîmes couverts,
  Ni desseigner du ciel la belle architecture.*
Je ne peins mes tableaux de si riche peinture, 5
  Et si hauts arguments ne recherche à mes vers :

If all that's born is destined to decay,
Why do you love the darkness of our day,   5
    My dreaming soul, imprisoned as you are,
    When to a brighter dwelling you might soar
    With such wide wings to bear you far away?
There is the good that every mind desires,
    There is the rest to which the world aspires,   10
    There is true love and uncorrupted mirth.
There, O my soul, in heaven's highest sphere,
    You will both see and know the pure Idea
    Of that one beauty I adore on earth.

The Regrets

4 TO HIS BOOK

My Book (I don't begrudge you this success),
    You're off to court alone to see my Prince.
    Poor me, I'd thank my stars if some good chance
    Could let my eyes share such great happiness!
If a man shows you courtesy and grace,   5
    Wish him long years of life at home in France;
    But if he acts with sly malevolence
    Wish him your tears and my ingrained distress.
Then you should wish him a long journey too,
    And that his home, however far from view,   10
    Be sadly present in his heart each day;
And that he should grow old in servitude,
    Find in the end only ingratitude,
    His goods devoured while he was away.

5 (1)

I don't go probing nature for what's hidden
    Or seek the spirit of the universe;
    I don't attempt to sound the sea's abyss
    Or plot the wondrous structure of the heavens.
I don't paint pictures in that splendid fashion,   5
    Exalted themes don't figure in my verse;

Mais suivant de ce lieu les accidents divers,
Soit de bien, soit de mal, j'écris à l'aventure.
Je me plains à mes vers, si j'ai quelque regret,
Je me ris avec eux, je leur dis mon secret,   10
Comme étant de mon cœur les plus sûrs secrétaires.
Aussi ne veux-je tant les pigner et friser,
Et de plus braves noms ne les veux déguiser,
Que de papiers journaux, ou bien de commentaires.

6 (2)

Un plus savant que moi (Paschal) ira songer
Aveques l'Ascréan dessus la double cime :
Et pour être de ceux dont on fait plus d'estime,
Dedans l'onde au cheval tout nu s'ira plonger.
Quant à moi, je ne veux pour un vers allonger,   5
M'accourcir le cerveau : ni pour polir ma rime,
Me consumer l'esprit d'une songneuse lime,
Frapper dessus ma table, ou mes ongles ronger.
Aussi veux-je (Paschal) que ce que je compose
Soit une prose en rime, ou une rime en prose,   10
Et ne veux pour cela le laurier mériter.
Et peut-être que tel se pense bien habile,
Qui trouvant de mes vers la rime si facile,
En vain travaillera, me voulant imiter.*

7 (4)

Je ne veux feuilleter les exemplaires Grecs.
Je ne veux retracer les beaux traits d'un Horace,
Et moins veux-je imiter d'un Pétrarque la grâce,
Ou la voix d'un Ronsard, pour chanter mes regrets.
Ceux qui sont de Phébus vrais poètes sacrés,   5
Animeront leurs vers d'une plus grand' audace :
Moi, qui suis agité d'une fureur plus basse,
Je n'entre si avant en si profonds secrets.
Je me contenterai de simplement écrire
Ce que la passion seulement me fait dire,   10
Sans rechercher ailleurs plus graves arguments.
Aussi n'ai-je entrepris d'imiter en ce livre

But in this place, for better or for worse,
   I find my subjects, and I write what's given.
If things go wrong, I grumble in these lines,
   I joke with them, confide what's on my mind   10
   As if to private secretaries of the heart.
So I won't tart them up with paint or powder
   Or veil their plainness with a name that's prouder
   Than daily records jotted down by clerks.

6 (2)

A wiser man than I, Paschal, will dream
   With Hesiod on Parnassus' double hill,
   And, seeking fame, hope to obtain his fill
   By diving naked in the Hippocrene.
That's not the way I write, for I don't mean   5
   To polish rhymes, wasting my wit as file,
   Shrinking my brain to lengthen verses while
   I gnaw my nails, pound tables, make a scene.
And so, Paschal, here is what I propose:
   Verses like prose in rhyme or rhyme in prose.   10
   For this I don't expect a laurel crown;
But that, perhaps, someone who thinks he's smart,
   Judging my rhymes an easy kind of art,
   Will work to copy me, and strive in vain.

7 (4)

I don't ape models that the Greeks have set
   Or seek in Horace lines I might retrace;
   Still less I care to copy Petrarch's grace
   Or Ronsard's voice in singing my regrets.
True poets sacred to Apollo get   5
   The quickening gift that makes a bolder race;
   My raving occupies a humbler place
   And there are secrets I won't penetrate.
I'm satisfied with simply writing down
   What passion makes me say and that alone,   10
   Not running elsewhere after graver themes.
For in this book I have not shared the boast

Ceux qui par leurs écrits se vantent de revivre,
Et se tirer tout vifs dehors des monuments.*

8 (6)

Las, où est maintenant ce mépris de Fortune ?
    Où est ce cœur vainqueur de toute adversité,
    Cet honnête désir de l'immortalité,
    Et cette honnête flamme au peuple non commune ?
Où sont ces doux plaisirs qu'au soir sous la nuit brune   5
    Les Muses me donnaient, alors qu'en liberté
    Dessus le vert tapis d'un rivage écarté
    Je les menais danser aux rayons de la Lune ?
Maintenant la Fortune est maîtresse de moi,
    Et mon cœur qui soulait être maître de soi,   10
    Est serf de mille maux et regrets qui m'ennuient.
De la postérité je n'ai plus de souci,
    Cette divine ardeur, je ne l'ai plus aussi,
    Et les Muses de moi, comme étranges, s'enfuient.

9 (9)

France, mère des arts, des armes, et des lois,*
    Tu m'as nourri du lait de ta mamelle :
    Ores, comme un agneau qui sa nourrice appelle,
    Je remplis de ton nom les antres et les bois.
Si tu m'as pour enfant avoué quelquefois,   5
    Que ne me réponds-tu maintenant, ô cruelle ?
    France, France, réponds à ma triste querelle :
    Mais nul, sinon Écho, ne répond à ma voix.
Entre les loups cruels j'erre parmi la plaine,
    Je sens venir l'hiver, de qui la froide haleine   10
    D'une tremblante horreur fait hérisser ma peau.
Las, tes autres agneaux n'ont faute de pâture,
    Ils ne craignent le loup, le vent, ni la froidure :
    Si ne suis-je pourtant le pire du troppeau.

10 (13)

Maintenant je pardonne à la douce fureur,
    Qui m'a fait consumer le meilleur de mon âge,
    Sans tirer autre fruit de mon ingrat ouvrage,
    Que le vain passe-temps d'une si longue erreur.*

Of those who think their writings will at last
Give them new life, fresh-risen from their tombs.

8 (6)

Alas, where's that contempt for Fortune now,
    The heart that conquered all adversity,
    The worthy quest for immortality,
    That worthy flame the masses seldom know?
Where did the sweet nocturnal pleasures go   5
    That the nine Muses gave when, young and free,
    I led their dance on the green carpet by
    Some lonely shore in Moonlight's lambent glow?
Now Fortune governs me; my subject heart,
    No longer the sole master of its fate,   10
    Is slave to sharp regrets and nagging pain.
I've lost all interest in posterity,
    That godlike fury's gone; the Muses see
    My state, and then, like strangers, run away.

9 (9)

Mother of arts, of arms, and of the laws,
    France, for so long you fed me at your breast;
    Now, as a lamb bleats to his nurse, distressed,
    I call your name to woods and savage lairs.
If in the past you counted me as yours,   5
    Where is your answer now when I protest?
    France, cruel France, answer my sad request.
    But only Echo answers to my voice.
A prey for ravening wolves, I roam the plain,
    Winter's cold breath sends shivers down my spine,   10
    Leaving me fearful, shuddering, and sick.
Your other lambs are fed within the fold,
    They have no fear of wolves or wind or cold;
    Yet I am not the worst in all the flock.

10 (13)

Now I forgive the sweet and mad endeavour
    That made me waste the best years of my life,
    A thankless work, fruitless save for the brief
    Joys of a pastime that was constant error.

Maintenant je pardonne à ce plaisant labeur.   5
    Puisque seul il endort le souci qui m'outrage,
    Et puisque seul il fait qu'au milieu de l'orage
    Ainsi qu'auparavant je ne tremble de peur.
Si les vers ont été l'abus de ma jeunesse,
    Les vers seront aussi l'appui de ma vieillesse,   10
    S'ils furent ma folie, ils seront ma raison,
S'ils furent ma blessure, ils seront mon Achille,
    S'ils furent mon venin, le scorpion* utile,
    Qui sera de mon mal la seule guérison.

11 (15)

Panjas, veux-tu savoir quels sont mes passe-temps ?
    Je songe au lendemain, j'ai soin de la dépense,
    Qui se fait chaque jour, et si faut que je pense
    A rendre sans argent cent créditeurs contents :
Je vais, je viens, je cours, je ne perds point le temps,   5
    Je courtise un banquier, je prends argent d'avance,
    Quand j'ai dépêché l'un, un autre recommence,
    Et ne fais pas le quart de ce que je prétends.
Qui me présente un compte, une lettre, un mémoire,
    Qui me dit que demain est jour de consistoire,   10
    Qui me rompt le cerveau de cent propos divers :
Qui se plaint, qui se deut, qui murmure, qui crie,
    Aveques tout cela, dis (Panjas) je te prie,
    Ne t'ébahis-tu point comment je fais des vers ?

12 (21)

Comte,* qui ne fis onc compte de la grandeur,
    Ton Dubellay n'est plus. Ce n'est plus qu'une souche
    Qui dessus un ruisseau d'un dos courbé se couche,
    Et n'a plus rien de vif, qu'un petit de verdeur.
Si j'écris quelquefois, je n'écris point d'ardeur,   5
    J'écris naïvement tout ce qu'au cœur me touche,
    Soit de bien, soit de mal, comme il vient à la bouche.
    En un style aussi lent, que lente est ma froideur.
Vous autres cependant peintres de la nature,*
    Dont l'art n'est pas enclos dans une portraiture,   10

Now I forgive what seems a pleasant labour,   5
   For that alone consoles my care and grief;
   Alone, amid the storm, it brings relief
   And when I quake with fear dissolves the terror.
If it was verse that led my youth astray,
   Verse in old age will be my strongest stay;   10
   What once was folly will be reason now.
What was my wound will be Achilles' spear,
   Past poison be the healing scorpion where
   My sickness finds the only cure I know.

11 (15)

You'd like to know, Panjas, how I spend my time?
   I think about tomorrow and its expense,
   How, without cash in hand, I can finance
   A hundred debts contracted in my name.
I go, I come, I run, I waste no time,   5
   I court a banker for a small advance;
   One debtor fixed, another tries his chance;
   I don't pay out a quarter of their claims.
Now here's a letter, an account, a bill;
   Tomorrow's the consistory with still   10
   More news to cause a headache, if not worse.
Here there's a clamour—protests, shouts, and cries;
   Tell me, my Panjas, are you not surprised
   At how, despite all that, I'm writing verse?

12 (21)

Count, who takes no account of what's called great,
   Hear that your Du Bellay's no more; he's like
   A barren stump leaning above a brook
   With nothing living but a small green shoot.
If sometimes I still write, it's without heat,   5
   Whatever strikes my heart I simply take
   For good or ill and write the way I speak,
   As slowly as befits my chilly state.
You painters of true nature's pure ideal,
   Who won't let portraiture restrict your art,   10

Contrefaites des vieux les ouvrages plus beaux.
Quant à moi je n'aspire à si haute louange,
 Et ne sont mes portraits auprès de vos tableaux
 Non plus qu'est un Janet auprès d'un Michel-Ange.*

13 (26)

Si celui qui s'apprête à faire un long voyage,
 Doit croire cestuy-là qui a jà voyagé,
 Et qui des flots marins longuement outragé,
 Tout moite et dégouttant* s'est sauvé du naufrage,
Tu me croiras (Ronsard) bien que tu sois plus sage,   5
 Et quelque peu encor (ce crois-je) plus âgé,*
 Puisque j'ai devant toi en cette mer nagé,
 Et que déjà ma nef découvre le rivage.
Donques je t'avertis, que cette mer Romaine,
 De dangereux écueils et de bancs toute pleine,   10
 Cache mille périls, et qu'ici bien souvent
Trompé du chant pipeur des monstres de Sicile
 Pour Charybde éviter tu tomberas en Scylle,
 Si tu ne sais nager d'une voile à tout vent.

14 (27)

Ce n'est ambition, ni le soin d'acquérir,
 Qui m'a fait délaisser ma rive paternelle,
 Pour voir ces monts couverts d'une neige éternelle,
 Et par mille dangers ma fortune quérir.
Le vrai honneur qui n'est coutumier de périr,   5
 Et la vraie vertu qui seule est immortelle,
 Ont comblé mes désirs d'une abondance telle
 Qu'un plus grand bien aux dieux je ne veux requérir.
L'honnête servitude, où mon devoir me lie,
 M'a fait passer les monts de France en Italie,   10
 Et demeurer trois ans sur ce bord étranger,
Où je vis languissant. Ce seul devoir encore
 Me peut faire changer France à l'Inde et au More,
 Et le ciel à l'enfer me peut faire changer.

15 (31)

Heureux qui,* comme Ulysse, a fait un beau voyage,
 Ou comme cestuy-là qui conquit la toison,

You copy the best works of long ago.
To such high praise I can make no appeal;
    Beside your work my portraits play the part
    Of Janet next to Michelangelo.

13 (26)

If there's a long hard journey he must make,
    A man should heed someone who's gone that way,
    And who, half drowned by waves and drenched with spray,
    Has dragged his dripping body from the wreck;
So you'll believe me, Ronsard, though I lack   5
    Your wisdom (and a few more years, I'd say)
    Because before you I have sailed this sea
    And glimpse the shore now from my leaking bark.
Be warned by me: this Roman sea is full
    Of menacing reefs and sandbanks that conceal   10
    A thousand dangers: often you will find,
After the sirens' song, because you dread
    Charybdis, you'll be Scylla's prey instead,
    Unless you've learned to sail with every wind.

14 (27)

It's not ambition, neither was it greed
    That made me leave my fathers' home and go
    To see those peaks clad in eternal snow
    And seek my fortune on that dangerous road.
True honour dies not; only virtue leads   5
    Truly to immortality, we know;
    They have fulfilled all my desires, so
    I do not ask the gods some greater good.
In honour's service duty ordered me
    To cross the Alps from France to Italy,   10
    An alien shore where, for a three-year spell,
I've lived and pined. Duty alone could make
    Me move from France to India or take
    An African trip, exchanging heaven for hell.

15 (31)

Happy the man who, with his journey done,
    Like Ulysses or him of the fleece, comes home

Et puis est retourné, plein d'usage et raison,
   Vivre entre ses parents le reste de son âge !
Quand reverrai-je, hélas, de mon petit village   5
   Fumer la cheminée,* et en quelle saison,
   Reverrai-je le clos de ma pauvre maison,
   Qui m'est une province, et beaucoup d'avantage ?
Plus me plaît le séjour qu'ont bâti mes aïeux,
   Que des palais Romains le front audacieux,   10
   Plus que le marbre dur me plaît l'ardoise fine :
Plus mon Loire Gaulois que le Tibre Latin,
   Plus mon petit Liré, que le mont Palatin,
   Et plus que l'air marin la douceur Angevine.

16 (32)

Je me ferai savant en la philosophie,*
   En la mathématique, et médecine aussi,
   Je me ferai légiste, et d'un plus haut souci
   Apprendrai les secrets de la théologie :
Du luth et du pinceau j'ébatterai ma vie,   5
   De l'escrime et du bal. Je discourais ainsi,
   Et me vantais en moi d'apprendre tout ceci,
   Quand je changeai la France au séjour d'Italie.
O beaux discours humains ! je suis venu si loin,
   Pour m'enrichir d'ennui, de vieillesse, et de soin,   10
   Et perdre en voyageant le meilleur de mon âge.
Ainsi le marinier souvent pour tout trésor
   Rapporte des harengs en lieu de lingots d'or,
   Ayant fait, comme moi, un malheureux voyage.

17 (33)

Que ferai-je, Morel ? dis-moi, si tu l'entends,
   Ferai-je encor ici plus longue demeurance,
   Ou si j'irai revoir les campagnes de France,
   Quand les neiges fondront au soleil du printemps ?
Si je demeure ici, hélas, je perds mon temps   5
   A me repaître en vain d'une longue espérance,
   Et si je veux ailleurs fonder mon assurance,
   Je fraude mon labeur du loyer que j'attends.

Well-stocked with wisdom and with seasoned calm
To live the remaining years with his kith and kin!
When shall I see the smoking chimney in 5
My little village? What will be the time
Of year when I see my humble house and farm,
A province and much more to me alone?
Dearer to me than some proud Roman wall
Is the grange my forebears built; fine slates are all 10
More pleasing than hard blocks of marble are,
Dearer than Tiber is my Gallic Loire,
Dearer than Palatine's Mount my Liré hill,
And dearer than sea-breeze soft Angevin air.

16 (32)

'I shall gain knowledge of philosophy,
Of mathematics, medicine as well,
I'll study law and, mounting higher still,
Learn all the secrets of theology.
With lute and brush I'll render life more gay, 5
With fencing, dancing.' So I told myself
And boasted loudly how I'd learn it all
When I exchanged our France for Italy.
Fine speeches that men make! I came so far
For riches of old age, trouble, and care, 10
While constant travelling consumed my prime.
Often the mariner, in his vessel's hold,
Brings herrings back instead of bars of gold
When he has made a fruitless voyage like mine.

17 (33)

Tell me, Morel, tell me what should I do?
Stay on in Rome or think of other plans,
Like going home to the fair fields of France
When spring's warm sunshine melts the winter's snow.
To stay would be a waste of time, I know, 5
Feeding on some vain hope of recompense;
Yet if I go elsewhere to try my chance,
I lose my labour, cheated of its due.

Mais faut-il vivre ainsi d'une espérance vaine ?
    Mais faut-il perdre ainsi bien trois ans de ma peine ?   10
    Je ne bougerais donc. Non, non, je m'en irai.
Je demeurrai pourtant, si tu le me conseilles.
    Hélas (mon cher Morel) dis-moi que je ferai,
    Car je tiens, comme on dit, le loup par les oreilles.*

18 (41)

N'étant de mes ennuis la fortune assouvie,
    Afin que je devinsse à moi-même odieux,
    M'ôta de mes amis celui que j'aimais mieux,*
    Et sans qui je n'avais de vivre nulle envie.
Donc l'éternelle nuit à ta clarté ravie,   5
    Et je ne t'ai suivi parmi les obscurs lieux ?
    Toi qui m'as plus aimé que ta vie et tes yeux,
    Toi, que j'ai plus aimé que mes yeux et ma vie.
Hélas, cher compagnon, que ne puis-je être encor
    Le frère de Pollux, toi celui de Castor,   10
    Puisque notre amitié fut plus que fraternelle ?
Reçois donques ces pleurs pour gage de ma foi,
    Et ces vers qui rendront, si je ne me déçois,
    De si rare amitié la mémoire éternelle.

19 (42)

C'est ores, mon Vineus, mon cher Vineus, c'est ore
    Que de tous les chétifs le plus chétif je suis,
    Et que ce que j'étais plus être je ne puis,
    Ayant perdu mon temps, et ma jeunesse encore.
La pauvreté me suit, le souci me dévore,   5
    Tristes sont mes jours, et plus tristes les nuits,
    O que je suis comblé de regrets, et d'ennuis !
    Plût à Dieu que je fusse un Pasquin ou Marphore.
Je n'aurais sentiment du malheur qui me point,
    Ma plume serait libre, et si ne craindrais point   10
    Qu'un plus grand contre moi pût exercer son ire.
Assure-toi Vineus que celui seul est Roi,
    À qui même les Rois ne peuvent donner loi,
    Et qui peut d'un chacun à son plaisir écrire.

But must I live like this when hope is vain?
    But must I lose what three years' toil should gain? 10
    So I won't budge. No! I'll get out of here,
Or else I'll stay if that's what you advise.
    Tell me, Morel, for as the proverb says,
    I stand in doubt, holding a wolf by the ears.

18 (41)

Fate had not done enough to make me grieve:
    To leave me with a self that I despise
    He took the friend that I most loved and prized
And without whom I have no wish to live.
Could endless night consume the light you give 5
    And I not go into the dark likewise?
    You who loved me more than your life and eyes
As I loved you more than my eyes and life.
Alas, my dear old friend, are we no longer
    Castor and Pollux, though our tie was stronger 10
    Than brotherly love could ever hope to be?
Accept these faithful tears as pledges which
    Shall in this verse endure to be of such
    Rare friendship the eternal memory.

19 (42)

It's now, dear Vineus, now that you can tell
    Who is the saddest wretch; it must be me;
    For I am not the man you used to see,
My wasted youth has gone for good and all.
My days are sad, my nights are sadder still, 5
    Consumed by care and dogged by poverty;
    With such regrets, how happy I would be
If I could be a Pasquin by God's will.
I would not feel the pangs that pierce me here;
    My pen would be quite free, I'd have no fear 10
    Of suffering the wrath of some great man.
He's a true King, my Vineus, whose hand
    Is never subject to a King's command,
    Who writes just what he thinks of anyone.

20 (49)

Si après quarante ans de fidèle service,
    Que celui que je sers* a fait en divers lieux,
    Employant, libéral, tout son plus et son mieux
    Aux affaires qui sont de plus digne exercice,
D'un haineux étranger* l'envieuse malice   5
    Exerce contre lui son courage odieux,
    Et sans avoir souci des hommes ni des dieux,
    Oppose à la vertu l'ignorance et le vice,
Me dois-je tormenter, moi qui suis moins que rien,
    Si par quelqu'un (peut-être) envieux de mon bien   10
    Je ne trouve à mon gré la faveur opportune ?
Je me console donc, et en pareille mer,
    Voyant mon cher Seigneur au danger d'abîmer,
    Il me plaît de courir une même fortune.

21 (53)

Vivons (Gordes)* vivons, vivons, et pour le bruit
    Des vieillards ne laissons à faire bonne chère :
    Vivons, puisque la vie est si courte et si chère,
    Et que même les Rois n'en ont que l'usufruit.
Le jour s'éteint au soir, et au matin reluit,   5
    Et les saisons refont leur course coutumière :
    Mais quand l'homme a perdu cette douce lumière,
    La mort lui fait dormir une éternelle nuit.
Donc imiterons-nous le vivre d'une bête ?
    Non, mais devers le ciel levant toujours la tête,   10
    Goûterons quelquefois la douceur du plaisir.
Celui vraiment est fol, qui changeant l'assurance
    Du bien qui est présent en douteuse espérance,
    Veut toujours contredire à son propre désir.

22 (59)

Tu ne me vois jamais (Pierre) que tu ne die
    Que j'étudie trop, que je fasse l'amour,
    Et que d'avoir toujours ces livres à l'entour,
    Rend les yeux éblouis, et la tête élourdie.
Mais tu ne l'entends pas: car cette maladie   5

20 (49)

The man I serve has given faithful service
   For forty years wherever there was need,
   Spending his strength, doing the best he could
   In matters that deserved such exercise:
If, after this, some hateful foreigner's malice   5
   Is exercised against him, with no heed
   For how it might be judged by man or God,
   Assaulting worth with ignorance and vice,
Why should I fret? Why should I care at all,
   If, because envy works for my downfall,   10
   I fail to gain the favour that I sought?
Some comfort's there; and seeing my dear Master
   Whelmed in the same rough sea and going under,
   I choose to run the risk and share his fate.

21 (53)

Let's live, Gordès, let's live; let not the spite
   Of crotchety old men spoil our good cheer;
   Let's live since life is short, so short and dear
   That even Kings have only borrowing rights.
Day dies each evening, morning brings the light;   5
   Seasons repeat their course with every year,
   But once man loses that sweet lucent air
   Death packs him off to sleep in endless night.
Shall we then live like beasts? Not so, but even
   As we raise pious heads to gaze on heaven,   10
   We still can taste how sweet are earthly pleasures.
The man's a fool who's ready to give up
   A good that's here and now for some vague hope,
   Denying all his natural desires.

22 (59)

Pierre, you keep insisting I'd be wise
   To study less and to make love instead;
   That poring over all these books has led
   To throbbing headaches and these bleary eyes.
You're wrong. It's not from reading that arise   5

Ne me vient du trop lire, ou du trop long séjour,
    Ains de voir le bureau, qui se tient chacun jour :
    C'est, Pierre mon ami, le livre où j'étudie.
Ne m'en parle donc plus, autant que tu as cher
    De me donner plaisir, et de ne me fâcher :   10
    Mais bien en cependant que d'une main habile
Tu me laves la barbe, et me tonds les cheveux,
    Pour me désennuyer, conte-moi si tu veux
    Des nouvelles du Pape, et du bruit de la ville.

23 (65)

Tu ne crains la fureur de ma plume animée,
    Pensant que je n'ai rien à dire contre toi,
    Sinon ce que ta rage a vomi contre moi,
    Grinçant comme un mâtin la dent envenimée.
Tu crois que je n'en sais que par la renommée,   5
    Et que quand j'aurai dit que tu n'as point de foi,
    Que tu es affronteur, que tu es traître au Roi,
    Que j'aurais contre toi ma force consommée.
Tu penses que je n'ai rien de quoi me venger,
    Sinon que tu n'es fait que pour boire et manger :   10
    Mais j'ai bien quelque chose encore plus mordante,
Et quoi ? L'amour d'Orphée?* Et que tu ne sus onc
    Que c'est de croire en Dieu ? Non. Quel vice est-ce donc ?
    C'est, pour le faire court, que tu es un pedante.

24 (68)

Je hais du Florentin l'usurière avarice,
    Je hais du fol Siennois le sens mal arrêté,
    Je hais du Genevois la rare vérité,
    Et du Vénitien la trop caute malice :
Je hais le Ferrarais pour je ne sais quel vice,   5
    Je hais tous les Lombards pour l'infidélité,
    Le fier Napolitain pour sa grand' vanité
    Et le poltron Romain pour son peu d'exercice :
Je hais l'Anglais mutin, et le brave Écossais,
    Le traître Bourguignon, et l'indiscret Français,   10
    Le superbe Espagnol, et l'ivrogne Thudesque :
Bref, je hais quelque vice en chaque nation,

Such maladies, nor that I may have stayed
Too long in Rome: this desk all day has made
Me ill, Pierre, and not the books I prize.
So if you really want to see me happy,
Just drop the subject since it makes me angry: 10
And while your agile fingers fuss around
My face, cutting my hair, washing my beard,
Regale me with some gossip that you've heard,
The Pope's affairs and what's the talk in town.

23 (65)

So you don't fear the fury of my pen,
Thinking there's nothing I can say to you,
Unless it's like the poison that you spew,
A rabid dog still snarling in his den.
You think that I'll say nothing but what men   5
Have said before: you're one whose word's untrue,
False to the king, traitor in all you do:
And with those shots, my powder will be spent.
Vengeance has nothing more to use, you think,
Except your slavery to food and drink;   10
But I've got something with a bit more bite.
What can it be? You're gay like Orpheus?
You don't believe in God? Something much worse:
That you're a pedant, that's the crowning vice.

24 (68)

I hate the Florentine's greed and usury,
I hate the thick slow-witted Sienese,
I hate the lying tongues of Genoese
And cold Venetian ways, hostile and sly.
I hate Ferrara folk (don't ask me why)   5
And Lombards who break any oath they please,
Fat lazy Romans, lolling at their ease,
Neapolitans puffed up with vanity.
I hate the rowdy English and the Scotch,
Burgundian traitors, French who talk too much,   10
The haughty Spaniard and the drunken German.
In short, I hate some vice in every nation,

Je hais moi-même encor mon imperfection.
Mais je hais par sur tout un savoir pédantesque.

25 (74)

Tu dis que Dubellay tient réputation,
    Et que de ses amis il ne tient plus de compte :
    Si ne suis-je Seigneur, Prince, Marquis, ou Comte,
    Et n'ai changé d'état ni de condition.
Jusqu'ici je ne sais que c'est d'ambition,   5
    Et pour ne me voir grand ne rougis point de honte,
    Aussi ma qualité ne baisse ni ne monte,
    Car je ne suis sujet qu'à ma complexion.
Je ne sais comme il faut entretenir son maître,
    Comme il faut courtiser, et moins quel il faut être   10
    Pour vivre entre les grands, comme on vit aujourd'hui.
J'honore tout le monde, et ne fâche personne,
    Qui me donne un salut, quatre je lui en donne,
    Qui ne fait cas de moi je ne fais cas de lui.

26 (80)

Si je monte au Palais, je n'y trouve qu'orgueil,
    Que vice déguisé, qu'une cérimonie,
    Qu'un bruit de tabourins, qu'une étrange harmonie,
    Et de rouge habits un superbe appareil :
Si je descends en banque, un amas et recueil   5
    De nouvelles je treuve, une usure infinie,
    De riches Florentins une troppe bannie,
    Et de pauvres Siennois* un lamentable deuil :
Si je vais plus avant, quelque part où j'arrive,
    Je treuve de Vénus la grand' bande lascive   10
    Dressant de tous côtés mille appas amoureux :
Si je passe plus outre, et de la Rome neuve
    Entre en la vieille Rome, adonques je ne treuve
    Que de vieux monuments un grand monceau pierreux.

27 (81)

Il fait bon voir (Paschal) un conclave serré,
    Et l'une chambre à l'autre également voisine
    D'antichambre servir, de salle, et de cuisine,

I hate myself for all my imperfection,
But most of all I hate pedantic learning.

25 (74)

You say that Du Bellay counts on promotion
    And that he holds his friends of no account;
    Yet I am not a Lord, a Prince, a Count,
    And neither have I changed my rank or station.
So far I've been a stranger to ambition,   5
    Not shame-faced that I've no great name to flaunt,
    And so my status doesn't fall or mount,
    Being subject only to my disposition.
I don't know how to butter up a master
    Or act in courtly fashion; I'm no better   10
    At copying the lifestyle of great men.
Polite to everyone, I give no trouble;
    All courteous greetings I return redoubled.
    Those who ignore me I ignore in turn.

26 (80)

If I frequent the Vatican, I see pride
    And secret vice disguised by ceremony,
    The martial noise of drums, strange harmony,
    And scarlet prelates, splendidly arrayed.
If the Exchange, it's news on every side,   5
    The latest gossip, endless usury,
    Rich Florentines, a banished company,
    And poor types from Siena, teary-eyed.
If I go further on, no matter where,
    I see the girls of Venus ready there,   10
    Dressed to display the thousand charms they own.
And if, at last, I leave new Rome behind
    And seek the old, there's nothing else to find
    But monuments reduced to heaps of stone.

27 (81)

It's fun to see a crowded conclave where
    No room is different from its next-door neighbour;
    Each serves as kitchen, hall, and antechamber

En un petit recoin de dix pieds en carré:*
Il fait bon voir autour du palais emmuré,   5
    Et briguer là-dedans cette troppe divine,
    L'un par ambition, l'autre par bonne mine,
    Et par dépit de l'un, être l'autre adoré :
Il fait bon voir dehors toute la ville en armes,
    Crier le Pape est fait,* donner de faux alarmes,   10
    Saccager un palais : mais plus que tout cela
Fait bon voir, qui de l'un, qui de l'autre se vante,
    Qui met pour cestui-ci, qui met pour cestui-là,
    Et pour moins d'un écu dix Cardinaux en vente.

28 (82)

Veux-tu savoir (Duthier) quelle chose c'est Rome ?
    Rome est de tout le monde un public échafaud,
    Une scène, un théâtre, auquel rien ne défaut
    De ce qui peut tomber ès actions de l'homme.
Ici se voit le jeu de la Fortune, et comme   5
    Sa main nous fait tourner ores bas, ores haut :
    Ici chacun se montre, et ne peut, tant soit caut,
    Faire que tel qu'il est, le peuple ne le nomme.
Ici du faux et vrai la messagère court,
    Ici les courtisans font l'amour et la cour,   10
    Ici l'ambition, et la finesse abonde :
Ici la liberté fait l'humble audacieux
    Ici l'oisiveté rend le bon vicieux,
    Ici le vil faquin discourt des faits du monde.

29 (83)

Ne pense (Robertet) que cette Rome-ci
    Soit cette Rome-là, qui te soulait tant plaire,
    On n'y fait plus crédit, comme l'on soulait faire,
    On n'y fait plus l'amour, comme on soulait aussi.
La paix, et le bon temps ne règnent plus ici,   5
    La musique et le bal sont contraints de s'y taire,
    L'air y est corrompu, Mars y est ordinaire,
    Ordinaire la faim, la peine, et le souci.
L'artisan débauché y ferme sa boutique,
    L'ocieux avocat y laisse sa pratique,   10

Crammed in a cell that measures ten-feet square.
It's fun to see that holy gang in there,   5
   Walled up and hatching plots against each other;
   One gets adored because they hate another;
   Some hide their game, some make it all too clear.
Outside it's fun to see the town in arms;
   They shout 'We've got a Pope!', spread false alarms,   10
   Or sack a palace; but the best of any
Such fun is hearing what they boast about,
   Who bets on this one and who bets on that,
   And how these Cardinals are ten a penny.

28 (82)

You want to know, Duthier, what Rome is like?
   It's like the whole wide world put on display,
   A stage, a scene, theatre for that great play
   Where nothing that men do on earth can lack.
Here you can witness Fortune's game that takes   5
   Us up on high, then down the following day;
   Here people can't be fooled, they'll see and say
   Who a man is, whatever show he makes.
Here news spreads quickly, whether false or true,
   And at the court courting is what they do;   10
   Here proud ambition favours cunning snares.
Here freedom makes the lowborn dare to rise,
   Here idleness turns honest men to vice,
   And porters spout their views on world affairs.

29 (83)

Don't think Rome's still the same, dear Robertet;
   It's nothing like the Rome that pleased you once.
   They give no credit here, that's gone long since,
   And making love's a custom in decay.
Peace and the good old times have had their day;   5
   Music is silent, no one joins the dance.
   The air is foul, it reeks of violence,
   Reeks too of famine, fear, and poverty.
The craftsman without work closes his shop;
   The lawyer has no clients and gives up;   10

Et le pauvre marchand y porte le bissac :
On ne voit que soldats, et morions en tête,
   On n'oit que tabourins, et semblable tempête,
   Et Rome tous les jours n'attend qu'un autre sac.*

30 (84)

Nous ne faisons la cour aux filles de Mémoire,*
   Comme vous, qui vivez libres de passion :
   Si vous ne savez donc notre occupation,
   Ces dix vers ensuivants vous la feront notoire :
Suivre son Cardinal au Pape, au consistoire,   5
   En capelle, en visite, en congrégation,
   Et pour l'honneur d'un prince, ou d'une nation,
   De quelque ambassadeur accompagner la gloire :
Être en son rang de garde auprès de son seigneur,
   Et faire aux survenants l'accoutumé honneur,   10
   Parler du bruit qui court, faire de l'habile homme :
Se pourmener en housse, aller voir d'huis en huis
   La Marthe, ou la Victoire,* et s'engager aux Juifs :
   Voilà, mes compagnons, les passe-temps de Rome.

31 (85)

Flatter un créditeur, pour son terme allonger,
   Courtiser un banquier, donner bonne espérance,
   Ne suivre en son parler la liberté de France,
   Et pour répondre un mot, un quart d'heure y songer :
Ne gâter sa santé par trop boire et manger,   5
   Ne faire sans propos une folle dépense,
   Ne dire à tout venant tout cela que l'on pense,
   Et d'un maigre discours gouverner l'étranger :
Connaître les humeurs, connaître qui demande,
   Et d'autant que l'on a la liberté plus grande,   10
   D'autant plus se garder que l'on ne soit repris :
Vivre aveques chacun, de chacun faire compte :
   Voilà, mon cher Morel (dont je rougis de honte)
   Tout le bien qu'en trois ans à Rome j'ai appris.

32 (86)

Marcher d'un grave pas, et d'un grave sourcil,
   Et d'un grave soubris à chacun faire fête,

The merchant has an alms-bag on his back.
Nothing to see but soldiers wearing helmets,
    Nothing to hear but only drums and trumpets:
    Rome every day awaits another sack.

30 (84)

We don't go courting Memory's daughters here,
    As you do who live free from agitation,
    So if you wonder what's our occupation,
    The next ten lines will make the matter clear:
There's following your Cardinal everywhere,   5
    To Pope, consistory, or congregation,
    And, for the honour of a prince or nation,
    Waiting on some puffed-up ambassador;
Keeping one's rank in service to my lord,
    Greeting all guests with the right courteous word   10
    And with some juicy gossip to take home;
Riding in style, passing from door to door,
    Getting in debt to Jews, finding a whore:
    That's how, my friends, we pass the time in Rome.

31 (85)

To put off creditors a little longer,
    To give a banker hope that one will pay,
    Not to speak freely in the old French way,
    But think for fifteen minutes about an answer;
To see when food and drink can be a danger,   5
    Never to splash the cash, not knowing why;
    Nor speak one's mind to every passer-by,
    But keep it short when speaking to a stranger;
To know men's humours, study their desires,
    And, with the greater freedom one acquires,   10
    Be still more careful to incur no blame;
Make friends all round, but take their measure well:
    That's all the good (I blush with shame, Morel)
    That I have learned from my three years in Rome.

32 (86)

To walk with solemn step and solemn brow
    And greet all comers with a solemn smile,

Balancer tous ses mots, répondre de la tête,
Avec un *Messer non*, ou bien un *Messer sì*:
Entremêler souvent un petit, *Et così*,   5
    Et d'un *son Servitor'* contrefaire l'honnête,
    Et comme si l'on eût sa part en la conquête,
    Discourir sur Florence, et sur Naples aussi :
Seigneuriser chacun d'un baisement de main,
    Et suivant la façon du courtisan Romain,   10
    Cacher sa pauvreté d'une brave apparence :
Voilà de cette cour la plus grande vertu,
    Dont souvent mal monté, mal sain, et mal vêtu,
    Sans barbe* et sans argent on s'en retourne en France.

33 (87)

D'où vient cela (Mauny) que tant plus on s'efforce
    D'échapper hors d'ici, plus le Démon du lieu
    (Et que serait-ce donc si ce n'est quelque Dieu ?)
    Nous y tient attachés par une douce force ?
Serait-ce point d'amour cette alléchante amorce,   5
    Ou quelque autre venin, dont après avoir beu
    Nous sentons nos esprits nous laisser peu à peu,
    Comme un corps qui se perd sous une neuve écorce ?
J'ai voulu mille fois de ce lieu m'étranger,
    Mais je sens mes cheveux en feuilles se changer,   10
    Mes bras en longs rameaux, et mes pieds en racine.
Bref, je ne suis plus rien qu'un vieil tronc animé,
    Qui se plaint de se voir à ce bord transformer,
    Comme le Myrte Anglois au rivage d'Alcine.*

34 (88)

Qui choisira pour moi la racine d'Ulysse ?*
    Et qui me gardera de tomber au danger
    Qu'une Circe en pourceau ne me puisse changer,
    Pour être à tout jamais fait esclave du vice ?
Qui m'étreindra le doigt de l'anneau de Mélisse,   5
    Pour me désenchanter comme un autre Roger ?
    Et quel Mercure encor me fera déloger,
    Pour ne perdre mon temps en l'amoureux service ?

To weigh each word, nod answers all the while
    With a brief *Messer sì* or *Messer no*;
To try a little *E così* (and so)   5
    And say 'Your Servant, sir'—it goes down well;
    Discuss how Florence and great Naples fell
    As if you'd been there and were in the know;
To flatter Everyman and kiss his hand;
    To hide your growing poverty behind   10
    A splendid cloak—a very Roman stance:
These are the virtues that this court loves best,
    From which, too often, sick and badly dressed,
    Beardless and broke, a man returns to France.

33 (87)

How comes it, Mauny, that the more we try
    To flee, the more the Daemon of this place
    (And what else but a God could have such force?)
    Keeps us bound fast with its enchanting tie?
Is love perhaps the bait we're tempted by   5
    Or has new poison brought us to this pass,
    To feel our wits slowly deserting us,
    As bodies, though with skin renewed, decay?
A thousand times I've sworn I mean to leave
    This place, but feel my hair change into leaves: 10
    My arms are branches, feet are rooted here.
I'm the complaining stump of some old tree,
    Like the poor Englishman transformed to be
    A Myrtle growing on Alcina's shore.

34 (88)

Who'll get for me the root that Ulysses had
    And save me from the trap a Circe lays
    To make of me a swine who spends his days
    Wallowing ever in his vice and mud?
Who'll disenchant me as Melissa did   5
    Ruggiero with a magic ring? Who'll be
    Another Mercury and find a way
    To get me off the amorous hook for good?

Qui me fera passer sans écouter la voix
   Et la feinte douceur des monstres d'Achelois ?   10
   Qui chassera de moi ces Harpies friandes ?
Qui volera pour moi encor un coup aux cieux,
   Pour rapporter mon sens, et me rendre mes yeux ?
   Et qui fera qu'en paix je mange mes viandes ?

35 (89)

Gordes, il m'est avis que je suis éveillé,
   Comme un qui tout ému d'un effroyable songe
   Se réveille en sursaut, et par le lit s'allonge,
   S'émerveillant d'avoir si longtemps sommeillé.
Roger devint ainsi (ce crois-je) émerveillé :   5
   Et crois que tout ainsi la vergogne me ronge,
   Comme lui, quand il eut découvert la mensonge
   Du fard magicien qui l'avait aveuglé.
Et comme lui aussi je veux changer de style,
   Pour vivre désormais au sein de Logistile,   10
   Qui des cœurs langoureux est le commun support.
Sus donc (Gordes) sus donc, à la voile, à la rame,
   Fuyons, gagnons le haut, je vois la belle Dame
   Qui d'un heureux signal nous appelle à son port.

36 (90)

Ne pense pas (Bouju) que les Nymphes Latines
   Pour couvrir leur traison d'une humble privauté,
   Ni pour masquer leur teint d'une fausse beauté,
   Me fassent oublier nos Nymphes Angevines.
L'Angevine douceur, les paroles divines,   5
   L'habit qui ne tient rien de l'impudicité,
   La grâce, la jeunesse, et la simplicité
   Me dégoûtent (Bouju) de ces vieilles Alcines.
Qui les voit par dehors, ne peut rien voir plus beau,
   Mais le dedans ressemble au-dedans d'un tombeau,   10
   Et si rien entre nous moins honnête se nomme.
Ô quelle gourmandise ! ô quelle pauvreté !
   Ô quelle horreur de voir leur immondicité !
   C'est vraiment de les voir le salut d'un jeune homme.

Who'll help me past the feigning siren voice
    Of some smooth daughter of Achelous? 10
    Who'll banish monstrous Harpies such as these?
Who'll fly for me once more as far as Heaven
    To bring back down to earth my sight and reason?
    Who'll grant that I may eat my meals in peace?

35 (89)

Gordes, I'm like a man who's had a dream,
    A ghastly nightmare, so that suddenly
    He starts upright in bed, amazed that he
    Has been so sound asleep for all that time.
Ruggiero, I believe, felt much the same 5
    When he discovered the magician's lie,
    The foul deceit that blinded him: so I
    Am gnawed, like him, by a deep sense of shame.
Like him, I mean to change my way of life
    And turn to Logistilla for relief, 10
    She who gives hearts that languish her support.
Rise up, Gordes, set sail and ply the oar,
    Already I behold the happy shore
    Where she awaits and calls us to her port.

36 (90)

Don't think these brazen Roman Nymphs, Bouju,
    For all their fake familiar charade,
    False charms and painted beauty, ever could
    Make me forget the Girls of our Anjou.
That lilting voice, the Angevin sweetness too, 5
    The dress that's never showy, never lewd,
    The youth, the simple grace—all these have made
    Me sick of what those old Alcinas do.
Viewed from outside, nothing could be more fair;
    Their inside's like a tomb: I wouldn't dare 10
    Go into detail, some things can't be named.
Such greed amid such abject poverty!
    And O such filth, so horrible to see!
    Show them to a young man and he'll be saved.

37 (91)

Ô beaux cheveux d'argent* mignonnement retors !
 Ô front crêpe, et serein ! Et vous face dorée !
 Ô beaux yeux de crystal ! Ô grand' bouche honorée,
 Qui d'un large repli retrousses tes deux bords !
Ô belles dents d'ébène ! Ô précieux trésors,   5
 Qui faites d'un seul ris toute âme enamourée !
 Ô gorge damasquine en cent plis figurée !
 Et vous beaux grands tétins, dignes d'un si beau corps !
Ô beaux ongles dorés ! Ô main courte et grassette !
 Ô cuisse délicate ! Et vous jambe grossette,   10
 Et ce que je ne puis honnêtement nommer !
Ô beau corps transparent ! Ô beaux membres de glace !
 Ô divines beautés ! Pardonnez-moi de grâce,
 Si pour être mortel, je ne vous ose aimer.

38 (92)

En mille crêpillons les cheveux se friser,
 Se pincer les sourcils, et d'une odeur choisie
 Parfumer haut et bas sa charnure moisie,
 Et de blanc et vermeil sa face déguiser :
Aller de nuit en masque, en masque deviser,   5
 Se feindre à tous propos être d'amour saisie,
 Siffler toute la nuit par une jalousie,
 Et par martel de l'un, l'autre favoriser :
Baller, chanter, sonner, folâtrer dans la couche,
 Avoir le plus souvent deux langues en la bouche, 10
 Des courtisans sont les ordinaires jeux.
Mais quel besoin est-il que je te les enseigne ?
 Si tu les veux savoir (Gordes) et si tu veux
 En savoir plus encor, demande à la Chassaigne.*

39 (93)

Douce mère d'amour, gaillarde Cyprienne,
 Qui fais sous ton pouvoir tout pouvoir se ranger,
 Et qui des bords de Xanthe, à ce bord étranger
 Guidas avec ton fils ta gent Dardanienne,
Si je retourne en France, ô mère Idalienne !*   5

37 (91)

O pretty crinkled curls in silver hair!
  O wrinkled forehead and serene gold face!
  O crystal eyes! O mouth whose wide grimace
  Makes two deep creases to be honoured there!
O splendid ebony teeth, treasures so rare   5
  That when she smiles no man resists her grace!
  O damask throat, a rugged mottled space!
  Big breasts to match the body that she bares!
O golden fingernails! Hands short and fat!
  O slender thighs, thick legs, and one thing that   10
  I can't describe: no decent words would do!
O lovely lucent body, limbs of ice!
  O form divine, forgive me: I confess
  That I'm a mortal man and dare not love you.

38 (92)

Curling her hair in ringlets round her head,
  Plucking her eyebrows, picking out a scent
  To hide her mouldy smell, and smearing paint
  Over her face, disguised with white and red:
Masked every night and talking as if mad   5
  With passionate love, although it's all pretence;
  A whistle through the lattice shows consent;
  She spites lost loves by making new loves glad.
Dancing and singing, bags of bedroom fun,
  Two tongues inside her mouth instead of one: 10
  For courtesans these are the standard games.
But Gordes, do I need to teach you this?
  If you are keen to know just how it is,
  You'll find the rest by asking la Chassaigne.

39 (93)

Love's mother, wanton Cyprian, and guide,
  Making all powers bend before your own,
  Who brought into this land, helped by your son,
  The Dardans exiled from Scamander's side;
If I return to France with my old hide   5

Comme je vins ici, sans tomber au danger
De voir ma vieille peau en autre peau changer,
Et ma barbe Française en barbe Italienne,
Dès ici je fais vœu d'appendre à ton autel
Non le lis, ou la fleur d'Amarante immortel,   10
Non cette fleur encor de ton sang colorée :
Mais bien de mon menton la plus blonde toison,
Me vantant d'avoir fait plus que ne fit Jason
Emportant le butin de la toison dorée.*

40 (94)

Heureux celui qui peut longtemps suivre la guerre
Sans mort, ou sans blessure, ou sans longue prison !
Heureux qui longuement vit hors de sa maison
Sans dépendre son bien, ou sans vendre sa terre !*
Heureux qui peut en cour quelque faveur acquerre   5
Sans crainte de l'envie, ou de quelque traison !
Heureux qui peut longtemps sans danger de poison*
Jouir d'un chapeau rouge, ou des clefs de saint Pierre !*
Heureux qui sans péril peut la mer fréquenter !
Heureux qui sans procès le palais peut hanter !   10
Heureux qui peut sans mal vivre l'âge d'un homme !
Heureux qui sans souci peut garder son trésor !
Sa femme sans soupçon, et plus heureux encor
Qui a pu sans peler vivre trois ans à Rome !

41 (95)

Maudit soit mille fois le Borgne de Libye,*
Qui le cœur des rochers perçant de part en part
Des Alpes renversa le naturel rempart,
Pour ouvrir le chemin de France en Italie.
Mars n'eût empoisonné d'une éternelle envie   5
Le cœur de l'Espagnol, et du Français soudard,
Et tant de gens de bien ne seraient en hasard
De venir perdre ici et l'honneur et la vie.
Le Français corrompu par le vice étranger
Sa langue et son habit n'eût appris à changer,   10
Il n'eût changé ses mœurs en une autre nature.
Il n'eût point éprouvé le mal qui fait peler.

Still safe from change into another skin,
And if, Idalian, I grow no thin
Italian bristles, but a good French beard,
I'll hang upon your altar when I'm there
  No Amaranth or lily (this I swear)   10
  Nor yet your blood-red flower: none of these;
But rather the fair fleece that decks my chin,
  Proud that in this I shall have far outdone
  That Jason who brought home the Golden Fleece.

40 (94)

Happy the man whose war comes to an end
  Before he's wounded, killed, or cast in prison;
  Who spends long years from home, yet finds no reason
  To waste his substance or to sell his land;
Happy the man who gains some favour and   5
  Is free from fear of envy or of treason;
  Happy who keeps without the threat of poison
  A scarlet cap or Peter's keys in hand;
Happy the sailor, safe though far from shore,
  The Vatican courtier who won't go to law,   10
  The man who lives old age in peace at home;
Happy the man who keeps his cash secure,
  His wife as well; but happiest for sure
  The man who keeps his hair three years in Rome.

41 (95)

My curses fall on Hannibal, for he,
  The One-Eyed Libyan, pierced from side to side
  The Alpine barrier and opened wide
  The road that leads from France to Italy.
Mars, but for him, with poisonous enmity   5
  Could not have stirred French hearts or Spanish pride;
  So many honest folk would not have died,
  Losing down here both life and dignity.
The Frenchman, now corrupt with foreign vice,
  Would not use dress so fine or speech so nice,   10
  Nor ape strange customs nature never set.
No sickness would have thinned his manly locks,

Il n'eût fait de son nom la vérole* appeler,
Et n'eût fait si souvent d'un buffle sa monture.

42 (97)

Doulcin, quand quelquefois je vois ces pauvres filles,
    Qui ont le diable au corps, ou le semblent avoir,
    D'une horrible façon corps et tête mouvoir,
    Et faire ce qu'on dit de ces vieilles Sibylles :*
Quand je vois les plus forts se retrouver débiles,   5
    Voulant forcer en vain leur forcené pouvoir :
    Et quand même j'y vois perdre tout leur savoir
    Ceux qui sont en votre art*tenus des plus habiles :
Quand effroyablement écrier je les ois,
    Et quand le blanc des yeux renverser je leur vois,   10
    Tout le poil me hérisse, et ne sais plus que dire.
Mais quand je vois un moine aveques son Latin
    Leur tâter haut et bas le ventre et le tétin,*
    Cette frayeur se passe, et suis contraint de rire.

43 (98)

D'où vient que nous voyons à Rome si souvent
    Ces garces forcener, et la plupart d'icelles
    N'être vieilles (Ronsard) mais d'âge de pucelles,
    Et se trouver toujours en un même couvent ?
Qui parle par leur voix ? Quel Démon leur défend   5
    De répondre à ceux-là qui ne sont connus d'elles ?
    Et d'où vient que soudain on ne les voit plus telles
    Ayant une chandelle éteinte de leur vent ?
D'où vient que les saints lieux telles fureurs augmentent ?
    D'où vient que tant d'esprits une seule tormentent ?   10
    Et que sortant les uns, le reste ne sort pas ?
Dis je te prie (Ronsard) toi qui sais leurs natures,*
    Ceux qui fâchent ainsi ces pauvres créatures,
    Sont-ils des plus hautains, des moyens, ou plus bas ?

44 (99)

Quand je vais par la rue, où tant de peuple abonde,
    De prêtres, de prélats, et de moines aussi,
    De banquiers, d'artisans, et n'y voyant, ainsi

Nor would his name be given to the pox,
His back so often bent by crippling debt.

42 (97)

When I see those poor girls, Doulcin, who seem
   Possessed by devils, how they jerk and quake,
   How horribly the head and members shake,
   Like the old Sibyls who were much the same;
And when I see those of the strongest frame   5
   Weakened by some mad urge they cannot slake,
   And when the best of your profession make
   No headway against force they cannot tame:
And when I hear the agonizing cries
   And see the ghastly white of rolling eyes,   10
   I'm stricken dumb with fear; I've had enough.
But when I see the exorcizing touch
   Some monk with Latin gives to breast or crotch,
   That fear dissolves and I can't help but laugh.

43 (98)

Why is it that you see in Rome so often
   These girls gone mad, and most of them, Ronsard,
   Not old, but of the age young virgins are,
   And always lodged together in one convent?
Who speaks through them? What Daemon can prevent   5
   Them answering any stranger who comes near?
   How is it that their troubled minds grow clear
   So quickly when they blow a candle out?
Why do the daemons choose such holy places?
   Why cram one body where so little space is?   10
   When one's chased out, why don't the others go?
Tell me, Ronsard, since you should know their nature,
   What's their daemonic rank who plague poor creatures:
   The highest or the middle or the low?

44 (99)

Out in the street, where there is such a horde
   Of prelates, priests, monks, bankers, tradesmen too,
   You'd know it isn't Paris because you

Qu'on voit dedans Paris, la femme vagabonde :
Pyrrhe, après le dégât de l'universelle onde,   5
   Ses pierres (dis-je alors) ne sema point ici :
   Et semble proprement, à voir ce peuple-ci,
   Que Dieu n'y ai formé que la moitié du monde.
Car la dame Romaine en gravité marchant,
   Comme la conseillère, ou femme du marchand   10
   Ne s'y pourmène point, et n'y voit-on que celles
Qui se sont de la cour l'honnête nom donné:*
   Dont je crains quelquefois qu'en France retourné,
   Autant que j'en verrai ne me ressemblent telles.

45 (100)

Ursin, quand j'ois nommer de ces vieux noms Romains,
   De ces beaux noms connus de l'Inde jusqu'au More,
   Non les grands seulement, mais les moindres encore,
   Voire ceux-là qui ont les ampoules aux mains :
Il me fâche d'ouïr appeler ces vilains   5
   De ces noms tant fameux, que tout le monde honore :
   Et sans le nom Chrétien, le seul nom que j'adore,
   Voudrais que de tels noms on appelât nos Saints.
Le mien sur tous me fâche, et me fâche un Guillaume,
   Et mille autres sots noms communs en ce royaume,   10
   Voyant tant de faquins indignement jouir
De ces beaux noms de Rome, et de ceux de la Grèce,
   Mais par sur tout (Ursin) il me fâche d'ouïr
   Nommer une Thaïs du nom d'une Lucrèce.

46 (101)

Que dirons-nous (Melin) de cette cour Romaine,
   Où nous voyons chacun divers chemins tenir,
   Et aux plus hauts honneurs les moindres parvenir,
   Par vice, par vertu, par travail, et sans peine ?
L'un fait pour s'avancer une dépense vaine,   5
   L'autre par ce moyen se voit grand devenir,
   L'un par sévérité se sait entretenir,
   L'autre gagne les cœurs par sa douceur humaine :
L'un pour ne s'avancer se voit être avancé,
   L'autre pour s'avancer se voit désavancé,   10

Wouldn't see any woman in the crowd.
It makes me say that after the Great Flood   5
    And its destruction, Pyrrha didn't sow
    Her stones round here, so that it seems as though
    Half of humanity wasn't framed by God.
The fact is that the proper Roman dame,
    The lawyer's or the banker's wife, won't deign   10
    To walk about, so we see only those
Who steal a decent name they take from court:
    I fear that back in France I shall suppose
    All women on the street are of that sort.

45 (100)

When I hear Roman names that every land
    Knows and reveres, Ursin, so misapplied
    By high and lower ranks on every side,
    And even by the plebs with horny hands,
The very thought is something I can't stand.   5
    Though Christian is a name to wear with pride,
    The names of Christian saints sound weak beside
    Those great old Romans: would they were so grand!
I loathe my own name; William I detest;
    Also the thousand names that common taste   10
    Sometimes prefers to those of Rome and Greece,
Now left to please the scoundrel and the lout.
    But most of all, Ursin, what gets my goat
    Is hearing some loose Thaïs called Lucrece.

46 (101)

This Roman court, what shall we say of it,
    Where men try various ways of rising up,
    And men of lowly birth can reach the top
    By virtue, vice, hard work, or with no effort?
One spends a fortune and it makes him great,   5
    Another spends as much and has no hope;
    One's cold stern purpose climbs the slippery slope,
    Another's human warmth wins every heart.
One's up because he seemed so unambitious,
    Another's down who couldn't hide his wishes,   10

Et ce qui nuit à l'un, à l'autre est profitable :
Qui dit que le savoir est le chemin d'honneur,
    Qui dit que l'ignorance attire le bonheur,
    Lequel des deux (Melin) est le plus véritable ?

47 (105)

De voir mignon du Roi un courtisan honnête,
    Voir un pauvre cadet l'ordre au col soutenir,
    Un petit compagnon aux états parvenir,
    Ce n'est chose (Morel) digne d'en faire fête.
Mais voir un estafier, un enfant, une bête,   5
    Un forfant, un poltron* Cardinal devenir,
    Et pour avoir bien su un singe entretenir
    Un Ganymède avoir le rouge sur la tête :
S'être vu par les mains d'un soldat Espagnol
    Bien haut sur une échelle avoir la corde au col   10
    Celui, que par le nom de Saint-Père l'on nomme :
Un bélitre en trois jours aux princes s'égaler,
    Et puis le voir de là en trois jours dévaler :*
    Ces miracles (Morel) ne se font point qu'à Rome.

48 (109)

Comme un, qui veut curer quelque Cloaque immonde,
    S'il n'a le nez armé d'une contresenteur,
    Étouffé bien souvent de la grand' puanteur
    Demeure enseveli dans l'ordure profonde :
Ainsi le bon Marcel ayant levé la bonde,   5
    Pour laisser écouler la fangeuse épaisseur
    Des vices entassés, dont son prédécesseur*
    Avait six ans devant empoisonné le monde :
Se trouvant le pauvret de telle odeur surpris,
    Tomba mort au milieu de son œuvre entrepris,   10
    N'ayant pas à demi cette ordure purgée.
Mais quiconque rendra tel ouvrage parfait,
    Se pourra bien vanter d'avoir beaucoup plus fait
    Que celui qui purgea les étables d'Augée.

49 (111)

Je n'ai jamais pensé que cette voûte ronde
    Couvrît rien de constant : mais je veux désormais,

And what harms one man benefits his neighbour.
Some say that knowledge is the path to honour,
   Some say that ignorance brings fortune closer:
   Which of the two, Mellin, strikes you as truer?

47 (105)

To see an honest courtier in the King's
   New-favoured pet, a younger son made noble,
   A nobody charged with state affairs—Morel,
   We wouldn't celebrate that sort of thing.
But then to see some scullion come along,   5
   Some beast, some wretch, who's made a Cardinal;
   A Ganymede who earns his red hat well
   Because he keeps a monkey safe and strong.
To see a man they'll call the Holy Father
   Hauled up a ladder by a Spanish soldier,   10
   A rope around his neck, exposed to shame;
To see it takes three little days to crown
   A scoundrel, and three more to pull him down:
   Such miracles only occur in Rome.

48 (109)

A man who wants to drain some filthy Pit
   Needs to protect his nose, for otherwise
   The fetid stench will choke him and he dies
   Buried for good beneath a pile of shit:
So good Marcellus perished, flushing out   5
   The sewer clogged by six long years of vice
   Left by Pope Julius, a stinking mess
   So foul that all the world was poisoned by it.
Shocked rigid by the smell of so much crap,
   He fell and died upon the spot, poor chap,   10
   Leaving the work he started incomplete.
But anyone who can prove that he is able
   To finish it will call the Augean Stable
   An easy task, not half so great a feat.

49 (111)

I never thought that this round vault hung over
   Much that is fixed; but now I must maintain,

Je veux (mon cher Morel) croire plus que jamais,
   Que dessous ce grand Tout rien ferme ne se fonde.
Puisque celui qui fut de la terre et de l'onde   5
   Le tonnerre et l'effroi, las de porter le faix
   Veut d'un cloître borner la grandeur de ses faits,
   Et pour servir à Dieu abandonner le monde.
Mais quoi ? que dirons-nous de cet autre vieillard,
   Lequel ayant passé son âge plus gaillard   10
   Au service de Dieu, ores César imite ?
Je ne sais qui des deux* est le moins abusé :
   Mais je pense (Morel) qu'il est fort mal aisé,
   Que l'un soit bon guerrier, ni l'autre bon ermite.

50 (121)

Se fâcher tout le jour d'une fâcheuse chasse,
   Voir un brave taureau se faire un large tour
   Etonné de se voir tant d'hommes alentour,
   Et cinquante piquiers affronter son audace :
Le voir en s'élançant venir la tête basse,   5
   Fuir et retourner d'un plus brave retour,
   Puis le voir à la fin pris en quelque détour
   Percé de mille coups ensanglanter la place :
Voir courir aux flambeaux, mais sans se rencontrer,
   Donner trois coups d'épée, en armes se montrer,   10
   Et tout autour du camp un rempart de Thudesques :
Dresser un grand apprêt, faire attendre longtemps,
   Puis donner à la fin un maigre passe-temps :
   Voilà tout le plaisir des fêtes Romanesques.

51 (123)

Nous ne sommes fâchés que la trêve* se fasse :
   Car bien que nous soyons de la France bien loin,
   Si est chacun de nous à soi-même témoin,
   Combien la France doit de la guerre être lasse.
Mais nous sommes fâchés que l'Espagnole audace,   5
   Qui plus que le Français de repos a besoin,
   Se vante avoir la guerre et la paix en son poing,
   Et que de respirer nous lui donnons espace.

My dear Morel, that the great Whole contains
   No stable thing; I hold this more than ever
Since he who was the terror and the thunder   5
   Of earth and sea, from warlike deeds withdrawn,
   Seeks in a cloister's calm to ease the strain,
   To serve his God and leave the world forever.
Another case: how about this old man
   Who in his prime served God, and now he's gone   10
   Off in his dotage to become a Caesar?
I can't say which is less deluded, but
   I doubt that one will make a pious hermit
   And cannot see the other as a soldier.

50 (121)

Maddened all day by the most maddening sight:
   To see a brave bewildered bull run round,
   Not understanding why there's such a crowd
   And fifty picadors daring him to fight;
To see him charge, head down, and lunging out,   5
   Boldly attacking after giving ground;
   To see his blood stream from a thousand wounds
   As, caught by some smart feint, he meets his fate.
To see them run with torches from all sides,
   Stabbing three times, just to display their swords,   10
   While a packed wall of Germans watch the play;
To see great preparations and then wait
   Hours on end for some cheap show, that's what
   The Romans like to call a holiday.

51 (123)

No, we're not angry at the truce. Though far
   Away from France, each one of us knows well
   And needs no other witness here to tell
   How weary France must be of this long war.
But still we feel annoyed that Spain should dare   5
   To say this truce is nothing but a lull,
   That she'll make peace or war just as she will,
   Although, in fact, Spain needs the respite more.

Il nous fâche d'ouïr nos pauvres alliés
    Se plaindre à tous propos qu'on les ait oubliés,   10
    Et qu'on donne au privé l'utilité commune :
Mais ce qui plus nous fâche, est que les étrangers
    Disent plus que jamais que nous sommes légers,
    Et que nous ne savons connaître la Fortune.

52 (127)

Ici de mille fards la traison se déguise,
    Ici mille forfaits pullulent à foison,
    Ici ne se punit l'homicide ou poison,
    Et la richesse ici par usure est acquise :
Ici les grands maisons viennent de bâtardise,   5
    Ici ne se croit rien sans humaine raison,
    Ici la volupté est toujours de saison,
    Et d'autant plus y plaît, que moins elle est permise.
Pense le demourant. Si est-ce toutefois
    Qu'on garde encor ici quelque forme de lois,   10
    Et n'en est point du tout la justice bannie :
Ici le grand seigneur* n'achète l'action,
    Et pour priver autrui de sa possession
    N'arme son mauvais droit de force et tyrannie.

53 (128)

Ce n'est pas de mon gré (Carle) que ma navire*
    Erre en la mer Tyrrhène : un vent impétueux
    La chasse maulgré moi par ces flots tortueux,
    Ne voyant plus le pol, qui sa faveur t'inspire.
Je ne vois que rochers, et si rien se peut dire   5
    Pire que des rochers le heurt audacieux :
    Et le phare jadis favorable à mes yeux
    De mon cours égaré sa lanterne retire.
Mais si je puis un jour me sauver des dangers
    Que je fuis vagabond par ces flots étrangers,   10
    Et voir de l'Océan les campagnes humides,
J'arrêterai ma nef au rivage Gaulois,
    Consacrant ma dépouille au Neptune François,
    A Glauque, à Mélicerte, et aux sœurs Néréides.*

And yes, it hurts when our poor allies come
   Complaining that we've quite forgotten them,   10
   Preferring our own ends to the common good.
But most of all we're irked when foreigners say
   That this has always been our careless way,
   And that we don't seize Fortune when we could.

52 (127)

Here's home for every crime, no matter which,
   No punishment for homicide or poison;
   Here masks abound to hide the face of treason,
   And usury's the way that men get rich:
Here bastards found great houses; there's not much   5
   Of faith in anything save human reason;
   Here lechery is never out of season—
   Illicit? Yes. They like it more as such.
I'll let you guess the rest. And yet perhaps
   Some forms of law have not entirely lapsed   10
   And justice, not quite banished, runs its course.
Here the great lord won't stoop to buy the session
   And win his feeble case with sheer oppression,
   Taking another man's estate by force.

53 (128)

To sail like this, dear Carle, was not my choice:
   Buffeted by the wild Tyrrhenian sea,
   Without a guiding star in the dark sky,
   My driven ship yields to the tempest's force.
The rocks are all I see, and what is worse   5
   I hear the clash of rocks as we pass by;
   The beaming lighthouse that once shone for me
   Withdraws its favour from my errant course.
But if, escaping from these alien waves,
   No longer wandering where the storm still raves,   10
   I reach the verdant Ocean of fresh fields,
I'll beach my boat upon that Gallic shore
   And leave my cast-offs to French Neptune or
   The sea-god Glaucus and the Nereids.

54 (130)

Et je pensais aussi ce que pensait Ulysse,*
    Qu'il n'était rien plus doux que voir encor un jour
    Fumer sa cheminée, et après long séjour
    Se retrouver au sein de sa terre nourrice.
Je me réjouissais d'être échappé au vice   5
    Aux Circés d'Italie, aux Sirènes d'amour,
    Et d'avoir rapporté en France à mon retour
    L'honneur que l'on s'acquiert d'un fidèle service.
Las mais après l'ennui de si longue saison,
    Mille soucis mordants je trouve en ma maison,   10
    Qui me rongent le cœur sans espoir d'allégeance.
Adieu donques (Dorat) je suis encor Romain,
    Si l'arc que les neuf sœurs te mirent en la main
    Tu ne me prête' ici, pour faire ma vengeance.

55 (133)

Il fait bon voir (Magny) ces Coïons magnifiques,*
    Leur superbe Arsenal, leurs vaisseaux, leur abord,
    Leur saint Marc, leur palais, leur Realte, leur port,
    Leurs changes, leurs profits, leur banque, et leurs trafiques :
Il fait bon voir le bec de leurs chapprons antiques,   5
    Leurs robes à grand' manche, et leurs bonnets sans bord,
    Leur parler tout grossier, leur gravité, leur port,
    Et leurs sages avis aux affaires publiques.
Il fait bon voir de tout leur Sénat ballotter,
    Il fait bon voir partout leurs gondoles flotter,   10
    Leurs femmes, leurs festins, leur vivre solitaire :
Mais ce que l'on en doit le meilleur estimer,
    C'est quand ces vieux cocus vont épouser la mer,*
    Dont ils sont les maris, et le Turc l'adultère.

56 (136)

Je les ai vus (Bizet) et si bien m'en souvient,
    J'ai vu dessus leur front la repentance peinte,
    Comme on voit ces esprits qui là-bas font leur plainte,
    Ayant passé le lac d'où plus on ne revient.*
Un croire de léger les fols y entretient   5

54 (130)

Ulysses thought—and I once thought the same—
    That the most pleasing thing a man can see
    Is his own chimney-smoke the day that he
    Regains at last the land that nurtured him.
And I was glad to have escaped the shame   5
    That wanton Sirens spread through Italy;
    Once back in France, I felt, my loyalty
    And service would bring honour to my name.
Alas, the long and wearisome years in Rome
    Were followed by a thousand cares at home   10
    That gnawed my heart and left no hope of change.
Adieu, Dorat, I'm still a Roman now
    Unless you lend me the nine sisters' bow,
    Their gift to you; I'll use it for revenge.

55 (133)

Magnificent old Cobblers, what a sight!
    Their splendid Arsenal, their ships, their docks,
    Their palace, their Rialto, their Saint Mark's,
    Their bank, their profits, their commercial might.
Their beak-shaped hairdos, Magny, what a sight!   5
    Their brimless bonnets and their wide-sleeved cloaks,
    Their uncouth speech, the ponderous way they walk,
    And their wise counsel in affairs of state.
And then what fun to see their Senate vote;
    Their wives, their feasts, their gondolas afloat,   10
    And how they live the way that they prefer:
But the best thing that anyone can see
    Is how these ancient cuckolds wed the sea—
    That bride who entertains a Turkish lover.

56 (136)

I've seen them, Bizet, and here's what remains
    If memory serves: repentance on each brow,
    Like those lost souls who weep and wail below,
    Crossing the lake from which there's no return.
A false pretext of liberty retains   5

Sous un prétexte faux de liberté contrainte :
Les coupables fuitifs y demeurent par crainte,
Les plus fins et rusés honte les y retient.
Au demeurant (Bizet) l'avarice et l'envie
  Et tout cela qui plus tormente notre vie,   10
  Domine en ce lieu là plus qu'en tout autre lieu.
Je ne vis onques tant l'un l'autre contredire,
  Je ne vis onques tant l'un de l'autre médire :
  Vrai est, que, comme ici, l'on n'y jure point Dieu.*

57 (148)

Autant comme l'on peut en un autre langage
  Une langue exprimer, autant que la nature
  Par l'art se peut montrer, et que par la peinture
  On peut tirer au vif un naturel visage :
Autant exprimes-tu, et encor davantage,   5
  Aveques le pinceau de ta docte écriture,
  La grâce, la façon, le port, et la stature
  De celui, qui d'Énée a décrit le voyage.
Cette même candeur, cette grâce divine,
  Cette même douceur, et majesté Latine   10
  Qu'en ton Virgile on voit, c'est celle même encore,
Qui Française se rend par ta céleste veine.
  Des-Masures sans plus a faute d'un Mécène,
  Et d'un autre César, qui ses vertus honore.*

58 (179)

Voyant l'ambition, l'envie, et l'avarice,
  La rancune, l'orgueil, le désir aveuglé,
  Dans cet âge de fer de vices tout rouglé
  A violé l'honneur de l'antique justice :
Voyant d'une autre part la fraude, la malice,   5
  Le procès immortel, le droit mal conseillé :
  Et voyant au milieu du vice déréglé
  Cette royale fleur, qui ne tient rien du vice,
Il me semble (Dorat) voir au ciel revolés
  Des antiques vertus les escadrons ailés   10
  N'ayant rien délaissé de leur saison dorée*
Pour réduire le monde à son premier printemps,

Gullible fools more captive than they know;
   Smart criminals with nowhere else to go
   Camp there with guilty outlaws on the run.
Moreover, Bizet, avarice and strife,
   Envy and everything that spoils our life,   10
   Thrive in that place more fully than elsewhere.
I never saw quarrels so deep and fierce,
   Nor slanders worse: it's true that, unlike us,
   They draw the line at 'By God!' when they swear.

57 (148)

As much as one tongue can express another,
   Or nature's truth be reproduced in art,
   As much as any painter can impart
   A living face exact in form and feature:
So much do you express and even more   5
   When with your learnèd pen you recreate
   The grace and bearing of the man who wrote
   Of how Aeneas reached the destined shore.
That very candour and the grace divine,
   The gentle and majestic Latin vein   10
   Of Virgil is precisely that which you
Make French by virtue of your heavenly skill.
   Now Des-Masures lacks only Maecenas still
   And a new Caesar's grant of honours due.

58 (179)

Seeing the ambition, envy, avarice,
   The rancour and the blind desire, the pride,
   Justice debauched, its honoured past denied
   By this our iron age, rusty with vice;
Seeing fraud and malice and the endless course   5
   Of trials where the right has no true guide,
   And amid all this vice on every side,
   Seeing one royal flower free from vice,
It seems, Dorat, that in the skies I see
   A host of ancient virtues wing away,   10
   Leaving no trace of golden age behind
To help restore the world back to its prime,

Fors cette Marguerite, honneur de notre temps,
Qui comme l'espérance, est seule demeurée.*

59 (180)

De quelque autre sujet, que j'écrive, Jodelle,
    Je sens mon cœur transi d'une morne froideur,
    Et ne sens plus en moi cette divine ardeur,
    Qui t'enflamme l'esprit de sa vive étincelle.
Seulement quand je veux toucher le los de celle   5
    Qui est de notre siècle et la perle* et la fleur,
    Je sens revivre en moi cette antique chaleur,
    Et mon esprit lassé prendre force nouvelle.
Bref, je suis tout changé, et si ne sais comment,
    Comme on voit se changer la vierge* en un moment, 10
    À l'approcher du Dieu qui telle la fait être.
D'où vient cela, Jodelle ? Il vient, comme je crois,
    Du sujet, qui produit naïvement en moi
    Ce que par art contraint les autres y font naître.

Les Antiquitez de Rome

60 (1)

Divins Esprits,* dont la poudreuse cendre
    Gît sous le faix de tant de murs couverts,
    Non votre los, que vif par vos beaux vers
    Ne se verra sous la terre descendre,
Si des humains la voix se peut étendre   5
    Depuis ici jusqu'au fond des enfers,
    Soient à mon cri les abîmes ouverts,
    Tant que d'abas vous me puissiez entendre.
Trois fois* cernant sous le voile des cieux
    De vos tombeaux le tour dévotieux,   10
    A haute voix trois fois je vous appelle :
J'invoque ici votre antique fureur,*
    En cependant que d'une sainte horreur
    Je vais chantant votre gloire plus belle.

Except that Margaret, honour of our time,
Remains on earth as the one hopeful sign.

59 (180)

Whatever else I write about, I find
  My weary heart numbed by a dreary chill,
  Lacking the fervent quickening fire, Jodelle,
  Whose vital heavenly spark inflames your mind.
Only when I attempt to turn my hand   5
  To praising her, this age's flower and pearl,
  That ancient heat returns and I can feel
  My tired spirit revive with strength regained.
One moment, and I'm changed, changed utterly,
  Just as the Pythia is transfigured by   10
  The approaching God who makes her what she is.
Jodelle, how can this happen? It must be
  The subject that by nature breeds in me
  What others bring to birth by artifice.

The Antiquities of Rome

60 (1)

Spirits Divine whose dusty ashes lie
  Beneath these ruined walls, there's nothing weighs
  Upon your verses, living in our praise,
  That are not buried since they cannot die,
If any human voice beneath the sky   5
  Can reach the Underworld, then let mine force
  Open the entrance to the dark abyss
  So that within its depths you hear my cry.
Beneath the veil of heaven I circle round
  Three times your tombs set in this sacred ground,   10
  Three times I call aloud upon your names:
And I invoke your ancient ecstasy here
  That I may be inspired with holy fear
  To sing the glory of your ancient fame.

61 (III)

Nouveau venu qui cherches Rome en Rome,
 Et rien de Rome en Rome n'aperçois,
 Ces vieux palais, ces vieux arcs que tu vois,
 Et ces vieux murs, c'est ce que Rome on nomme.
Vois quel orgueuil, quelle ruine : et comme   5
 Celle qui mit le monde sous ses lois
 Pour dompter tout, se dompta quelquefois,
 Et devint proie au temps, qui tout consomme.
Rome de Rome est le seul monument,
 Et Rome Rome a vaincu seulement,   10
 Le Tibre seul, qui vers la mer s'enfuit,
Reste de Rome. O mondaine inconstance !
 Ce qui est ferme, est par le temps détruit,
 Et ce qui fuit, au temps fait résistance.

62 (V)

Qui voudra voir* tout ce qu'ont pu nature,
 L'art, et le ciel (Rome) te vienne voir :
 J'entends s'il peut ta grandeur concevoir
 Par ce qui n'est que ta morte peinture.
Rome n'est plus : et si l'architecture   5
 Quelque ombre encor de Rome fait revoir,
 C'est comme un corps par magique savoir
 Tiré de nuit hors de sa sépulture.
Le corps de Rome en cendre est dévallé,
 Et son esprit rejoindre s'est allé   10
 Au grand esprit de cette masse ronde.
Mais ses écrits,* qui son los le plus beau
 Malgré le temps arrachent du tombeau,
 Font son idole errer parmi le monde.

63 (VIII)

Par armes et vaisseaux Rome dompta le monde,
 Et pouvait-on juger qu'une seule cité
 Avait de sa grandeur le terme limité
 Par la même rondeur de la terre, et de l'onde.
Et tant fut la vertu de ce peuple féconde   5

61 (III)

Newcomer, eager to find Rome in Rome
  And finding there's no Rome in Rome to see,
  Old palaces, this crumbling masonry
  Of walls and arches, that's what men call Rome.
See here what pride, what ruin; how it came   5
  That the wide world's sole lawgiver should be
  Conquered, the last of all her conquests, prey
  To her own self and all-consuming time.
Rome is the only monument to Rome,
  And Rome by Rome alone was overcome: 10
  Only the Tiber, running to the sea,
Remains of Rome. O world's inconstant stay!
  For time destroys whatever's standing firm
  And time's resisted by what runs away.

62 (V)

Whoever longs to see what nature, art
  And heaven can do, let him come see you, Rome,
  If he can conjure up that greatness from
  A painted portrait where life has no part.
Rome is no more, and if her ruined site   5
  Still grants some shadow of what once was Rome,
  It seems a body raised up from the tomb
  By magic powers in the dark of night.
Rome's body now is ashes, and its soul
  Has gone to join the spirit that moves the whole,   10
  The great soul of the rounded universe.
But still, in spite of time, her writings live
  To wrest her fairest praises from the grave
  And keep her image wandering through the earth.

63 (VIII)

With arms and ships, Rome tamed the world, and we
  Must think how did a single city find
  Bounds set so wide they only were defined
  By the circumference of land and sea.
That race had virtue whose fertility   5

En vertueux neveux, que sa postérité
    Surmontant ses aïeux en brave autorité,
    Mesura le haut ciel à la terre profonde ;
Afin qu'ayant rangé tout pouvoir sous sa main,
    Rien ne pût être borne à l'empire Romain :   10
    Et que, si bien le temps détruit les Républiques,
Le temps ne mit si bas la Romaine hauteur,
    Que le chef déterré* aux fondements antiques,
    Qui prirent nom de lui, fût découvert menteur.

64 (XIII)

Ni la fureur de la flamme enragée,*
    Ni le tranchant du fer victorieux,
    Ni le dégât du soldat furieux,
    Qui tant de fois (Rome) t'a saccagée,
Ni coup sur coup ta fortune changée,   5
    Ni le ronger des siècles envieux,
    Ni le dépit des hommes et des Dieux,
    Ni contre toi ta puissance rangée,
Ni l'ébranler des vents impétueux,
    Ni le débord de ce Dieu tortueux,*   10
    Qui tant de fois t'a couvert de son onde,
Ont tellement ton orgueil abaissé,
    Que la grandeur du rien,* qu'ils t'ont laissé,
    Ne fasse encor émerveiller le monde.

65 (XVIII)

Ces grands monceaux pierreux, ces vieux murs que tu vois,
    Furent premièrement le clos d'un lieu champêtre:*
    Et ces braves palais dont le temps s'est fait maître,
    Cassines de pasteurs ont été quelquefois.
Lors prindrent les bergers les ornements des Rois,   5
    Et le dur laboureur de fer arma sa dextre :
    Puis l'annuel pouvoir le plus grand se vit être,
    Et fut encor plus grand le pouvoir de six mois :
Qui, fait perpétuel, crût en telle puissance,
    Que l'aigle Impérial de lui print sa naissance :   10
    Mais le Ciel s'opposant à tel accroissement,
Mit ce pouvoir ès mains du successeur de Pierre,

Created offspring of a bolder kind
    Who, to surpass ancestral exploits, mined
    The depth of earth and mounted to the sky:
So that, with all the power in her hands,
    The Roman Empire would know no bounds;   10
    And that, though passing time destroys great nations,
Yet time would not diminish Roman pride
    Or contradict the Capitol's foundations
    And say the head discovered there had lied.

64 (XIII)

Neither the furious rage of searing flame,
    Nor the sharp edge of the victorious sword,
    Nor the wild soldier from some savage horde
    Who have so often sacked the city, Rome,
Nor the incessant changes wrought by time,   5
    Nor what the envious centuries corrode,
    Nor the hostility of man or God,
    Nor ingrown power working its own doom,
Nor the impetuous buffeting of wind,
    Nor floods from that meandering stream divine   10
    That overflows time and again your land
Have yet so shrunk your pride that all the world
    Does not still come and marvel to behold
    How great the nothing is they left behind,

65 (XVIII)

These heaps of stone, these old walls that you see
    Once closed the fields some farmer called his own;
    These palaces that time has overthrown
    Were shepherds' cottages in days gone by.
Then shepherds donned the pomp of Royalty,   5
    Ploughmen took arms of steel, and later came
    The annual consulate and the six-month reign
    Of the dictators with far greater sway;
This, made perpetual and fully grown,
    Hatched forth the eagle of Imperial Rome: 10
    But this increase provoked high Heaven's ban,
Which gave that power to Peter's heirs who go

Qui sous nom de pasteur, fatal à cette terre,
Montre que tout retourne à son commencement.

66 (XXVII)

Toi qui de Rome émerveillé contemples
    L'antique orgueil, qui menaçait les cieux,
    Ces vieux palais, ces monts audacieux,
    Ces mures, ces arcs, ces thermes, et ces temples,
Juge, en voyant ces ruines si amples,   5
    Ce qu'a rongé le temps injurieux,
    Puisqu'aux ouvriers les plus industrieux
    Ces vieux fragments encor servent d'exemples.
Regarde après, comme de jour en jour
    Rome fouillant son antique séjour,   10
    Se rebâtit de tant d'œuvres divines :
Tu jugeras, que le démon Romain
    S'efforce encor d'une fatale main
    Ressusciter ces poudreuses ruines.*

67 (XXX)

Comme le champ semé en verdure foisonne,
    De verdure se hausse en tuyau verdissant,
    Du tuyau se hérisse en épi florissant,
    D'épi jaunit en grain, que le chaud assaisonne :
Et comme en la saison le rustique moissonne   5
    Les ondoyants cheveux du sillon blondissant,
    Les met d'ordre en javelle, et du blé jaunissant
    Sur le champ dépouillé mille gerbes façonne :
Ainsi de peu à peu crût l'empire Romain,
    Tant qu'il fut dépouillé par la Barbare main,   10
    Qui ne laissa de lui que ces marques antiques,
Que chacun va pillant : comme on voit le glaneur
    Cheminant pas à pas recueillir les reliques
    De ce qui va tombant après le moissonneur.

68 (XXXII)

Espérez-vous que la postérité
    Doive (mes vers) pour tout jamais vous lire ?
    Espérez-vous que l'œuvre d'une lyre
    Puisse acquérir telle immortalité ?

Under the shepherd's destined name and show
That everything returns where it began.

66 (XXVII)

You who behold Rome's ancient pride and marvel
    At arrogance that dared to menace heaven,
    Old palaces, presumptuous hills uprisen,
    These walls, these baths, these arches, and these temples,
Judge, as you see the ruined sites so ample,   5
    What ravenous time has gnawed away, since even
    Our most proficient artisans are given
    To using these old fragments as a model.
Then see how with each passing day new Rome,
    Through excavation in its ancient home,   10
    Rebuilds itself with works that are divine.
You'll judge that here the spirit of Rome commands
    A city that still strives with destined hands
    To make these dusty ruins rise again.

67 (XXX)

Just as the field that's sown gets clothed with green
    And from that green we see a stalk appear,
    And from that stalk a bristly flowering ear
    Which the warm weather turns to yellow grain;
And as the farmer sees his harvest grown   5
    And from the furrow crops the golden hair,
    Then, on the field his sickle has left bare,
    Lays out a thousand sheaves of yellow corn;
So, step by step, did Rome's great empire grow
    Until Barbarians who laid it low   10
    Left only ancient ruins free for all
To pillage, like poor fellows that are seen
    Stepping behind the harvester to glean
    Whatever careless remnants he lets fall.

68 (XXXII)

My verses, do you think posterity
    Will keep on reading you for evermore?
    And do you think the lyre's work is sure
    To reach such heights of immortality?

Si sous le ciel fût quelque éternité,   5
    Les monuments que je vous ai fait dire,*
    Non en papier, mais en marbre et porphyre,
    Eussent gardé leur vive antiquité.
Ne laisse pas toutefois de sonner,
    Luth, qu'Apollon m'a bien daigné donner :   10
    Car si le temps ta gloire ne dérobe,
Vanter te peux, quelque bas que tu sois,
    D'avoir chanté, le premier des François,
    L'antique honneur du peuple à longue robe.*

Divers Jeux Rustiques

69 (3) D'UN VANNEUR DE BLÉ, AUX VENTS

À vous, troppe légère,
    Qui d'aile passagère
    Par le monde volez,
    Et d'un sifflant murmure
    L'ombrageuse verdure   5
    Doucement ébranlez,

J'offre ces violettes,
    Ces lis et ces fleurettes
    Et ces roses ici,
    Ces vermeillettes roses   10
    Tout fraîchement écloses
    Et ces œillets aussi.

De votre douce haleine
    Éventez cette plaine,
    Éventez ce séjour: 15
    Cependant que j'ahanne
    A mon blé que je vanne
    A la chaleur du jour.

70 (20) CONTRE LES PÉTRARQUISTES*

J'ai oublié l'art de pétrarquiser,
Je veux d'amour franchement deviser
Sans vous flatter et sans me déguiser :
    Ceux qui font tant de plaintes

If anything could last eternally,   5
    The monuments that I make you speak of here
    Would not have needed paper; they'd endure
    Alive in marble and in porphyry.
Yet for all that, you should not cease to sound,
    Lute that Apollo deigned to make my own,   10
  . For if your glory is not dimmed by time,
Lowly though you may be, you still can boast
    That among all the French, you were the first
    To sing the long-robed people's honoured name.

Rustic Amusements

69 (3) A WINNOWER OF WHEAT, TO THE WINDS

To you, light company,
    Who take your airy way
    Swiftly above the earth,
    Who shake the leaves and grass
    That tremble as you pass   5
    With your soft-whispering breath,

I offer these sweet posies
    Of violets and roses
    In their fresh-blooming prime,
    Lilies from rustic bowers,   10
    Red poppies and wild flowers
    That grow at harvest time;

With cooling breath again
    Refresh the burning plain,
    Refresh me while I stay   15
    To toil and pant and sweat,
    A winnower of wheat
    In the heat of the day.

70 (20) AGAINST THE PETRARCHISTS

I've long forgotten how to Petrarchize,
A franker mode is what I now advise,
 Not flattering you, and wearing no disguise;
   There's not an ounce of love

N'ont pas le quart d'une vraie amitié,   5
Et n'ont pas tant de peine la moitié
Comme leurs yeux, pour vous faire pitié,
    Jettent de larmes feintes.

Ce n'est que feu de leurs froides chaleurs,
Ce n'est qu'horreur de leurs feintes douleurs,   10
Ce n'est encor de leurs soupirs et pleurs
    Que vents, pluie et orages :
En bref, ce n'est à ouïr leurs chansons
De leurs amours que flammes et glaçons,
Flèches, liens, et mille autres façons   15
    De semblables outrages.

De vos beautés, ce n'est que tout fin or,
Perles, cristal, marbre et ivoire encor,
Et tout l'honneur de l'indique trésor,
    Fleurs, lis, œillets et roses :   20
De vos douceurs ce n'est que sucre et miel,
De vos rigueurs n'est qu'aloès et fiel,
De vos esprits, c'est tout ce que le ciel
    Tient de grâces encloses.

Puis tout soudain ils vous font mille torts,   25
Disant que voir vos blonds cheveux retors,
Vos yeux archers, auteurs de mille morts,
    Et la forme excellente
De ce que peut l'accoutrement couver,
Diane en l'onde il vaudrait mieux trouver,   30
Ou voir Méduse, ou au cours s'éprouver
    Aveques Atalante.

S'il faut parler de votre jour natal,
Votre ascendant heureusement fatal
De votre chef écarta tout le mal   35
    Qui aux humains peut nuire.
Quant au trépas, sa' vous quand ce sera

In poets who write all those sad complaints,   5
And in their hearts there isn't half the pain
Shown by their weeping eyes in hope to gain
    The pity that they crave.

Their lukewarm passions always start a fire,
Oppressed by fictive sorrows they expire,   10
Their simulated sighs and tears inspire
    Torrents of rain and tempest,
If you believe their songs (I'll be concise)
Their loves are nothing else but fire and ice,
Arrows and chains and a few other nice   15
    Conceits no less far-fetched.

As for your beauties, they must be fine gold,
Pearls, crystal, ivory, marble, the untold
Abundant treasures that the Indies hold;
    And violets, lilies, roses;   20
Sugar or honey's what they always call
Your sweet days; when you're bitter then it's gall:
Your mind and manners surely mirror all
    The graces heaven encloses.

Then suddenly they blame the harm you've spread: 25
Enough to see the curls on your fair head,
Your murderous eyes that leave a thousand dead,
    And the surpassing grace
Of all those perfect parts your garments cover!
Better to spy Diana in the water,   30
Gaze on Medusa, challenge Atalanta
    In her next running race.

What of the day when you were born? They are
Firmly convinced a most propitious star
Reigned high above your head and kept afar   35
    All mortal harm and spite.
As for your death, when your pure soul shall flee

Que votre esprit le monde laissera ?
Ce sera lorsque là-haut on verra
     Un nouvel astre luire.   40

Si pour sembler autre que je ne suis
Je me plaisais à masquer mes ennuis,
J'irais au fond des éternelles nuits
     Plein d'horreur inhumaine :
Là d'un Sisyphe et là d'un Ixion   45
J'éprouverais toute l'affliction
Et l'estomac qui pour punition
     Vit et meurt à sa peine.

De vos beautés sa' vous que j'en dirais ?
De vos deux yeux deux astres je ferais,   50
Vos blonds cheveux en or je changerais
     Et vos mains en ivoire.
Quant est du teint, je le peindrais trop mieux
Que le matin ne colore les cieux.
Bref, vous seriez belles comme les dieux,   55
     Si vous me vouliez croire.

Mais cet Enfer de vaines passions,
Ce Paradis de belles fictions,
Déguisements de nos affections,
     Ce sont peintures vaines   60
Qui donnent plus de plaisir aux lisants
Que vos beautés à tous vos courtisans
Et qu'au plus fol de tous ces bien-disants
     Vous ne donnez de peines.

Vos beautés donc leur servent d'arguments,   65
Et ne leur faut de meilleurs instruments
Pour les tirer tous vifs des monuments :
     Aussi comme je pense,
Sans qu'autrement vous les récompensez
De tant d'ennuis mieux écrits que pensés,   70
Amour les a de peine dispensés,
     Et vous de récompense.

This wicked world, you know when that will be?
The day when in the vault of heaven we see
    A new star shining bright.   40

If, to seem other than I am, I chose
The stock poetic dressing for my woes,
You'd see me plunging headlong into those
    Depths of eternal torment:
I'd suffer all the pains inflicted on   45
Mythical Sisyphus or Ixion
And, with my liver's living death, I'd groan
    At such harsh punishment.

And of your beauties what then would I write?
Your eyes would be two stars diffusing light: 50
Blond hair must be fine gold when I indite,
    Your hands pure ivory.
I'd say your radiant complexion vies
With heaven when fresh morning gilds the skies:
In short, with gods above you'd share the prize, 55
    If only you'd believe me.

But this imagined Hell of vain afflictions,
This Heaven of the most resplendent fictions
Adds up to nothing more than vain depictions
    Of false or shallow feelings: 60
It's readers who enjoy this long pretence
And do so with a feeling more intense
Than any pains and joys that touch the sense
    Of suitors in their pleading.

Your beauties thus provide their arguments,   65
They have no need of better instruments
To quicken their poetic monuments;
    And therefore it's my view
That since, by Love's decree, they have been spared
So many ills best written, not endured,   70
You should not offer any more reward,
    Nor they expect it from you.

Si je n'ai peint les miens dessus le front
Et les assauts que vos beautés me font,
Si sont-ils bien gravés au plus profond   75
    De ma volonté franche :
Non comme un tas de vains admirateurs
Qui font ainsi par leurs soupirs menteurs
Et par leurs vers honteusement flatteurs
    Rougir la carte blanche.   80

Il n'y a roc qui n'entende leur voix,
Leurs piteux cris ont fait cent mille fois
Pleurer les monts, les plaines et les bois,
    Les antres et fontaines :
Bref, il n'y a ni solitaires lieux   85
Ni lieux hantés, voire mêmes les cieux,
Qui çà et là ne montrent à leurs yeux
    L'image de leurs peines.

Cestui-là porte en son cœur fluctueux
De l'Océan les flots tumultueux,   90
Cestui l'horreur des vents impétueux
    Sortant de leur caverne :
L'un d'un Caucase et Montgibel se plaint,
L'autre en veillant plus de songes se peint
Qu'il n'en fût onc en cet orme qu'on feint   95
    En la fosse d'Averne.

Qui contrefait ce Tantale mourant
Brûlé de soif au milieu d'un torrent,
Qui repaissant un aigle dévorant
    S'accoutre en Prométhée :   100
Et qui encor par un plus chaste vœu,
En se brûlant, veut Hercule être veu,
Mais qui se mue en eau, air, terre et feu,
    Comme un second Protée.

L'un meurt de froid et l'autre meurt de chaud,   105
L'un vole bas et l'autre vole haut,
L'un est chétif, l'autre a ce qu'il lui faut,

If I don't wear my feelings on my brow,
Or use the pain of love to make a show,
Yet nonetheless love's graven down below   75
   Deep in my dearest wish:
Not like that heap of suitors who devise
Those verses studded with mendacious sighs
And such outrageous shameless flattering lies
   That make the white page blush.   80

There's not a rock that hasn't heard their moans;
A hundred thousand times their piteous groans
Have made the mountains weep, the woods, the stones.
   And secret springs below.
In short, you cannot find a place that lies   85
Near or far off, or even in the skies,
That does not send an image to their eyes,
   Reflecting their own woe.

To this man's stormy heart the Ocean gave
The fury of its wild tumultuous waves,   90
And for another, from their sea-dark cave,
   Surged winds tempestuous:
One seethes like Caucasus or Mongibel
Another paints more waking dreams than dwell
Within that elm of which the ancients tell   95
   In fabled deep Avernus.

One sees himself in Tantalus' dying throes,
Plunged in the stream, thirsting where water flows,
Another spies the eagle's flight and knows
   That he's Prometheus: 100
Yet one more looks to Hercules, no less,
Burning himself in Dejanira's dress:
With water, air, fire, and earth, you'll guess
   Who thinks he's Proteus.

One dies of cold, the other dies of heat,   105
One's flight is low, the other loves the heights,
One man is shy, the other knows his rights:

   L'un sur l'esprit se fonde,
L'autre s'arrête à la beauté du corps :
On ne vit onc si horribles discords   110
En ce chaos qui troublait les accords
   Dont fut bâti le monde.

Quelque autre après, ayant subtilement
Trouvé l'accord de chacun élément,*
Façonne un rond tendant également   115
   Au centre de son âme :
Son firmament est peint sur un beau front,
Tous ses désirs sont balancés en rond,
Son pôle Artiq et Antartiq, ce sont
   Les beaux yeux de sa dame.   120

Cestui, voulant plus simplement aimer,
Veut un Properce et Ovide exprimer
Et voudrait bien encor se transformer
   En l'esprit d'un Tibulle :
Mais cestui-là, comme un Pétrarque ardent,   125
Va son amour en son style fardant :
Cet autre après va le sien mignardant
   Comme un second Catulle.

Quelque autre encor la terre dédaignant
Va du tiers ciel les secrets enseignant,   130
Et de l'amour, où il se va baignant,
   Tire une quinte essence.
Mais quant à moi, qui plus terrestre suis
Et n'aime rien que ce qu'aimer je puis,
Le plus subtil qu'en amour je poursuis   135
   S'appelle jouissance.

Je ne veux point savoir si l'amitié
Prit du facteur, qui jadis eut pitié
Du pauvre Tout fendu par la moitié,
   Sa céleste origine :   140
Vous souhaiter autant de bien qu'à moi,
Vous estimer autant comme je dois,

For one the body's all,
Another thinks the soul should be adored:
Never was seen such horrible discords   110
As in this chaos, troubling the accords
    That framed the turning world.

The next along, finding a subtle way
Of making all the elements agree,
Fashions a sphere that by some mystery   115
    At his soul's centre lies:
On her fair brow his firmament appears,
All his desires enclosed within a sphere:
His poles, both Arctic and Antarctic, are
    His lady's lovely eyes.   120

A man whose love demands a plainer way
Brings Ovid and Propertius into play
And, if he could, would have his verse display
    The spirit of Tibullus;
While yet another who like Petrarch burns   125
Thinks a more florid style will serve his turn:
And, with a daintier manner, one can learn
    To be a new Catullus.

Some others scorn the earth and teach the lore
Of the third secret heaven, and what's more,   130
Bathe in love's magic fount from which they draw
    A perfect quintessence.
But as for me, with my more earthbound frame,
I only love what's there to love; my aim
Is simply what love's lexicon would name   135
    The pleasure of the senses.

They say we once were Whole and then divided;
In pity for two halves, the Lord decided
To join them up, and that's why love is guided
    By origin divine.   140
I wouldn't know: to love you as I do,
To see your worth and give that worth its due,

Avoir de vous le loyer de ma foi,
  Voilà mon Androgyne.

Nos bons aïeux, qui cet art démenaient,   145
Pour en parler Pétrarque n'apprenaient,
Ains franchement leur dame entretenaient
  Sans fard ou couverture :
Mais aussitôt qu'Amour s'est fait savant,
Lui, qui était Français auparavant,   150
Est devenu flatteur et décevant
  Et de thusque nature.

Si vous trouvez quelque importunité
En mon amour, qui votre humanité
Préfère trop à la divinité   155
  De vos grâces cachées,
Changez ce corps, objet de mon ennui ;
Alors je crois que de moi ni d'autrui,
Quelque beauté que l'esprit ait en lui,
  Vous ne serez cherchées.   160

Et qu'ainsi soit, quand les hivers nuisants
Auront séché la fleur de vos beaux ans,
Ridé ce marbre, éteint ces feux luisants,
  Quand vous voirez encore
Ces cheveux d'or en argent se changer,   165
De ce beau sein l'ivoire s'allonger,
Ces lis fanir et de vous s'étranger
  Ce beau teint de l'aurore,

Qui pensez-vous qui vous aille chercher,
Qui vous adore, ou qui daigne toucher   170
Ce corps divin, que vous tenez tant cher ?
  Votre beauté passée
Ressemblera un jardin à nos yeux,
Riant naguère aux hommes et aux dieux,
Ores fâchant de son regard les cieux   175
  Et l'humaine pensée.

And have the wages of my faith from you:
   That's all my Androgyne.

Our forefathers, in practising this art,   145
Needed no Petrarch to dictate their part,
But freely sought to win the lady's heart,
   Plainly and without guile:
But Love, though proudly French in days gone by,
When he became a scholar, chose to be   150
A paragon of fraud and flattery,
   In perfect Tuscan style.

Now if you think there's something not quite proper
About this human love I choose to offer
Because I make no effort to discover   155
   A nature that's divine,
Change that fair body, cause of all this care:
Then neither I nor other men, I swear,
Will seek the beauties that lie hidden there
   Under the spirit's sign.   160

And when that happens, when the wintertime
Has shrivelled up the flowers of your prime,
Defiled your marble and put out your flame:
   When slowly you discern
Silver encroaching on your golden hair,   165
The ivory breast that droops, the fading air
Of lilies on the skin that used to share
   The pearly tint of dawn,

Tell me who then will venture out in search
Of your adored sweet self, who'll want to touch   170
The sacred body that you prize so much?
   The beauty we once sought
Will seem a garden long decayed, for when
It bloomed in spring, it smiled on gods and men,
But now it frowns and will not please again   175
   Divine or human thought.

N'attendez donc que la grand faux du temps
Moissonne ainsi la fleur de vos printemps
Qui rend les dieux et les hommes contents :
    Les ans, qui peu séjournent,   180
Ne laissent rien que regrets et soupirs,
Et empennés de nos meilleurs désirs
Aveques eux emportent nos plaisirs,
    Qui jamais ne retournent.

Je ris souvent, voyant pleurer ces fous,   185
Qui mille fois voudraient mourir pour vous,
Si vous croyez de leur parler si doux
    Le parjure artifice :
Mais quant à moi, sans feindre ni pleurer,
Touchant ce point je vous puis assurer   190
Que je veux sain et dispos demeurer
    Pour vous faire service.

De vos beautés je dirai seulement
Que si mon œil ne juge follement
Votre beauté est jointe également   195
    A votre bonne grâce :
De mon amour, que mon affection
Est arrivée à la perfection
De ce qu'on peut avoir de passion
    Pour une belle face.   200

Si toutefois Pétrarque vous plaît mieux,
Je reprendrai mon chant mélodieux
Et volerai jusqu'au séjour des dieux
    D'une aile mieux guidée.
Là dans le sein de leurs divinités   205
Je choisirai cent mille nouveautés,
Dont je peindrai vos plus grandes beautés
    Sur la plus belle Idée.*

So do not wait for passing time to bring
Its scythe to reap the flower of your spring
That gods and men enjoy above all things.
    Brief is the years' sojourn,   180
Sighs and regrets are all they leave behind:
Winged with the best desires of our mind,
They carry off our pleasures, every kind
    Of joy that won't return.

I can't help laughing when, in hollow rhymes,   185
Men swear they'd die for you a thousand times:
Don't say you heed such false preposterous claims
    Because I won't believe you.
But touching on this point, I'd have you know
That, without feigning or fake tears, I vow   190
To keep a strong and healthy body so
    That I can better serve you.

And of your beauties I will say just this:
Unless my eyes are dim and judge amiss,
I see a harmony where that beauty is   195
    Combined with your good grace;
As for my love, I'll say that my affection
Has reached a point that must be the perfection
Of what a man can feel when seized by passion
    For woman's lovely face.   200

But if you still prefer old Petrarch's mode,
I'll try my hand at a melodious ode
And soar again up to the gods' abode
    On stronger wings; and there
Amid the throng of massed divinities,   205
I'll choose a hundred thousand novelties
With which to paint the finest of your beauties
    On the most fair Idea.

Pierre de Ronsard

Les Amours

Le Premier Livre des Amours (Cassandre)

1 (1)

Qui voudra voir* comme Amour me surmonte,
    Comme il m'assaut, comme il se fait vainqueur,
    Comme il renflamme et renglace mon cœur,
    Comme il reçoit un honneur de ma honte :
Qui voudra voir une jeunesse prompte   5
    A suivre en vain l'objet de son malheur,
    Me vienne lire : il verra la douleur,
    Dont ma Déesse et mon Dieu ne font compte.
Il connaîtra qu'Amour est sans raison,
    Un doux abus, une belle prison,
    Un vain espoir qui de vent nous vient paître :   10
 Et connaîtra que l'homme se déçoit,
    Quand plein d'erreur un aveugle il reçoit
    Pour sa conduite, un enfant pour son maître.

2 (3)

Entre les rais de sa jumelle flamme
    Je vis Amour qui son arc débandait,
    Et dans mon cœur le brandon épandait,
    Qui des plus froids les moelles enflamme :
Puis en deux parts près les yeux de ma Dame,   5
    Couverts de fleurs un rets d'or* me tendait,
    Qui tout crépu sur sa face pendait
    A flots ondés pour enlacer mon âme.
Qu'eussé-je fait ? l'Archer était si doux,
    Si doux son feu, si doux l'or de ses nouds,   10
    Qu'en leurs filets encore je m'oublie :
Mais cet oubli ne me travaille point,
    Tant doucement le doux Archer me point,
    Le feu me brûle, et l'or crêpe me lie.

3 (9)

Le plus touffu d'un solitaire bois,*
    Le plus aigu d'une roche sauvage,

The Love Poems

The First Book of Love Poems (Cassandra)

1 (1)

If you would see how Love has mastered me,
    How he attacks, subjecting every part,
    How he will kindle and then freeze my heart,
    How he exploits my shame to swell his glory;
If you would see rash youth so readily   5
    Follow what caused its misery from the start,
    Then come and read me: you will see the smart
    To which my God and Goddess pay no heed.
Then you will learn that Love is without reason,
    It is a splendid jail, a sweet deception,   10
    A hope that's futile, feeding us on wind.
And you will learn how deeply man deceives
    Himself when in his ignorance he receives
    No other master than a child who's blind.

2 (3)

Between the twin bright fires of her eyes
    I saw the God of Love bending his bow,
    And in my heart the brand began to glow
    That heats the coldest marrow with its blaze.
To frame her face Love knowingly devised   5
    A cunning net, covered with flowers, so
    That he could hang it where those ringlets flow
    And tangle up my soul to be his prize.
What could I do? The Archer was so sweet,
    So sweet his flame, so sweet each golden knot   10
    That captured I forgot myself again.
But this forgetting is no cause for care,
    So sweetly does the Archer pierce me there,
    And sweet the curls that bind, the searing flame.

3 (9)

The lonely wood that hides the thickest grove,
    The sharpest pinnacle that rears its head,

Le plus désert d'un séparé rivage,
Et le frayeur des antres les plus cois,
Soulagent tant mes soupirs et ma voix,   5
    Qu'au seul écart d'un plus secret ombrage
    Je sens guarir cette amoureuse rage,
    Qui me raffole au plus vert de mes mois.
Là renversé dessus la terre dure,
    Hors de mon sein je tire une peinture,   10
    De tous mes maux le seul allègement :
Dont les beautés par Denisot encloses
    Me font sentir mille métamorphoses
    Tout en un coup d'un regard seulement.

4 (20)

Je voudrais bien richement jaunissant
    En pluie d'or* goutte à goutte descendre
    Dans le giron de ma belle Cassandre,
    Lorsqu'en ses yeux le somme va glissant.
Puis je voudrais en taureau blanchissant   5
    Me transformer pour sur mon dos la prendre,
    Quand en Avril par l'herbe la plus tendre
    Elle va fleur mille fleurs ravissant.
Je voudrais bien pour alléger ma peine,
    Être un Narcisse et elle une fontaine,   10
    Pour m'y plonger une nuit à séjour :
Et si voudrais que cette nuit encore
    Fût éternelle et que jamais l'Aurore
    Pour m'éveiller ne rallumât le jour.

5 (36)

Pour la douleur qu'Amour veut que je sente,
    Ainsi que moi Phébus* tu lamentais,
    Quand amoureux et banni tu chantais
    Près d'Ilion sur les rives de Xanthe.
Pinçant en vain ta lyre blandissante,   5
    Fleuves et fleurs et bois tu enchantais,
    Non la beauté qu'en l'âme tu sentais,
    Qui te navrait d'une plaie aigrissante.

The most deserted shoreline, wild and wide,
    And the uncanny silence of the caves,
All calm my sighs and soothe me when I grieve,   5
    For only when I find some secret shade
    I seem to heal the madness that has made
    My flourishing youth into a waste of love.
There, lying on the naked earth, I draw
    A painting from my breast and keep it sure   10
    As the sole remedy for my mischance;
For Denisot has framed such beauties that
    A thousand metamorphoses break out
    And overcome me at a single glance.

4 (20)

I wish I could grow yellow and devise
    To be a golden shower that drop by drop
    Would fall into my fair Cassandra's lap
    As sleep comes stealing softly in her eyes.
I wish I were a bull, for in that guise   5
    I'd bend my broad white back and take her up
    In April when around her every step
    The fresh young grass and ravished flowers rise.
I wish that I could ease the pains I feel
    As if I were Narcissus, she the pool;   10
    I'd dive straight in and please myself all night;
And what is more, I wish that night would last
    Forever so Aurora could not cast
    Her rays to wake me with the morning light.

5 (36)

The pains decreed by Love that now I try
    Are those that caused, Phoebus, your own lament
    When sick with love, condemned to banishment,
    You sang on Xanthus' banks, with Troy hard by.
You plucked the lyre in vain; your melody   5
    Charmed woods and streams but never could enchant
    The beauty who possessed your soul and sent
    The festering wound of your long agony.

Là de ton teint tu pâlissais les fleurs,
    Là les ruisseaux s'augmentaient de tes pleurs,   10
    Là tu vivais d'une espérance vaine.
Pour même nom Amour me fait douloir
    Près de Vendôme au rivage du Loir,
    Comme un Phénix renaissant de ma peine.

6 (41)

Quand au matin ma Déesse s'habille,
    D'un riche or crêpe ombrageant ses talons,
    Et les filets de ses beaux cheveux blonds
    En cent façons énonde et entortille :
Je l'accompare à l'écumière fille*   5
    Qui or' peignant les siens brunement longs,
    Or' les frisant en mille crêpillons,
    Passait la mer portée en sa coquille.
De femme humaine encore ne sont pas
    Son ris, son front, ses gestes, ne ses pas,   10
    Ne de ses yeux l'une et l'autre étincelle.
Rocs, eaux, ne bois, ne logent point en eux
    Nymphe qui ait si folâtres cheveux,
    Ni l'œil si beau, ni la bouche si belle.

7 (43)

Ores la crainte et ores l'espérance*
    De tous côtés se campent en mon cœur :
    Ni l'un ni l'autre au combat n'est vainqueur,
    Pareils en force et en persévérance.
Ores douteux, ores plein d'assurance,   5
    Entre l'espoir, le soupçon et la peur,
    Pour être en vain de moi-même trompeur,
    Au cœur captif je promets délivrance.
Verrai-je point avant mourir le temps,
    Que je tondrai la fleur de son printemps,   10
    Sous qui ma vie à l'ombrage demeure ?
Verrai-je point qu'en ses bras enlacé,
    Recru d'amour tout pantois et lassé,
    D'un beau trépas entre ses bras je meure?*

There your pale looks drained colour from the flowers,
 There streams were swollen with your tearful showers,   10
 There your life-giving hope was hope in vain.
Now Love torments me with that very name
 Where the Loir flows, close to my own Vendôme,
 Seeming reborn, a Phoenix, with my pain.

6 (41)

·When in the morning my fair Goddess wears
 A rich gold crêpe that reaches to her heels,
 And when she gathers up her stray blond curls
 And twines a hundred ways her waving hair;
Only the sea-foam's daughter can compare   5
 When she combs out her flowing locks unfurled,
 Or sails the sea, naked upon a shell,
 Those ringlets lifted by the lovesick air.
No mortal woman ever had that smile,
 The brow, the bearing, gestures that beguile,   10
 Nor yet the sparkling glance her eyes dart forth.
Never was found in waters, woods, and rocks
 A nymph with such enchanting wanton locks,
 Or such a lovely eye or lovelier mouth.

7 (43)

Now fear, now hope, invade from every side,
 To set up camp and occupy my heart;
 Neither can be a victor in the fight,
 Equally strong and stubborn to abide.
Assailed by hope, by deep mistrust and dread,   5
 Now full of confidence, now plagued with doubt,
 I promise freedom to my captive heart,
 Vain self-deceit by which the truth's denied.
Shall I not see, before I die, the time
 When I shall pluck the flower of her prime —   10
 She who now casts a shadow on my youth?
Shall I not see myself, when that day comes,
 Breathless and spent, exhausted in her arms,
 Dying in her embrace a lovely death?

8 (44)

Je voudrais être Ixion et Tantale,*
    Dessus la roue et dans les eaux là-bas,
    Et nu à nu presser entre mes bras
    Cette beauté qui les anges égale.
S'ainsin était, toute peine fatale   5
    Me serait douce et ne me chaudrait pas
    Non d'un vautour fussé-je le repas,
    Non, qui le roc remonte et redévale.*
Voir ou toucher le rond de son tétin
    Pourrait changer mon amoureux destin   10
    Aux majestés des Princes de l'Asie :
Un demi-dieu me ferait son baiser,
    Et sein sur sein mon feu désembraser,
    Un de ces Dieux qui mangent l'Ambroisie.

9 (52)

Avant qu'Amour du Chaos ocieux*
    Ouvrît le sein qui couvait la lumière
    Avec la terre, avec l'onde première,
    Sans art, sans forme étaient brouillés les Cieux.
Tel mon esprit à rien industrieux,   5
    Dedans mon corps, lourde et grosse matière,
    Errait sans forme et sans figure entière,
    Quand l'arc d'Amour le perça par tes yeux.
Amour rendit ma nature parfaite,
    Pure par lui mon essence s'est faite,   10
    Il me donna la vie et le pouvoir,
Il échauffa tout mon sang de sa flamme,
    Et m'agitant de son vol fit mouvoir
    Aveque lui mes pensers et mon âme.

10 (78)

Petit barbet,* que tu es bienheureux,
    Si ton bonheur tu savais bien entendre,
    D'ainsi ton corps entre ses bras étendre,
    Et de dormir en son sein amoureux !
Où moi je vis chétif et langoureux,   5

8 (44)

Would I were Tantalus or Ixion,
    Neck-high in water or upon the wheel,
    If, flesh to naked flesh, my hands might feel
    A beauty such as heavenly angels own.
For all such cruel sentences would then   5
    Become a pleasure; I'd not care at all;
    Not if a vulture took me for his meal
    Nor if my rock, pushed up, rolled down again.
To see or touch the roundness of her breast
    Would change my fate, raise me above the rest   10
    Of lovers like some stately Asian Prince.
I would be made a demigod by her kiss,
    Our bodies joined, my fire quenched in bliss,
    A God who has Ambrosia to drink.

9 (52)

Before Love opened up the brooding womb
    Of idle Chaos whence the light would rise
    Together with the primal earth and seas,
    The Heavens were vague and turbid, without form.
My soul within my body was the same,   5
    Bogged down in matter, wandering aimless ways,
    Unfinished, shapeless, until your sharp eyes,
    Love's arrows, pierced it with a perfect aim.
Now by Love's work my nature is perfected,
    Through him my essence has been purified,   10
    I have been given life and power by Love:
My blood is heated by his potent flame,
    And with his flight he urges me to move
    My soul and all my thoughts to follow him.

10 (78)

If only you could know your happiness,
    How happy, little spaniel, you would be,
    Your body in her arms so tenderly
    And sleeping softly on her loving breast!
While I live here, enfeebled and depressed   5

Pour savoir trop ma fortune comprendre.
Las ! pour vouloir en ma jeunesse apprendre
Trop de raisons, je me fis malheureux.
Je voudrais être un pitaut de village,
   Sot, sans raison et sans entendement,   10
   Ou fagoteur qui travaille au bocage :
Je n'aurais point en amour sentiment.
   Le trop d'esprit me cause mon dommage,
   Et mon mal vient de trop de jugement.

11 (94)

Soit que son or se crêpe lentement,
   Ou soit qu'il vague en deux glissantes ondes,
   Qui ça, qui là par le sein vagabondes,
   Et sur le col nagent folâtrement :
Ou soit qu'un noud illustré richement   5
   De maints rubis et maintes perles rondes,
   Serre les flots de ses deux tresses blondes,
   Mon cœur se plaît en son contentement.
Quel plaisir est-ce, ainçois quelle merveille,
   Quand ses cheveux troussés dessus l'oreille,   10
   D'une Vénus imitent la façon ?
Quand d'un bonnet sa tête elle Adonise,
   Et qu'on ne sait s'elle est fille ou garçon*
   Tant sa beauté en tous deux se déguise?

12 STANCES*

Quand au temple nous serons
Agenouillés, nous ferons
Les dévots selon la guise
De ceux qui pour louer Dieu
Humbles se courbent au lieu   5
Le plus secret de l'Église.

   Mais quand au lit nous serons
Entrelacés, nous ferons
Les lascifs selon les guises
Des Amants qui librement   10
Pratiquent folâtrement
Dans les draps cent mignardises.

Because I sought to know my destiny.
As a young man, I far too cleverly
Reasoned myself into this deep distress.
I wish I were a rustic village clod
    With neither sense nor reason of my own,   10
    Who scours the forest floor for firewood:
Then I'd feel nothing of love's joy and pain.
    My ills are caused by all the wit I had
    And judgement in excess has been my bane.

11 (94)

Whether she softly curls her golden hair
    Or lets it fall in two great waves that slide
    Over her breasts, swaying from side to side,
    Or on her neck with such a wanton air:
Or, perhaps, gathered in a knot that bears   5
    Round pearls and glowing rubies multiplied,
    She seeks to hold in check that flooding tide,
    It pleases me to take my pleasure there.
What pleasure, what a marvel have we here
    When she tucks up her hair above her ear,   10
    Copying Venus who looks just that way!
Or when, Adonis-like, she wears a bonnet,
    Her face so well disguised (I'd bet upon it)
    You can't tell whether she's a girl or boy.

12 STANZAS

When we're in church we'll seek to please,
Devoutly kneeling on our knees,
Good pious folk who choose that way
To praise the Lord by bending low
In some dark corner where they go   5
To find a quiet place and pray.

But when we come back home to bed,
We'll try another act instead,
As Lovers do who freely meet,
And twined together only aim   10
To play a hundred wanton games
And frolic free between the sheets.

Pourquoi donque quand je veux
Ou mordre tes beaux cheveux,
Ou baiser ta bouche aimée,   15
Ou toucher à ton beau sein,
Contrefais-tu la nonnain
Dedans un cloître enfermée ?

Pour qui gardes-tu tes yeux
Et ton sein délicieux,   20
Ton front, ta lèvre jumelle ?
En veux-tu baiser Pluton
Là-bas, après que Charon
T'aura mise en sa nacelle ?

Après ton dernier trépas,   25
Grêle, tu n'auras là-bas
Qu'une bouchette blêmie :
Et quand mort je te verrais
Aux Ombres je n'avouerais
Que jadis tu fus m'amie.   30

Ton test n'aura plus de peau,
Ni ton visage si beau
N'aura veines ni artères :
Tu n'auras plus que les dents
Telles qu'on les voit dedans   35
Les têtes de cimetières.

Donque tandis que tu vis,
Change, Maîtresse, d'avis,
Et ne m'épargne ta bouche :
Incontinent tu mourras,   40
Lors tu te repentiras
De m'avoir été farouche.

Ah je meurs ! ah baise-moi !
Ah, Maîtresse, approche-toi !
Tu fuis comme un Faon qui tremble :   45

Why is it then that when I dare
To bite a bunch of your lush hair
Or kiss your mouth or take just one 15
Soft-stealing touch of your sweet breast,
You start to shudder and protest
As if you were some cloistered nun?

Those precious charms that you preserve,
The sparkling eyes, the gentle curve 20
Of that fine breast, the tempting lip:
Who are they for? Will you kiss Pluto
Down in the Underworld you'll go to
When Charon's had you in his ship?

There you'll be scrawny, pale and gaunt, 25
You'll have no rosy lips to vaunt,
Once you are dead and life's all over.
And if, when dead myself, I spy
You with the Shades, I shall deny
That you have ever been my lover. 30

There'll be no skin upon your head;
Your lovely face will then have shed
Its web of arteries and veins.
You'll still have teeth, but they will be
Like stumps inside the skulls you see 35
Amid the charnel-house remains.

And therefore, while you live these days,
Change, my dear Mistress, change your ways,
Do not disjoin your mouth from mine;
Soon death will come to seal your fate 40
And then you will repent too late
That you were ever so unkind.

I'm dying. Ah! Give me a kiss,
Come close to me, closer than this;
You're trembling like a Fawn that flees. 45

Au moins souffre que ma main
S'ébatte un peu dans ton sein,
Ou plus bas, si bon te semble.

13 (146)

Tout effrayé* je cherche une fontaine
    Pour expier un horrible songer,
    Qui toute nuit ne m'a fait que ronger
    L'âme effrayée au travail de ma peine.
Il me semblait que ma douce-inhumaine   5
    Criait, Ami, sauve-moi du danger,
    À toute force un larron étranger
    Par les forêts prisonnière m'emmène.
Lors en sursaut, où me guidait la voix,
    Le fer au poing je brossai dans le bois :   10
    Mais en courant après la dérobée,
Du larron même assaillir me suis veu,
    Qui me perçant le cœur de mon épée,
    M'a fait tomber dans un torrent de feu.

14 (152)

Lune à l'œil brun, Déesse* aux noirs chevaux,
    Qui ça, qui là, qui haut, qui bas te tournent,
    Et de retours qui jamais ne séjournent,
    Traînent ton char éternel en travaux :
À tes désirs les miens ne sont égaux,   5
    Car les amours qui ton âme époinçonnent,
    Et les ardeurs qui la mienne aiguillonnent,
    Divers souhaits désirent à leurs maux.
Toi mignotant ton dormeur de Latmie,
    Voudrais toujours qu'une course endormie   10
    Retînt le train de ton char qui s'enfuit :
Mais moi qu'Amour toute la nuit dévore,
    Depuis le soir je souhaite l'Aurore,
    Pour voir le jour, que me celait ta nuit.

15 (168)

Puisque je n'ai pour faire ma retraite
    Du Labyrinth', qui va me séduisant,

Allow, at least, my hand to rest
And play a little on your breast;
Or even lower, as you please.

13 (146)

In terror I seek out a spring to free
　My mind from the atrocious dream I had
　All night without relief: it drove me mad,
　Gnawing the soul it plunged in agony.
I heard my sweet inhuman lady cry:　　　　　　5
　'Come save me, Friend; some ruffian has laid
　Strange hands on me, and through the forest glade
　Will haul me off into captivity.'
I leapt to follow where that voice might lead,
　And sword in hand rushed headlong through the wood,　10
　Seeking my stolen lady; but the same
Strange ruffian was there, lying in wait,
　Who with my own sword pierced me to the heart,
　And dropped me in an avalanche of flame.

14 (152)

Brown-eyed Goddess, bright moon whose sable horses
　Draw you now here, now there, and high and low,
　Appearing but not stopping as they go,
　Pulling your chariot round in cyclic courses,
Your fierce desires are not like mine; what causes　　5
　The passion that torments your soul has no
　Resemblance to the ardour that I know:
　To ease our pain we look to different forces.
While on Mount Latmos you caress your sleeper
　Your only hope is that a lucky slumber　　　　　10
　Will slow your chariot as it speeds away.
But I, whom Love devours all night long,
　From evening on yearn for the Dawn to bring
　What your night hid from me, the light of day.

15 (168)

Since I'm not Theseus and have no thread
　To help me find a path out of the Maze,

Comme Thésée, un filet conduisant
Mes pas douteux dans les erreurs de Crète :
Eussé-je au moins une poitrine faite   5
Ou de cristal, ou de verre luisant,
Ton œil irait dedans mon cœur lisant
De quelle foi mon amour est parfaite.
Si tu savais de quelle affection
Je suis captif de ta perfection,   10
La mort serait un confort à ma plainte :
Et lors peut-être éprise de pitié,
Tu pousserais sur ma dépouille éteinte,
Quelque soupir de tardive amitié.*

16 (172)

Je veux brûler, pour m'envoler aux cieux,
Tout l'imparfait de mon écorce humaine.
M'éternisant comme le fils d'Alcmène,*
Qui tout en feu s'assit entre les Dieux.
Jà mon esprit désireux de son mieux,   5
Dedans ma chair, rebelle, se promène,
Et jà le bois de sa victime amène
Pour s'immoler aux rayons de tes yeux.
Ô saint brasier, ô flamme entretenue
D'un feu divin, advienne que ton chaud   10
Brûle si bien ma dépouille connue,
Que libre et nu je vole d'un plein saut
Outre le ciel, pour adorer là-haut
L'autre beauté* dont la tienne est venue.

17 (174)

Or' que le ciel,* or' que la terre est pleine
De glas, de grêle éparse en tous endroits,
Et que l'horreur des plus froidureux mois
Fait hérisser les cheveux de la plaine :
Or' que le vent qui mutin se promène,   5
Rompt les rochers, et déplante les bois,
Et que la mer redoublant ses abois,
Sa rage enflée aux rivages amène :

Spellbound I stay, lost in the Cretan ways,
    Without a guide for my uncertain tread;
Had I at least a breast that had been made   5
    Of lucent crystal or transparent glass,
    Into my heart your eye would surely pass
    And read the love and faith that there abide.
If you could know how your perfection makes
    Me captive to the passion it awakes,   10
    Then Death might soothe the pain of my complaint,
And moved perhaps by pity you'd bestow
    Upon my poor remains interred below
    Some passing sigh of love that comes too late.

16 (172)

I long to burn away all imperfections
    That plague this mortal coil so that I rise
    And make myself immortal in the skies,
    As, with the Gods, Alcmene's fiery son.
Within my body, seeking to obtain   5
    Its highest good, the rebel soul supplies
    Wood for the victim's final sacrifice,
    An immolation that your eyes ordain.
O holy pyre, flame forever fed
    By fire divine, may your consuming heat   10
    Burn so completely my familiar shroud
That free and naked, to a greater height
    Beyond the heavens I leap, and there adore
    The other beauty from which yours was born.

17 (174)

Now when the earth and skies are clogged with ice
    And unremitting hail falls everywhere,
    When grasses of the field bristle like hair
    In horror at the coldest month's duress;
Now when the wind, in its disruptive course,   5
    Breaks rocks, uproots the woods and strips them bare,
    And when the sea, surging towards the shore,
    Ramps on the beaches with redoubled force:

Amour me brûle, et l'hiver froidureux
    Qui gèle tout, de mon feu chaleureux   10
    Ne gèle point l'ardeur qui toujours dure.
Voyez, Amants, comme je suis traité,
    Je meurs de froid au plus chaud de l'été,
    Et de chaleur au cœur de la froidure.

18 (177)

Au même lit où pensif je repose,
    Presque ma Dame en langueur trépassa
    Devant-hier, quand la fièvre effaça
    Son teint d'œillets, et sa lèvre de rose.
Une vapeur avec sa fièvre éclose,   5
    Dedans le lit son venin me laissa,
    Qui par destin, diverse m'offensa
    D'une autre fièvre en mes veines enclose.
L'un après l'autre elle avait froid et chaud :
    Ne l'un ne l'autre à mon mal ne défaut :   10
    Et quand l'un croît, l'autre ne diminue.
L'accès fiévreux toujours ne la tentait,
    De deux jours l'un sa chaleur s'alentait :
    Je sens toujours la mienne continue.

19 (192)

Il faisait chaud,* et le somme coulant
    Se distillait dans mon âme songearde,
    Quand l'incertain d'une idole gaillarde
    Fut doucement mon dormir affolant.
Penchant sous moi son bel ivoire blanc,   5
    Et m'y tirant sa langue frétillarde,
    Me baisotait d'une lèvre mignarde,
    Bouche sur bouche, et le flanc sur le flanc.
Que de coral, que de lis, que de roses,
    Ce me semblait à pleines mains décloses   10
    Tâtais-je lors entre deux maniements ?
Mon Dieu, mon Dieu, de quelle douce haleine,
    De quelle odeur était sa bouche pleine,
    De quels rubis, et de quels diamants ?

Love burns me, and the winter's bitter chill
    That freezes all things, cannot ever cool   10
    An ardour over which it has no hold.
Lovers, now see the contraries I meet:
    I die of cold in summer's torrid heat
    And die of heat here in the heart of cold.

18 (177)

In this same bed where pensive I repose
    The other day my Lady almost died;
    She languished as a feverish pallor preyed
    On her carnation cheeks and lips' red rose.
Her fever left a toxic vapour whose   5
    Poison lay waiting for me in this bed,
    Yet fate has willed that in my veins should spread
    Another fever, not the one she knows.
First she was cold, then hot—one, then the other;
    But in my sickness I have both together,   10
    The growth of one won't ease the other pain.
She was not always subject to the fever
    And every second day the heat would leave her;
    I always feel that mine goes on and on.

19 (192)

The day was hot, my drowsy sense was lost
    In dreams when some vague spirit softly stole,
    Like my fair idol's ghost, into my soul,
    And settled there, a trouble to my rest.
Leaning above me, tenderly she pressed   5
    Down with her agile tongue and ivory smile,
    With dainty lips kissing me all the while,
    Mouth upon mouth and naked breast on breast.
What coral wealth, what blooming lily and rose,
    Or so it seemed, could I at last enclose,   10
    Pressing, caressing them with two full hands?
O God, O God, the sweetness of her breath
    The fine aroma wafting from her mouth,
    And with what rubies and what diamonds!

20 (227)

Le Jeu, la Grâce, et les Frères Jumeaux
    Suivent ma Dame, et quelque part qu'elle erre,
    Dessous ses pieds fait émailler la terre,
    Et des hivers fait des printemps nouveaux.
En sa faveur jargonnent les oiseaux,   5
    Ses vents Éole en sa caverne enserre,
    Le doux Zéphyr un doux soupir desserre,
    Et tous muets s'accoisent les ruisseaux.
Les Éléments se remirent en elle,
    Nature rit de voir chose si belle :   10
    Je tremble tout, que quelqu'un de ces Dieux
Ne passionne après son beau visage,
    Et qu'en pillant le trésor de notre âge,
    Ne la ravisse et ne l'emporte aux cieux.

21 ÉLÉGIE À JANET PEINTRE DU ROI

    Peins-moi, Janet,* peins-moi je te supplie,
Sur ce tableau les beautés de m'amie
De la façon que je te les dirai.
Comme importun je ne te supplierai
D'un art menteur quelque faveur lui faire.   5
Il suffit bien si tu la sais portraire
Telle qu'elle est, sans vouloir déguiser
Son naturel pour la favoriser :
Car la faveur n'est bonne que pour celles
Qui se font peindre, et qui ne sont pas belles.   10
    Fais-lui premier les cheveux ondelés,
Serrés, retors, recrêpés, annelés,
Qui de couleur le cèdre représentent :
Ou les allonge, et que libres ils sentent
Dans le tableau, si par art tu le peux,   15
La même odeur de ses propres cheveux :
Car ses cheveux comme fleurettes sentent,
Quand les Zéphyrs au printemps les éventent.
    Que son beau front ne soit entre-fendu
De nul sillon en profond étendu,   20
Mais qu'il soit tel qu'est l'eau de la marine

20 (227)

Play joined with Grace and the Fraternal Twins
    Follow my Lady everywhere she goes,
    Under her feet a flowery carpet grows,
    Converting all the winters to new springs.
For her alone the jargoning birds will sing,   5
    The garrulous brook falls silent as it flows,
    Zephyr exhales the sweetest of his sighs
    And in his cave Aeolus chains the winds.
The Elements come to see themselves in her
    And Nature smiles to see a thing so fair.   10
    I tremble, fearing that some God like these,
Impassioned by that face with lust divine,
    In pillaging the treasure of our time,
    Will catch her up and snatch her to the skies.

21 ELEGY FOR JANET, PAINTER TO THE KING

    Paint for me, Janet, paint me, I implore
The beauties of the girl that I adore
And follow me as I describe each part.
I won't keep nagging for mendacious art
To do her any favours; all I say   5
Is that it will be fine if you portray
Her as she is and bring before our eyes
A natural beauty that needs no disguise;
For girls with whom such favours go down well
Love painting since they are not beautiful.   10
    So let's begin: first paint her waving hair,
Its coils and curls, its ringlets twined with care,
Reddish like wood cut from a cedar tree;
Or else spread fully out and floating free;
And, if you can, paint it so that we feel,   15
Wafting across, as if that hair were real,
A scent like early flowers blossoming
When gentle Zephyr fans them in the spring.
    Don't let her lovely brow be lined or stained
By wrinkles or by furrows deep ingrained,   20
But make it smooth like the unruffled seas

Quand tant soit peu le vent ne la mutine,
Et que gisante en son lit elle dort,
Calmant ses flots sillés d'un somme mort.

Tout au milieu par la grève descende   25
Un beau rubis, de qui l'éclat s'épande
Par le tableau, ainsi qu'on voit de nuit
Briller les rais de la Lune qui luit
Dessus la neige au fond d'un val coulée,
De trace d'homme encore non foulée.   30

Après fais-lui son beau sourcil voûtis
D'Ébène noir, et que son plis tortis
Semble un Croissant, qui montre par la nue
Au premier mois sa voûture cornue :
Ou si jamais tu as vu l'arc d'Amour,   35
Prends le portrait dessus le demi-tour
De sa courbure à demi-cercle close :
Car l'arc d'Amour et lui n'est qu'une chose.

Mais las ! Janet, hélas je ne sais pas
Par quel moyen, ni comment tu peindras   40
(Voire eusses-tu l'artifice d'Apelle)
De ses beaux yeux la grâce naturelle,
Qui font vergogne aux étoiles des Cieux.
Que l'un soit doux, l'autre soit furieux,
Que l'un de Mars, l'autre de Vénus tienne :   45
Que du bénin toute espérance vienne,
Et du cruel vienne tout désespoir :
L'un soit piteux et larmoyant à voir,
Comme celui d'Ariane laissée
Aux bords de Die, alors que l'insensée   50
Près de la mer, de pleurs se consumait,
Et son Thésée en vain elle nommait :
L'autre soit gai, comme il est bien croyable
Que l'eut jadis Pénélope louable
Quand elle vit son mari retourné   55
Ayant vingt ans loin d'elle séjourné.

Après fais-lui sa rondelette oreille
Petite, unie, entre blanche et vermeille,
Qui sous le voile apparaisse à l'égal
Que fait un lis enclos dans un cristal,   60

When there's no breath of a rebellious breeze,
The waveless waters lying in their bed,
Sleeping as calmly as if they were dead.

    Between the hair and brow be sure to place 25
A ruby whose great shining fills the space
Of the whole picture, as one sees at night
The Moonshine spreading out its radiant light
Over a valley where the virgin snow
Lies pure and human footsteps never go. 30

    Then trace the ebony eyebrow's lovely line,
A perfect arching curve that calls to mind
The Crescent moon revealing through a cloud
Its slender horn when the new month comes round;
Or, if you ever chanced to see Love's bow, 35
That memory should help the portrait now:
Preserve that semicircle in your frame
For bow and brow are, in this case, the same.

    But O, alas, Janet, alas, I can't
Imagine how or with what means you'll paint 40
(Even if you were gifted like Apelles)
The natural grace that dwells in eyes like these
That put to shame the stars that stud the Heavens.
If one eye reassures, the other threatens,
If one eye's Venus, then the other's Mars; 45
The mild eye tells of hope that could be ours,
The cruel one speaks only of despair;
One has a piteous and tearful air
Like wretched Ariadne left alone
On Naxos' sandy shore to weep and moan 50
Beside the sea, half-senseless with the pain,
And calling on her Theseus in vain;
The other's no less happy, you might say,
Than was Penelope upon the day
She saw her absent husband reappear, 55
Not having been with him for twenty years.

    Then you should trace her little ear, I think,
Rounded and even, between white and pink,
Whose aspect, glimpsed beneath the veil can rival
A lily's fragile form encased in crystal 60

Ou tout ainsi qu'apparaît une rose
Tout fraîchement dedans un verre enclose.

   Mais pour néant tu aurais fait si beau
Tout l'ornement de ton riche tableau,
Si tu n'avais de la linéature   65
De son beau nez bien portrait la peinture.
Peins-le moi donc ni court, ni aquilin,
Poli, traitis, où l'envieux malin
Quand il voudrait n'y saurait que reprendre,
Tant proprement tu le feras descendre   70
Parmi la face, ainsi comme descend
Dans une plaine un petit mont qui pend.

   Après au vif peins-moi sa belle joue
Pareille au teint de la rose qui noue
Dessus du lait, ou au teint blanchissant   75
Du lis qui baise un œillet rougissant.

   Dans le milieu portrais une fossette,
Fossette, non, mais d'Amour la cachette,
D'où ce garçon de sa petite main
Lâche cent traits et jamais un en vain,   80
Que par les yeux droit au cœur il ne touche.

   Hélas ! Janet, pour bien peindre sa bouche,
À peine Homère en ses vers te dirait
Quel vermillon égaler la pourrait :
Car pour la peindre ainsi qu'elle mérite,   85
Peindre il faudrait celle d'une Charite.
Peins-la moi donc, qu'elle semble parler,
Ores sourire, ores embaumer l'air
De ne sais quelle ambrosienne haleine :
Mais par sur tout fais qu'elle semble pleine   90
De la douceur de persuasion.
Tout à l'entour attache un million
De ris, d'attraits, de jeux, de courtoisies,
Et que deux rangs de perlettes choisies
D'un ordre égal en la place des dents   95
Bien poliment soient arrangés dedans.

   Peins tout autour une lèvre bessonne,
Qui d'elle-même en s'élevant semonne
D'être baisée, ayant le teint pareil

Or else a fresh-plucked rose whose transient grace
Lives on a little longer under glass.
    But you'll have wasted all the time you've spent
To give your picture such rich ornament
Unless the portrait quite precisely shows   65
The perfect outline of her lovely nose;
Let it be neither short nor aquiline,
So neat and shapely that the most malign
And envious critics seek to make amends
And praise the way the dainty nose descends,   70
Surmounting that smooth face without a stain
Just as a little hill surmounts a plain.
    Now for her cheek a colour that would seem
A red rose floating in a bowl of cream,
Or else a lily blushing with the bliss   75
Her whiteness gains from a carnation's kiss.
    Then, in the middle of that cheek, a dimple.
A dimple? No, a hideout for the nimble
Archer who with his little hand takes aim;
A hundred arrows fly, not one in vain,   80
Directly through the eyes to strike the heart.
    Alas, Janet, next comes the mouth. What art
Could find vermilion to match its red
I don't think even Homer could have said.
One of the Graces, at a pinch, might serve   85
As model for the painting it deserves.
So make it seem that she is speaking there,
Smiling at times and perfuming the air
With what ambrosian breath I cannot tell;
But above all, as if the mouth were full   90
Of sweet persuasive power that beguiles,
Give it an escort of a million smiles,
With games and charms and every courteous grace;
Two rows of chosen pearls should take the place
Of teeth, each row being perfect like its twin,   95
Standing on guard in orderly ranks within.
    Then paint a pair of lips that can't resist
(See how they rise!) a longing to be kissed,
Having a special hue that makes one think

Ou de la rose, ou du coural vermeil :   100
Elle flambante au Printemps sur l'épine,
Lui rougissant au fond de la marine.

    Peins son menton au milieu fosselu,
Et que le bout en rondeur pommelu
Soit tout ainsi que l'on voit apparoître   105
Le bout d'un coin qui jà commence à croître.

    Plus blanc que lait caillé dessus le jonc
Peins-lui le col, mais peins-le un petit long,
Grêle et charnu, et sa gorge douillette
Comme le col soit un peu longuette.   110

    Après fais-lui par un juste compas,
Et de Junon les coudes et les bras,
Et les beaux doigts de Minerve, et encore
La main égale à celle de l'Aurore.

    Je ne sais plus, mon Janet, où j'en suis :   115
Je suis confus et muet : je ne puis
Comme j'ai fait, te déclarer le reste
De ces beautés qui ne m'est manifeste :
Las ! car jamais tant de faveurs je n'eus,
Que d'avoir vu ses beaux tétins à nu.   120
Mais si l'on peut juger par conjecture,
Persuadé de raisons je m'assure
Que la beauté qui ne s'apparaît, doit
Être semblable à celle que l'on voit,
Donque peins-la, et qu'elle me soit faite   125
Parfaite autant comme l'autre est parfaite.

    Ainsi qu'en bosse élève-moi son sein
Net, blanc, poli, large, entre-ouvert et plein,
Dedans lequel mille rameuses veines
De rouge sang tressaillent toutes pleines.   130

    Puis quand au vif tu auras découvert
Dessous la peau les muscles et les nerfs,
Enfle au-dessus deux pommes nouvelettes
Comme l'on voit deux pommes verdelettes
D'un oranger, qui encore du tout   135
Ne font qu'à l'heure à se rougir au bout.

    Tout au plus haut des épaules marbrines,
Peins le séjour des Charites divines,

Either of springtime rose or coral pink: 100
One from the thorn raises its flaming head,
The other blushes on the ocean bed.

    Now for the dimpled chin; show how its shape
Ends with the curve an apple has when ripe,
Or do it in a way that gently hints 105
At something like the swelling of a quince.

    Whiter than curds of milk on beds of straw,
Portray her slim soft neck, but then be sure
To make it somewhat long; likewise her throat
May seem more charming slightly lengthened out. 110

    Next find the right proportions that will show
Elbows and arms as fine as those of Juno,
The lovely fingers of Minerva and
Aurora's elegance in the slender hand.

    What's left? Janet, I don't know where I am; 115
Dumbstruck, confused. There's no way that I can
Describe with such familiarity
Beauties I've never had the luck to see.
Alas, for I have never been so blest
As to have seen her splendid naked breasts. 120
But, if we take conjecture for a guide,
I'm sure I have good reason on my side
When I affirm the beauty that's concealed
Can't be inferior to what's revealed.
So when you paint such beauty let me find 125
It's just as perfect as the other kind.

    So let her breast appear before my eyes,
Smooth, white, and broad, a plain two hills divide,
To which a thousand veins convey a flood
Of ever-flowing red pulsating blood. 130

    Next, when you've shown the life vibrating in
The muscles and the nerves beneath the skin,
Make two fresh apples swell above, whose sheen
Recalls the orange trees you may have seen
With unripe fruits so young that until now 135
Only the tips had any red to show.

    Between two domes of marble you can trace
A dwelling that the Graces love to grace,

Et que l'Amour sans cesse voletant
Toujours les couve et les aille éventant,   140
Pensant voler avec le Jeu son frère
De branche en branche ès vergers de Cythère.

   Un peu plus bas en miroir arrondi,
Tout potelé, grasselet, rebondi,
Comme celui de Vénus, peins son ventre :   145
Peins son nombril ainsi qu'un petit centre,
Le fond duquel paraisse plus vermeil
Qu'un bel œillet favori du Soleil.

   Qu'attends-tu plus ? portrais-moi l'autre chose
Qui est si belle, et que dire je n'ose,   150
Et dont l'espoir impatient me point :
Mais je te prie, ne me l'ombrage point,
Si ce n'était d'un voile fait de soie
Clair et subtil, afin qu'on l'entrevoie.

   Ses cuisses soient comme faites au Tour   155
À pleine chair, rondes tout à l'entour,
Ainsi qu'un Terme arrondi d'artifice
Qui soutient ferme un royal édifice.

   Comme deux monts enlève ses genoux,
Douillets, charnus, ronds, délicats et mous,   160
Dessous lesquels fais-lui la grève pleine,
Telle que l'ont les vierges de Lacène,
Quand près d'Eurote en s'accrochant des bras
Luttent ensemble et se jettent à bas :
Ou bien chassant à meutes découplées   165
Quelque vieil cerf ès forêts Amyclées.

   Puis pour la fin portrais-lui de Thétis
Les pieds étroits, et les talons petits.

   Ha, je la vois ! elle est presque portraite :
Encore un trait, encore un, elle est faite.   170
Lève tes mains, ha mon Dieu, je la vois !
Bien peu s'en faut qu'elle ne parle à moi.

And let Love ceaselessly fly round and bring
His brooding care and fan them with his wing,   140
Imagining he's flitting all the while
From branch to branch upon Cythera's isle.

    Formed like a convex mirror, further down,
Observe her belly, smooth and plump and round
Like that of Venus; paint her navel too,   145
That lovely little centre with a hue
In its recesses richer than the one
Found in carnations favoured by the Sun.

    You ask what's next? I want you to portray
A lovely part whose name I dare not say,   150
A part I've long been eager to invade;
I beg you, do not leave it in the shade.
Perhaps a silk transparent veil will do
So that at least we get a stealthy view.

    Then let your brush fill out her shapely thighs;   155
Sturdy and strong, well-rounded, they arise,
Much like those statues carved with artifice
Whose bulk sustains some regal edifice.

    Now draw her knees like little hills; your craft
Should show them smooth and dainty, round and soft;   160
Below the knee, the calf should be robust
With all the strength that Spartan virgins boast
When, wrestling naked on Eurotas' strand,
One strives to throw the other on the ground,
Or when they chase some poor old stag who flees   165
Their unleashed hounds in woods of Amycles.

    And last, to make this portraiture complete,
Let her have Thetis' heel and slender feet.

    Ah, now I see her! One more touch, just one!
That's almost it. One brushstroke! Now she's done!   170
Hands off! O God above, it's her I see!
It won't take much to make her speak with me.

Le Second Livre des Amours (Marie)

22 (1)

Tyard, on me blâmait* à mon commencement,
   De quoi j'étais obscur au simple populaire :
   Mais on dit aujourd'hui que je suis au contraire,
   Et que je me démens parlant trop bassement.
Toi de qui le labeur enfante doctement   5
   Des livres immortels, dis-moi, que dois-je faire ?
   Dis-moi (car tu sais tout) comme dois-je complaire
   À ce monstre têtu divers en jugement ?
Quand je tonne en mes vers il a peur de me lire :
   Quand ma voix se désenfle il ne fait qu'en médire,   10
   Dis-moi de quel lien, force, tenaille, ou clous
Tiendrai-je ce Protée qui se change à tous coups ?
   Tyard, je t'entends bien, il le faut laisser dire,
   Et nous rire de lui, comme il se rit de nous.

23 (4)

Le vingtième d'Avril* couché sur l'herbelette,
   Je vis ce me semblait en dormant, un Chevreuil,
   Qui ça, qui là marchait où le menait son vueil,
   Foulant les belles fleurs de mainte gambelette.
Une corne et une autre encore nouvelette   5
   Enflait son petit front d'un gracieux orgueil :
   Comme un Soleil luisait la rondeur de son œil,
   Et un carcan pendait sous sa gorge douillette.
Sitôt que je le vis, je voulais courre après,
   Et lui qui m'avisa prit sa fuite ès forêts,   10
   Où se moquant de moi ne me voulut attendre :
Mais en suivant son trac, je ne m'avisai pas
   D'un piège entre les fleurs, qui me lia le pas :
   Ainsi pour prendre autrui moi-même me fis prendre.

24 (19)

Marie levez-vous* ma jeune paresseuse,
   Jà la gaie Alouette au ciel a fredonné,
   Et jà le Rossignol doucement jargonné

The Second Book of Love Poems (Marie)

22 (1)

Tyard, they blamed me in my early days
  For being too obscure for simple folk,
  But now they find the contrary mistake,
  That I debase my speech in common ways.
Tell me, my friend, whose learned labours raise   5
  Immortal works, what action should I take?
  Tell me, since you must know, how can I make
  This fickle monster constant in my praise?
When my verse thunders he's afraid to read,
  And when I tone it down I'm damned instead.   10
  Tell me, have I no fetters, chain, or rope
To bind this Proteus who keeps changing shape?
  Tyard, I hear you, let him make a fuss,
  We'll laugh at him just as he laughs at us.

23 (4)

The twentieth of April as I lay
  Sleeping upon the grass I thought I saw
  A carefree Roebuck treading here and there
  Among the flowers in his wanton play.
Two dainty horns in graceful proud display   5
  New-formed upon his little brow he bore
  While at his downy throat a chain he wore
  And the Sun gave his eyes their fulgent ray.
No sooner was I roused by that fair sight
  Than I gave chase; he through the woods took flight,   10
  Turning to mock me, and refused to wait.
I followed, knowing not that I would meet
  Amid the flowers a snare that trapped my feet;
  So seeking to catch another, I was caught.

24 (19)

Marie, get up! Get up, young sleepyhead,
  The merry Lark has carolled to the sky;
  The lovesick Nightingale has trilled already

Dessus l'épine assis sa complainte amoureuse.
Sus debout allons voir l'herbelette perleuse,   5
    Et votre beau rosier de boutons couronné,
    Et vos œillets mignons auxquels aviez donné
    Hier au soir de l'eau d'une main si songneuse.
Harsoir en vous couchant vous jurâtes vos yeux
    D'être plus tôt que moi ce matin éveillée :   10
    Mais le dormir de l'Aube aux filles gracieux
Vous tient d'un doux sommeil encor les yeux sillée.
    Çà, çà que je les baise et votre beau tétin
    Cent fois pour vous apprendre à vous lever matin.

25 (44)

Marie, baisez-moi:* non, ne me baisez pas,
    Mais tirez-moi le cœur de votre douce haleine :
    Non, ne le tirez pas, mais hors de chaque veine
    Sucez-moi toute l'âme éparse entre vos bras :
Non, ne la sucez pas : car après le trépas   5
    Que serais-je sinon une semblance vaine,
    Sans corps dessur la rive, où l'amour ne démène
    (Pardonne-moi Pluton) qu'en feinte ses ébats ?
Pendant que nous vivons, entr'aimons nous, Marie,
    Amour ne règne point sur la troupe blêmie   10
    Des morts, qui sont sillés d'un long somme de fer.
C'est abus que Pluton ait aimé Proserpine,
    Si doux soin n'entre point en si dure poitrine :
    Amour règne en la terre et non point en enfer.

26 CHANSON

    Comme la cire* peu à peu,
Quand près de la flamme on l'approche,
Se fond à la chaleur du feu :
Ou comme au faîte d'une roche
La neige encore non foulée   5
Au Soleil se perd écoulée :

    Quand tu tournes tes yeux ardents
Sur moi d'une œillade gentille,
Je sens tout mon cœur au-dedans

A sad lament within its thorny bed.
Up then! We'll see the pearls that dew the mead,   5
   And what new buds your roses now display,
   And those carnations that but yesterday
   Your careful hands watered at eventide.
At bedtime yesterday by your eyes you swore
   That in the morning you'd be first to rise,   10
   But sleep that's kind to girls, sweet sleep of Dawn,
Still keeps you slumbering. I'll kiss those eyes
   A hundred times (your breasts as well), a warning
   That you should get up early in the morning.

25 (44)

Kiss me, Marie; or rather, do not kiss,
   But with your sweet breath draw my heart from me;
   Yet not my heart, for it had better be
   My soul sucked from each vein in your embrace;
No, not my soul, for would not death make this   5
   Body of mine a vacant entity
   On that far shore where only fantasy
   (Pardon me, Pluto) thinks love has a place?
So let us love each other while we live,
   Death's pallid troop knows not the reign of Love;   10
   Sleep binds them ironfast; their eyes are sealed.
Pluto loved Proserpine, lying tales attest;
   But no sweet pain could pierce so hard a breast:
   Love reigns on earth, not in the Underworld.

26 SONG

As, when the flame is brought too near,
The hardened wax is liquefied,
Unable to resist the heat;
Or as, upon a mountainside,
The Sunshine warms the untrodden snow   5
Until it thaws and streams below,

So, when you turn your ardent eyes
Upon me with a gentle glance,
I feel my heart within me fail,

Qui se consomme et se distille,   10
Et ma pauvre âme n'a partie
Qui ne soit en feu convertie.

    Comme une rose qu'un amant
Cache au sein de quelque pucelle
Qu'elle enferme bien chèrement   15
Près de son sein qui pommelle,
Puis chet fanie sur la place
Au soir quand elle se délace.

    Et comme un lis par trop lavé
De quelque pluie printanière,   20
Penche à bas son chef aggravé
Dessus la terre nourricière,
Sans que jamais il se relève,
Tant l'humeur pesante le grève :

    Ainsi ma tête à tous les coups   25
Se penche de tristesse à terre.
Sur moi ne bat veine ni pouls,
Tant la douleur le cœur me serre :
Je ne puis parler, et mon âme
Engourdie en mon corps se pâme.   30

    Adonques pâmé je mourrais,
Si d'un seul baiser de ta bouche
Mon âme tu ne secourais,
Et mon corps froid comme une souche :
Me ressoufflant en chaque veine   35
La vie par ta douce haleine.

    Mais c'est pour être tourmenté
De plus longue peine ordinaire,
Comme le cœur de Prométhé,
Qui se renaît à sa misère,   40
Éternel repas misérable
De son vautour insatiable.

Dissolved and self-consumed at once;   10
And in my soul I cannot claim
A part that does not feel the flame;

Or, like the rose a lover hides
Between the breasts of some young maid,
Who keeps it safe and guarded by   15
Those ripening apples, undisplayed
Until the night when she'll unlace
And find it withered in its place;

Or as a lily washed too much
By rain in spring will bend its head,   20
Weary and heavy-laden to
The bounteous earth where it was bred;
So burdensome the moisture lies
That it can never hope to rise:

Likewise my head at every blow   25
Is bent with sadness to the ground;
There is no throb in vein or pulse,
So firmly sorrow has me bound;
I cannot speak, my soul is numb,
My fainting body overcome.   30

And so, thus fainting, I must die
Unless you choose to cure my soul
With just one kiss from your dear mouth,
Enough to warm my body's cold,
Your sweet breath filling every vein   35
To bring me back to life again.

But this is for my greater pain
And a far longer torment brings,
Like sad Prometheus whose heart
Revived each day his sufferings,   40
With a deep wound that night would heal
To be the unsated vulture's meal.

27 (60)

Marie tout ainsi* que vous m'avez tourné
   Ma raison qui de libre est maintenant servile,
   Ainsi m'avez tourné mon grave premier style
   Que pour chanter si bas n'était point ordonné.
Au moins si vous m'aviez pour ma perte donné   5
   Congé de manier votre cuisse gentile,
   Ou bien si vous étiez à mes désirs facile,
   Je n'eusse regretté mon style abandonné.
Las ! ce qui plus me deult, c'est que n'êtes contente
   De voir que ma Muse est si basse et si rampante,   10
   Qui soulait apporter aux Français un effroi :
Mais votre peu d'amour ma loyauté tourmente,
   Et sans aucun espoir d'une meilleure attente
   Toujours vous me liez et triomphez de moi.

28 AMOURETTE

Or que l'hiver* roidit la glace épaisse,
Réchauffons-nous ma gentille maîtresse,
Non accroupis près le foyer cendreux,
Mais aux plaisirs des combats amoureux.
Assisons-nous sur cette molle couche :   5
Sus baisez-moi, tendez-moi votre bouche,
Pressez mon col de vos bras dépliés,
Et maintenant votre mère oubliez.
   Que de la dent votre tétin je morde,
Que vos cheveux fil à fil je détorde :   10
Il ne faut point en si folâtres jeux,
Comme au dimanche arranger vos cheveux.
   Approchez donc, tournez-moi votre joue.
Vous rougissez ? il faut que je me joue.
Vous souriez : avez-vous point ouï   15
Quelque doux mot qui vous ait réjoui ?
Je vous disais que la main j'allais mettre
Sur votre sein : le voulez-vous permettre ?
Ne fuyez pas sans parler : je vois bien
À vos regards que vous le voulez bien.   20
Je vous connais en voyant votre mine.

27 (60)

Just as, Marie, you have transformed my mind,
   Making my reason that was free your slave,
   So you have changed my style, once high and grave
   And for such lowly matter not designed.
If, to make up this loss, you were inclined   5
   To let me feel your thigh or give me leave
   To try some other pleasures that I crave,
   I would not mourn the style I left behind.
What grieves me most is that it's not enough
   To have debased my Muse, slouching and rough,   10
   That Muse that kept the French in awe of me;
But that I'm tortured by your loveless scorn
   As, with no prospect of a better dawn,
   You keep me bound and vaunt your victory.

28 LOVE SONG

When deep midwinter makes the waters freeze,
We'll warm ourselves, my love, the way we please,
Not crouched around the embers of a fire,
But hot from bouts of amorous desire.
So let's sit down upon this cosy couch: 5
Come, kiss me, let me feast upon your mouth,
Come clasp me round the neck with arms outspread,
And now forget all that your mother said.
   A nibble on your nipple's what I've planned,
And then I'll let your hair down, strand by strand;   10
Your proper tidy Sunday sort of hair
Is hardly suited to the games we'll share.
   Come here to me then, let me see your cheek.
You're blushing? Well, it's true, I've got some cheek.
You're smiling now, so can it be you've heard   15
Something that pleases you, some charming word?
I was just saying that I meant to touch
Your lovely breast: will you allow that much?
Don't run away without a word, I know
You really want it, and you tell me so   20
With that strange look that comes into your eye.

Je jure Amour que vous êtes si fine,
Que pour mourir de bouche ne diriez
Qu'on vous baisât bien que le désirez :
Car toute fille encor qu'elle ait envie   25
Du jeu d'aimer désir être ravie.
Témoin en est Hélène qui suivit
D'un franc vouloir Pâris qui la ravit.
     Je veux user d'une douce main forte.
Ha, vous tombez : vous faîtes jà la morte.   30
Ha, quel plaisir dans le cœur je reçois :
Sans vous baisez vous moqueriez de moi
En votre lit quand vous seriez seulette,
Or sus, c'est fait ma gentille brunette :
Recommençons afin que nos beaux ans   35
Soient réchauffés de combats si plaisants.

Seconde Partie

Sur la mort de Marie*

29 (4)

Comme on voit sur la branche* au mois de Mai la rose
En sa belle jeunesse, en sa première fleur
Rendre le ciel jaloux de sa vive couleur,
Quand l'Aube de ses pleurs au point du jour l'arrose :
     La grâce dans sa feuille, et l'amour se repose,   5
Embaumant les jardins et les arbres d'odeur :
Mais battue ou de pluie, ou d'excessive ardeur,
Languissante elle meurt feuille à feuille déclose.
     Ainsi en ta première et jeune nouveauté,
Quand la terre et le ciel honoraient ta beauté,   10
La Parque t'a tuée, et cendres tu reposes.
     Pour obsèques reçois mes larmes et mes pleurs,
Ce vase plein de lait, ce panier plein de fleurs,
Afin que vif et mort ton corps ne soit que roses.

30 (12)

Aussitôt que Marie en terre fut venue,
Le Ciel en fut marri, et la voulut ravoir :

I swear by Love itself that you're so sly
That even for your life's sweet sake you can't
Ask for a kiss, although it's what you want.
For every girl who'd like to play love's game   25
Is eager to be ravished just the same.
Take Helen: Paris ravished her, but still
She followed him to Troy of her free will.
    I'd like to use a little gentle force.
Aha! You faint: a little death, of course.   30
Oh what a pleasure floods into my heart!
If I don't kiss you on the spot, you'll start
To mock me once you're in your bed alone.
So there, my pretty dark-haired girl, it's done.
When all our amorous struggles have such charm,   35
Be sure we'll spend our best years keeping warm.

Part Two

On the Death of Marie

29 (4)

    As on its stem in May we see the rose
In its fair youth and in its earliest flower
Shame and outshine the envious skies that lour
As it is dewed with tears that Dawn bestows;
    Within its petals grace and love repose,   5
Perfuming trees, embalming every bower;
But spoiled by sultry heat or sudden shower,
Its petals droop, it wastes away and dies.
    So, in your fresh and blossoming prime of youth,
That beauty honoured by both heaven and earth   10
Was slain by Fate; as dust it now reposes.
    For your last rites receive this tearful shower,
This bowl of milk, this basket full of flowers,
So that your body live and die all roses.

30 (12)

    As soon as Heaven saw Marie alight
On earth, it vowed to take her back again;

À peine notre siècle eut loisir de la voir,
Qu'elle s'évanouit comme un feu dans la nue.

    Des présents de Nature elle vint si pourvue,   5
Et sa belle jeunesse avait tant de pouvoir,
Qu'elle eût pu d'un regard les rochers émouvoir,
Tant elle avait d'attraits et d'amours en la vue.

    Ores la Mort jouit des beaux yeux que j'aimais,
La boutique et la forge, Amour, où tu t'armais.   10
Maintenant de ton camp cassé je me retire:*

    Je veux désormais vivre en franchise et tout mien :
Puisque tu n'as gardé l'honneur de ton empire,
Ta force n'est pas grande, et je le connais bien.

Sonnets et Madrigals pour Astrée

31 MADRIGAL I

L'homme est bien sot qui aime sans connaître.
J'aime et jamais je ne vis ce que j'aime :
D'un faux penser je me déçois moi-même.
Je suis esclave et ne connais mon maître.

    L'imaginer seulement me fait être   5
Comme je suis en une peine extrême.
L'œil peut faillir, l'oreille fait de même,
Mais nul des sens mon amour n'a fait naître.

    Je n'ai vu, ni ouï, ni touché :
Ce qui m'offense à mes yeux est caché :   10
La plaie au cœur à crédit m'est venue.

    Ou nos esprits se connaissent au Cieux
Ains que d'avoir notre terre vêtue,
Qui vont gardant la même affection
Dedans les corps qu'au Ciel ils avaient eue :   15

    Ou je suis fol : encore vaut-il mieux
Aimer en l'air une chose inconnue
Que n'aimer rien, imitant Ixion
Qui pour Junon embrassait une nue.

Our age had scarcely time to see her when
She passed like lightning in a cloudy night.

 The gifts that Nature gave her were so great   5
With youth and beauty's force one glance alone
Could have moved rocky mountains, split a stone,
Such charms and loves were offered to our sight.

 Now Death enjoys those eyes I loved to see,
Workshop and forge, Love, of your armoury.   10
Now I shall leave your camp, broken and ill:

 Freely I mean to live, as my own man;
Since all the honour of your empire's gone,
Your power cannot be great, I know it well.

Sonnets and Madrigals for Astraea

31   MADRIGAL I

 Only a fool knows not to whom he gave
His heart. I love, yet never saw her face,
Myself deceiving with a thought that's false,
I know no master, yet am I a slave.

 Only imagination makes me live   5
The way I do, beset by many woes;
The eye may fail, even the ear may close,
It's not my senses that gave birth to love.

 I have not heard or touched the one I prize;
What wounds my heart is hidden from my eyes;   10
I'm harmed by what I'm told, not what I see.

 It may be that our spirits met in Heaven
Before we came to wear this mortal clay
And that on earth the bodies we are given
May still preserve the same celestial passion;   15

 Or else I'm mad, in which case it might be
Better to love some insubstantial void
Than not to love, to copy Ixion
Who looked for Juno and embraced a cloud.

32 (14)

À mon retour* (hé, je m'en désespère)
Tu m'as reçu d'un baiser tout glacé,
Froid, sans saveur, baiser d'un trépassé,
Tel que Diane en donnait à son frère,
   Tel qu'une fille en donne à sa grand-mère,   5
La fiancée en donne au fiancé,
Ni savoureux, ni moiteux ni pressé :
Et quoi, ma lèvre est-elle si amère ?
   Ha, tu devrais imiter les pigeons
Qui bec en bec de baisers doux et longs   10
Se font l'amour sur le haut d'une souche.
   Je te suppli', maîtresse désormais
Ou baise-moi la saveur en la bouche,
Ou bien du tout ne me baise jamais.

Le Premier Livre des Sonnets pour Hélène

33 (19)

   Tant de fois s'appointer, tant de fois se fâcher,*
Tant de fois rompre ensemble et puis se renouer,
Tantôt blâmer Amour et tantôt le louer,
Tant de fois se fuir, tant de fois se chercher,
   Tant de fois se montrer, tant de fois se cacher,   5
Tantôt se mettre au joug, tantôt le secouer,
Avouer sa promesse et la désavouer,
Sont signes que l'Amour de près nous vient toucher.
   L'inconstance amoureuse est marque d'amitié.
Si donc tout à la fois avoir haine et pitié,   10
Jurer, se parjurer, serments faits et défaits,
   Espérer sans espoir, confort sans réconfort,
Sont vrais signes d'amour, nous entr'aimons bien fort :
Car nous avons toujours ou la guerre, ou la paix.

34 (20)

Quoi ? me donner congé de servir toute femme,
Et mon ardeur éteindre au premier corps venu,
Ainsi qu'un vagabond sans être retenu,

32 (14)

On my return (in deep despair I shiver!)
You greeted me with such an icy kiss,
Cold, savourless, a corpse would taste like this,
The sort of kiss Diana gave her brother,

Or that a girl might give to her grandmother   5
Or promised spouse get from his frigid miss,
Passionless, dry, and with no taste of bliss.
Come on! And tell me: is my lip so bitter?

Ah, imitate the pigeons, how they seek
To show their love, embracing beak to beak,   10
With kisses long drawn out and sweet of savour.

The time has come, dear mistress, when you should
Kiss with a mouth that's moist and full of flavour,
Or else have done with kissing me for good.

The First Book of Sonnets for Helen

33 (19)

Now breaking off, now coming back together,
Now quarrelling and promptly making peace,
Now blaming Love and crowning him with praise,
Now running off, now searching for each other,

Now putting on, now shaking off the tether,   5
Hiding away and standing face to face,
Making and breaking vows—signs such as these
Reveal us pierced by arrows from Love's quiver.

True Love is marked by mutability.
If then to feel at once both hate and pity,   10
To break firm vows, to swear and then forswear,

To find hope's comfort in a hopeless state,
Are signs of love, then our love must be great
For we have always either peace or war.

34 (20)

What? So you give me leave to quench my flame
With the first woman who might come my way,
Like some poor vagrant seeking to allay

Abandonner la bride au vouloir de ma flamme :
    Non, ce n'est pas aimer. L'Archer ne vous entame   5
Qu'un peu le haut du cœur d'un trait faible et menu.
Si d'un coup bien profond il vous était connu,
Ce ne serait que soufre et braise de votre âme.
    En soupçon de votre ombre en tous lieux vous seriez :
À toute heure, en tous temps jalouse me suivriez,   10
D'ardeur et de fureur et de crainte allumée.
    Amour au petit pas non au galop vous court,
Et votre amitié n'est qu'une flamme de Cour,*
Où peu de feu se trouve et beaucoup de fumée.

35 (22)

    Puisqu'elle est tout hiver, toute la même glace,
Toute neige, et son cœur tout armé de glaçons,
Qui ne m'aime sinon pour avoir mes chansons,
Pourquoi suis-je si fol que je ne m'en délace ?
    De quoi me sert son nom, sa grandeur et sa race,*   5
Que d'honnête servage et de belles prisons ?
Maîtresse, je n'ai pas les cheveux si grisons,
Qu'une autre de bon cœur ne prenne votre place.
    Amour, qui est enfant, ne cèle vérité.
Vous n'êtes si superbe, ou si riche en beauté,   10
Qu'il faille dédaigner un bon cœur qui vous aime.
    Rentrer en mon Avril désormais je ne puis :
Aimez-moi, s'il vous plaît, grison comme je suis,
Et je vous aimerai quand vous serez de même.*

36 (33)

    Nous promenant tous seuls, vous me dîtes, Maîtresse,
Qu'un chant vous déplaisait, s'il était doucereux :
Que vous aimiez les plaints des tristes amoureux,
Toute voix lamentable et pleine de tristesse.
    Et pour ce (disiez-vous) quand je suis loin de presse,   5
Je choisis vos Sonnets qui sont plus douloureux :
Puis d'un chant qui est propre au sujet langoureux,
Ma nature et Amour veulent que je me paisse.
    Vos propos sont trompeurs. Si vous aviez souci
De ceux qui ont un cœur larmoyant et transi,   10

A lust no bridle ever thought to tame;
    No, that's not love. The Archer missed his aim,   5
The arrow grazed your heart but did not stay;
If it had pierced you and not gone astray
Your soul would be a pit of burning lime:
    You'd look on your own shadow and beware,
You'd follow me at all times everywhere   10
With jealous flames that fear and fury stoke.
    A trot but not a gallop, that's your passion,
A love that's nothing but a courtly fashion,
With not much fire and a lot of smoke.

35 (22)

    Since she's all winter, all sheer ice and snow,
And rows of icicles protect her heart
That loves me only for the songs I write,
Fool that I am, why can't I let her go?
    What can her old and noble name bestow   5
But gilded prison or a servant's right?
Lady, I'm not so grey that others might
Not take with joy the place that you forgo.
    Love is a child and cannot hide what's true.
You're not so beautiful and grand that you   10
Can treat a loving heart with such disdain.
    I can't retrieve the April of my days:
Grey as I am, give me your love, I pray,
And I'll love you when you look much the same.

36 (33)

    Once, Lady, as we walked alone, you said
That you disliked a song if it was sweet,
That you preferred lovers who mourn their plight,
All such complaints, unutterably sad.
    'And so', you said, 'when I have fled the crowd,   5
I choose the saddest Sonnets that you write,
For Love and my own nature both invite
Indulgence in such melancholy food.'
    Hypocrisy! For if you cared at all
For stricken hearts, my words would make you feel   10

Je vous ferais pitié par une sympathie:*
    Mais votre œil cauteleux, trop finement subtil,
Pleure en chantant mes vers, comme le Crocodil,
Pour mieux me dérober par feintise la vie.

37 (36)

    Vous me dîtes, Maîtresse, étant à la fenêtre,
Regardant vers Montmartre et les champs d'alentour :
La solitaire vie, et le désert séjour
Valent mieux que la Cour, je voudrais bien y être.

    À l'heure mon esprit de mes sens serait maître,   5
En jeûne et oraison je passerais le jour,
Je défierais les traits et les flammes d'Amour :
Ce cruel de mon sang ne pourrait se repaître.

    Quand je vous répondis, Vous trompez de penser
Qu'un feu ne soit pas feu pour se couvrir de cendre :   10
Sur les cloîtres sacrés la flamme on voit passer :

    Amour dans les déserts, comme aux villes s'engendre.
Contre un Dieu si puissant, qui les Dieux peut forcer,
Jeûnes ni oraisons ne se peuvent défendre.

Le Second Livre des Sonnets pour Hélène

38 (1)

    Soit qu'un sage amoureux ou soit qu'un sot me lise,
Il ne doit s'ébahir voyant mon chef grison,*
Si je chante d'amour : toujours un vieil tison
Cache un germe de feu sous une cendre grise.

    Le bois vert à grand' peine en le soufflant s'attise,   5
Le sec sans le souffler brûle en toute saison.
La Lune se gagna d'une blanche toison,
Et son vieillard Tithon l'Aurore ne méprise.

    Lecteur, je ne veux être écolier de Platon,
Qui la vertu nous prêche, et ne fait pas de même :   10
Ni volontaire Icare ou lourdaud Phaéton,

    Perdus pour attenter une sottise extrême :
Mais sans me contrefaire ou Voleur ou Charton,
De mon gré je me noie et me brûle moi-même.

By sympathy some pity for my grief.
    But you are like the cunning Crocodile:
You sing my verse, your eyes shed tears; such guile
More easily to cheat me of my life!

37 (36)

    As you were at the window, looking out
Towards Montmartre and its fields, you said:
'That's where I'd rather live, far from the crowd,
In solitude, rather than here at Court.
    My soul would teach my senses to submit,   5
And every day I'd fast and pray aloud;
Far from that cruel lord who drank my blood,
I would defy Love's flame and scorn his dart.'
    I answered: 'You are wrong to think that fire
Is fire no longer under blackened cinders.   10
Even the sacred cloisters know desire,
    Love's born in desert wastes as well as cities.
A God whose power makes the Gods obey
Won't be deterred because you fast and pray.'

The Second Book of Sonnets for Helen

38 (1)

    My reader, sage in love or some poor fool,
Should hardly wonder that from my grey head
Come songs of love: a smouldering log will hide
A stubborn fire while its ashes cool;
    Green wood won't kindle, blow it as you will,   5
You need no breath to fire up dry wood;
A white fleece won the moon, or so it's said;
Aurora loves her old Tithonus still.
    Reader, I'm not a follower of Plato
Who preaches virtue that he doesn't practise;   10
Dull Phaeton and rash Icarus I scorn,
    Both victims of excessive foolishness;
But they're not models that I need to go to
Since of my own free will I drown and burn.

39 (9)

Ni la douce pitié, ni le pleur lamentable
Ne t'ont baillé ton nom : ton nom Grec* vient d'ôter,
De ravir, de tuer, de piller, d'emporter
Mon esprit et mon cœur, ta proie misérable.

Homère en se jouant de toi fit une fable,   5
Et moi l'histoire au vrai. Amour, pour te flatter,
Comme tu fis à Troie, au cœur me vient jeter
Le feu qui de mes os se paît insatiable.

La voix, que tu feignais à l'entour du Cheval*
Pour décevoir les Grecs, me devait faire sage :   10
Mais l'homme de nature est aveugle à son mal,

Qui ne peut se garder ni prévoir son dommage.
Au pis aller je meurs pour ce beau nom fatal,
Qui mit toute l'Asie et l'Europe en pillage.

40 (26)

Au milieu de la guerre, en un siècle sans foi,
Entre mille procès, est-ce pas grand' folie
D'écrire de l'Amour ? De menottes on lie
Les fols qui ne sont pas si furieux que moi.

Grison et maladif rentrer dessous la loi   5
D'Amour, ô quelle erreur ! Dieux, merci je vous crie.
Tu ne m'es plus Amour, tu m'es une Furie,
Qui me rends fol enfant* et sans yeux comme toi :

Voir perdre mon pays, proie des adversaires,
Voir en nos étendards les fleurs de lis* contraires,   10
Voir une Thébaïde* et faire l'amoureux !

Je m'en vais au Palais : adieu vieilles Sorcières.
Muses je prends mon sac, je serai plus heureux
En gagnant mes procès, qu'en suivant vos rivières.

41 (32)

J'avais été saigné,* ma Dame vient me voir
Lorsque je languissais d'une humeur froide et lente :
Se tournant vers mon sang, comme toute riante
Me dit en se jouant, Que votre sang est noir !

Le trop penser en vous a pu si bien mouvoir   5

39 (9)

Not from sad tears and pity, as men say,
You took your name; the Greek word means to seize,
To kill and rob, to ravish and to raze,
To steal my mind and heart, your wretched prey.

Homer made you a fable, just in play,   5
Mine's the true story. Love, to flatter and please,
Copied your Trojan tale and kindled these
Unsated flames that eat my bones away.

The story should have warned me; how she came
And spoke false words to the Horse when Troy was lost;   10
But that's the way men are, we're all the same,

And fail to see the impending ill: at worst
I shall have died for that fair fatal name
That ruined Asia and laid Europe waste.

40 (26)

At war and in a faithless century,
Plagued by a thousand lawsuits, is it not
Folly to write of Love? They chain a lot
Of lunatics who aren't as mad as me.

Greying and sick, to choose Love's mastery!   5
'O Gods, forgive my error,' I cry out,
'Love's now become a Fury who's about
To make me too a child who cannot see.'

To see my country lost, to foes a prey,
To see our lilies pitched against each other,   10
To see a Theban War and play the lover!

Muses, farewell, you old bewitching dreams,
The Law Court waits; I'll spend a happier day
Winning my case than following your streams.

41 (32)

My lady came when I had just been bled
And languished in a humour slow and cold:
Then, having seen the blood, she turned and smiled
And said: 'How black is all this blood you've shed!

Thinking too deeply has confused your head: 5

L'imagination, que l'âme obéissante
A laissé la chaleur naturelle impuissante
De cuire, de nourrir, de faire son devoir.

   Ne soyez plus si belle, et devenez Médée :
Colorez d'un beau sang ma face jà ridée,   10
Et d'un nouveau printemps faites-moi ranimer.

   Aeson vit rajeunir son écorce ancienne :
Nul charme ne saurait renouveler la mienne.
Si je veux rajeunir il ne faut plus aimer.

42 (42)

   Ces longues nuits* d'hiver, où la Lune ocieuse
Tourne si lentement son char tout à l'entour,
Où le Coq si tardif nous annonce le jour,
Où la nuit semble un an à l'âme soucieuse :

   Je fusse mort d'ennui sans ta forme douteuse,   5
Qui vient par une feinte alléger mon amour,
Et faisant toute nue entre mes bras séjour,
Me pipe doucement d'une joie menteuse.

   Vraie tu es farouche, et fière en cruauté :
De toi fausse on jouit en toute privauté.   10
Près ton mort, je m'endors, près de lui je repose :

   Rien ne m'est refusé. Le bon sommeil ainsi
Abuse par le faux mon amoureux souci.
S'abuser en amour n'est pas mauvaise chose.

43 (43)

   Quand vous serez bien vieille, au soir à la chandelle,
Assise auprès du feu, dévidant et filant,*
Direz chantant mes vers, en vous émerveillant,
Ronsard me célébrait du temps que j'étais belle.

   Lors vous n'aurez servante oyant telle nouvelle,   5
Déjà sous le labeur à demi sommeillant,
Qui au bruit de mon nom ne s'aille réveillant,
Bénissant votre nom de louange immortelle.

   Je serai sous la terre et fantôme sans os
Par les ombres myrteux* je prendrai mon repos :   10
Vous serez au foyer une vieille accroupie,

   Regrettant mon amour et votre fier dédain.

Imagination overrules the soul
Which, without natural heat, failing its role,
No longer warms or nourishes as it should.'

  Discard your beauty, take Medea's place:
With fine fresh blood colour my wrinkled face,   10
And with a second spring give me new life.

  Old Aeson saw his skin grow young again:
But no charm works for me; if I regain
My youth, it must be by renouncing love.

42 (42)

  These winter nights when, weary of its round,
The Moon's slow chariot dawdles on its way,
When the dull Cock is late to greet the day,
When one night seems a year to the troubled mind,

  I would have died of sadness had your kind   5
Illusory shape not come at night to stay
Naked within my arms and thus allay
With a deceptive joy this love of mine.

  Though you in truth are pitiless and proud,
This spectral you is privily enjoyed,   10
Together with the sleep that shadow brings.

  There's nothing that's denied. So that sweet sleep
Deceives the pains of love, however deep.
In love such self-deception's no bad thing.

43 (43)

  When you are old, croodled beside the fire,
Spinning by candlelight, you'll sing, and say,
Still marvelling, 'Ronsard wrote that for me
Back in the days when I was young and fair.'

  Then you won't find a single servant there,   5
However tired and dozy she may be,
Who will not wake to hear my name and cry
Immortal blessings on the name you bear.

  I'll be a boneless phantom buried deep,
At rest beneath the myrtles, sound asleep: 10
You will be hunched and housebound, old and grey,

  Regretting my lost love and your disdain.

Vivez, si m'en croyez, n'attendez à demain :
Cueillez dès aujourd'hui les roses de la vie.*

44 (49)

Le soir qu'Amour vous fit en salle descendre
Pour danser d'artifice un beau ballet d'Amour,*
Vos yeux, bien qu'il fût nuit, ramenèrent le jour,
Tant ils surent d'éclairs par la place répandre.

Le ballet fut divin, qui se soulait reprendre,   5
Se rompre, se refaire, et tour dessus retour
Se mêler, s'écarter, se tourner à l'entour,
Contre-imitant le cours du fleuve de Méandre.

Ores il était rond, ores long, or' étroit,
Or' en pointe, en triangle en la façon qu'on voit   10
L'escadron de la Grue évitant la froideur.

Je faux, tu ne dansais, mais ton pied voletait
Sur le haut de la terre : aussi ton corps s'était
Transformé pour ce soir en divine nature.

45 (57)

De Myrte et de Laurier* feuille à feuille enserrés
Hélène entrelaçant une belle Couronne,
M'appela par mon nom : Voilà que je vous donne,
De moi seule, Ronsard, l'écrivain vous serez.

Amour qui l'écoutait, de ses traits acérés   5
Me pousse Hélène au cœur, et son Chantre m'ordonne :
Qu'un sujet si fertil votre plume n'étonne :
Plus l'argument est grand, plus Cygne vous mourrez.*

Ainsi me dit Amour, me frappant de ses ailes :
Son arc fit un grand bruit, les feuilles éternelles   10
Du Myrte je sentis sur mon chef tressaillir.

Adieu Muses adieu, votre faveur me laisse :
Hélène est mon Parnasse : ayant telle Maîtresse,
Le Laurier est à moi je ne saurais faillir.

46 (65)

Je ne serais marri si tu comptais ma peine,
De compter tes degrés recomptés tant de fois :
Tu loges au sommet du Palais de nos Rois :*
Olympe n'avait pas la cime si hautaine.

Live now and listen, do not wait in vain
Until tomorrow; pluck life's rose today.

44 (49)

That evening when Love chose to send you down
Into the hall to lead his exquisite dance,
Though it was night, the splendour of your glance
Restored the day, flashing such beams around:
    Divine ballet, resuming time and again,   5
Forming, reforming, radiating thence,
Merging, diverging, but to recommence
Like sinuous Meander on its plain:
    Now it was round, and now a long thin line,
Now with a point, triangular in design,   10
Taking a shape like Cranes who fly from winter.
    But no: you did not dance, rather your feet
Fluttered above the earth; for that one night
Your body had become divine in nature.

45 (57)

As twining leaf with leaf she made a Crown
Of Laurel and of Myrtle, Helen called
My name: 'Ronsard, accept this gift, behold
You are my poet now and mine alone.'
    Love who was listening thrust Helen down   5
Into my heart and that appointment sealed:
'Let not this subject check the pen you hold;
With such rich matter you will die a Swan.'
    Then, as he struck me with his wings, I heard
His bow twang loud and felt upon my head   10
The everlasting Myrtle's trembling spell.
    Muses, farewell, Helen is my Parnassus:
Your favour leaves me, but with such a Mistress
The Laurel must be mine, I cannot fail.

46 (65)

If only you could count my griefs as I
Count and recount the stony steps that bring
Me up to where you lodge above our King;
Olympus was not nearer to the sky.

Je perds à chaque marche et le pouls et l'haleine :   5
J'ai la sueur au front, j'ai l'estomac pantois,
Pour ouïr un nenni, un refus, une voix
De dédain, de froideur et d'orgueil toute pleine.

Tu es comme Déesse assise en très haut lieu.
Pour monter en ton ciel je ne suis pas un Dieu.   10
Je ferai de la Cour* ma plainte coutumière,

T'envoyant jusqu'en haut mon cœur dévotieux.
Ainsi les hommes font à Jupiter prière :
Les hommes sont en terre, et Jupiter aux cieux.

47 ÉLÉGIE

Six ans étaient coulés, et la septième année
Était presques entière en ses pas retournée,
Quand loin d'affection, de désir et d'amour,
En pure liberté je passais tout le jour,
Et franc de tout souci qui les âmes dévore,   5
Je dormais dès le soir jusqu'au point de l'aurore.
Car seul maître de moi j'allais plein de loisir,
Où le pied me portait, conduit de mon désir,
Ayant toujours ès mains pour me servir de guide
Aristote ou Platon, ou le docte Euripide,   10
Mes bons hôtes muets, qui ne fâchent jamais :
Ainsi que je les prends, ainsi je les remets.
Ô douce compagnie et utile et honnête !
Un autre en caquetant m'étourdirait la tête.

Puis du livre ennuyé, je regardais les fleurs,   15
Feuilles, tiges, rameaux, espèces et couleurs,
Et l'entrecoupement de leurs formes diverses,
Peintes de cent façons, jaunes, rouges et perses,
Ne me pouvant soûler, ainsi qu'en un tableau,
D'admirer la Nature, et ce qu'elle a de beau :   20
Et de dire en parlant aux fleurettes écloses :
Celui est presque Dieu qui connaît toutes choses,
Éloigné du vulgaire, et loin des courtisans,
De fraude et de malice impudents artisans.

Tantôt j'errais seulet par les forêts sauvages   25
Sur les bords enjonchés des peinturés rivages,

At every step I gasp for breath and sigh;   5
My pulse beats fast, I sweat, my innards sting;
And all to hear a sharp cold voice that rings
With scorn and pride as you reject my plea.

You're like a Goddess on your lofty seat;
I'm not a God to climb and meet you there,   10
But from the Court down here my song shall rise,
    The old lament of my devoted heart.
For that's how Jupiter receives man's prayer:
Men dwell on earth and Jupiter in the skies.

47 ELEGY

Six years had passed and now the time was near
For turning earth to close the seventh year
When, with love's lust and frenzy far from me,
I spent the hours in perfect liberty;
Free from all cares that eat men's souls away,   5
I slept from evening till the dawn of day.
For master of myself, I walked at leisure
Wherever my feet took me for my pleasure,
Always in hand to guide me one of these:
Sage Aristotle and Euripides   10
And Plato too, guests who don't grumble when
I pick them up and put them down again.
Sweet troupe by whom my steps were fairly led!
Another's blathering would dull my head.

Then, weary of the book, I turned to flowers,   15
Leaves, stems, and shoots in variegated bowers;
And the sweet blending of their forms and hues,
Painted a hundred ways—reds, yellows, blues:
I could not get enough. As in some pictures,
I marvelled there at Nature's loveliest features,   20
And said to all those flowers blossoming:
'That man is almost God who knows such things',
Far from the clamour of the common sort,
Shunning the fraud and malice of the court.

Often I roamed wild forests far and wide   25
Or walked along the rushy riverside;

Tantôt par les rochers reculés et déserts,
Tantôt par les taillis, verte maison des cerfs.
　J'aimais le cours suivi d'une longue rivière,
Et voir onde sur onde allonger sa carrière,　　　　　30
Et flot à l'autre flot en roulant s'attacher,
Et pendu sur le bord me plaisait d'y pêcher,
Étant plus réjoui d'une chasse muette
Troubler des écaillés la demeure secrète,
Tirer avec la ligne en tremblant emporté　　　　　35
Le crédule poisson pris à l'hain appâté,
Qu'un grand Prince n'est aise ayant pris à la chasse
Un cerf qu'en haletant tout un jour il pourchasse.
Heureux, si vous eussiez d'un mutuel émoi
Pris l'appât amoureux aussi bien comme moi,　　　　　40
Que tout seul j'avalai, quand par trop désireuse
Mon âme en vos yeux but la poison amoureuse.
　Puis alors que Vesper vient embrunir nos yeux,
Attaché dans le ciel je contemple les cieux,
En qui Dieu nous écrit* en notes non obscures　　　　　45
Les sorts et les destins de toutes créatures.
Car lui, en dédaignant (comme font les humains)
D'avoir encre et papier et plume entre les mains,
Par les astres du ciel qui sont ses caractères,
Les choses nous prédit et bonnes et contraires :　　　　　50
Mais les hommes chargés de terre et du trépas
Méprisent tel écrit, et ne le lisent pas.
Or le plus de mon bien pour décevoir ma peine,
C'est de boire à longs traits les eaux de la fontaine
Qui de votre beau nom se brave, et en courant　　　　　55
Par les prés vos honneurs va toujours murmurant,
Et la Reine se dit des eaux de la contrée :
Tant vaut le gentil soin d'une Muse sacrée,
Qui peut vaincre la mort, et les sorts inconstants,
Sinon pour tout jamais, au moins pour un long temps.　　　　　60
Là couché dessus l'herbe en mes discours je pense
Que pour aimer beaucoup j'ai peu de récompense,
Et que mettre son cœur aux Dames si avant,
C'est vouloir peindre en l'onde et arrêter le vent :
M'assurant toutefois qu'alors que le vieil âge　　　　　65

Sometimes I scaled the rocky heights alone,
Or trod through thickets to the deer's green home.
   I loved long rivers flowing on their course,
Wave upon wave, with undiminished force; 30
And all those rolling billows brought one wish:
To lean out from the grassy bank and fish;
For there it pleased me so to stop and trace
The secret dwellings of the scaly race,
Straining the taut and tremulous line that took 35
The credulous victim with its baited hook—
The pleasures of that capture far outweigh
Those of a Prince who hunts the deer all day.
If only you, drawn to a mutual fate,
Had joined with me in swallowing Love's bait! 40
But all alone, too ardent to be wise,
I drank the amorous poison from your eyes.
   At length, when gentle Vesper veils our sight,
I look up to the heavens and contemplate
The sky where God has written for us to read 45
The fate of all the creatures He has made;
For He, who needs no tools of mortal men
And scorns to handle paper, ink, and pen,
Writes with the stars of heaven to foretell
Events that lie in wait for good or ill: 50
But man, by death and dusty earth oppressed,
Disdains that book and will not read the text.
Now when I seek to soothe my suffering
I drink long draughts of water from the spring
That vaunts your name to the meads and sweetly flows, 55
Trilling your virtues everywhere it goes,
Calling itself the Queen of that land's waters:
Such is the worth the sacred Muse confers,
That conquers death and our uncertain fate
For years on end, if not of endless date. 60
Stretched there upon the grass, I think out loud
That my great love has gained but small reward:
Whoever trusts his heart to Women strives
To still the winds and paint the foaming waves.
Yet I look forward to the day when age 65

Aura comme un sorcier changé votre visage,
Et lorsque vos cheveux deviendront argentés,*
Et que vous yeux, d'amour ne seront plus hantés,
Que toujours vous aurez, si quelque soin vous touche,
En l'esprit mes écrits, mon nom en votre bouche.   70

    Maintenant que voici l'an septième venir,
Ne pensez plus Hélène en vos lacs me tenir.
La raison m'en délivre, et votre rigueur dure,
Puis il faut que mon âge obéisse à Nature.

48 (75)

    Je m'enfuis du combat mon armée est défaite :
J'ai perdu contre Amour la force et la raison :
Jà dix lustres passés, et jà mon poil grison
M'appellent au logis, et sonnent la retraite.

    Si comme je voulais ta gloire n'est parfaite.   5
N'en blâme point l'esprit, mais blâme la saison :
Je ne suis ni Paris, ni déloyal Jason :
J'obéis à la loi que la Nature a faite.*

    Entre l'aigre et le doux, l'espérance et la peur,
Amour dedans ma forge a poli cet ouvrage.   10
Je ne me plains du mal, du temps ni du labeur,

    Je me plains de moi-même et de ton faux courage.
Tu t'en repentiras, si tu as un bon cœur,
Mais le tard repentir n'amende le dommage.

Les Amours Diverses

49 (9)

    Je voudrais bien n'avoir jamais tâté
Si follement le tétin de m'amie :*
Sans ce malheur l'autre plus grande envie
Ne m'eût jamais le courage tenté.

    Comme un poisson pour s'être trop hâté,   5
Par un appât suit la fin de sa vie :
Ainsi je vais où la mort me convie,
D'un beau tétin doucement appâté.

    Qui eût pensé que le cruel destin

Will wreak upon your face its magic change,
When streaks of silver will bestrew your hair
And in your eyes no trace of love appear;
Then, if some touch of feeling still remain,
Your mind will hold my works, your lips my name.   70

    Now, Helen, as we close this seventh year,
You must not think to keep in me your snare.
My reason and your rigour set me free;
My age must bow to Nature's firm decree.

48 (75)

    I quit the field, my army knows defeat:
By fighting Love I've wasted strength and reason:
Fifty years gone and greying hair now summon
Me home already, sounding the retreat.

    And if my praise of you proves incomplete,   5
Blame not my wit, but blame life's autumn season:
I'm neither Paris nor unfaithful Jason,
For Nature gives the law and I submit.

    With fearful hope and bitter sweetness, Love
Forged in my smithy this, his work of art.   10
Not for the pains and time and toil I grieve;

    I grieve for my own self and you, false friend.
You will repent, if you still have a heart,
But late repentance does not make amends.

Various Love Poems

49 (9)

    I wish to God I had not placed my hand
So foolishly upon my darling's breast:
I never would have dared the greater quest
That tempts me to perform what I intend;

    Just as a fish hurries towards its end,   5
Lured by the bait to act with too great haste,
So I keep pressing on at death's behest,
Whose bait's a nipple daintily designed.

    Who would have ever thought that cruel fate

Eût enfermé sous un si beau tétin   10
Un si grand feu pour m'en faire la proie?
     Avisez donc quel serait le coucher
Quand le péché d'un seul petit toucher
Ne me pardonne, et les mains me foudroie?

50 (12)

     Petit nombril, que mon penser adore,
Et non mon œil qui n'eut onques le bien
De te voir nu, et qui mérites bien
Que quelque ville on te bâtisse encore.
     Signe amoureux, duquel Amour s'honore,   5
Représentant l'Androgyne* lien,
Et le courroux du grand Saturnien,
Dont le nombril toujours se remémore.
     Ni ce beau chef ni ces yeux ni ce front,
Ni ce beau sein où les flèches se font,   10
Que les beautés diversement se forgent,
     Ne me pourraient ma douleur conforter,
Sans espérer quelque jour de tâter
Ton compagnon où les amours se logent.

51 (18)

     Chacun me dit, Ronsard, ta Maîtresse n'est telle
Comme tu la décris. Certes je n'en sais rien :
Je suis devenu fol, mon esprit n'est plus mien,
Je ne puis discerner la laide de la belle.
     Ceux qui ont en amour et prudence et cervelle,   5
Poursuivant les beautés, ne peuvent aimer bien.
Le vrai amant est fol, et ne peut être sien,
S'il est vrai que l'amour une fureur s'appelle.
     Souhaiter la beauté que chacun veut avoir,
Ce n'est humeur de sot, mais d'homme de savoir,   10
Qui prudent et rusé cherche la belle chose.
     Je ne saurais juger,* tant la fureur me suit :
Je suis aveugle et fol : un jour est une nuit,
Et la fleur d'un Chardon m'est une belle Rose.

Could hide inside that nipple fire so great   10
As to make me the prey that burns within?
   Imagine what to lie with her would do
When from mere touch such torments then ensue—
Thunderstruck hands for that unpardoned sin!

50 (12)

   Sweet little navel that my thoughts acclaim,
But not my eyes that never had the luck
To see you naked; truly we should make
A splendid city worthy of your name;
   Navel, the site and symbol of Love's fame,   5
A memory of the Androgyne, a mark
Of how we were before Jove's anger broke
The ancient oneness that we can't reclaim.
   Neither that noble brow, that head, those eyes,
Nor the fair breast where two small darts arise,   10
Nor all the blend of beauties that they form,
   Have any force to comfort my distress,
Unless there's still some hope I might caress
That friend of yours below, where Love's at home.

51 (18)

   They say: 'Ronsard, your Mistress cannot be
As you describe her.' Well, I wouldn't know:
I've lost my wits and I'm half crazy now.
What's beautiful? What's ugly? Don't ask me.
   Those who pursue a beauty cautiously   5
And keep their wits don't feel the love they show.
True lovers must be raving mad, and so
When love is called a frenzy, I know why.
   It's not a fool's behaviour, but a grave
And serious motion when a wise man craves   10
A beauty all the world desires and knows.
   But I'm so mad my judgement can't be right;
I'm blind and foolish; day to me is night;
To me a Thistle's flower is a Rose.

52 ÉLÉGIE 2

Cherche, Maîtresse, un Poète nouveau
Qui après moi se rompe le cerveau
À te chanter : il aura bien affaire,
Et fût-ce un Dieu, s'il peut aussi bien faire.
Si notre Empire avait jadis été   5
Par nos Français aussi avant planté
Que le Romain, tu serais autant lue
Que si Tibull' t'avait pour sienne élue :
Et néanmoins tu te dois contenter
De voir ton nom par la France chanter,   10
Autant que Laure en Tuscan anoblie
Se voit chanter par la belle Italie.

Or pour t'avoir consacré mes écrits,
Je n'ai gagné sinon les cheveux gris,
La ride au front, la tristesse en la face,   15
Sans mériter un seul bien de ta grâce :
Bien que mon nom, mes vers, ma loyauté
Eussent d'un Tigre ému la cruauté.
Et toutefois je m'assure, quand l'âge
Aura dompté l'orgueil de ton courage,   20
Que de mon mal tu te repentiras,
Et qu'à la fin tu te convertiras :
Et cependant je souffrirai la peine,
Toi le plaisir comme Dame inhumaine,
De trop me voir languir en ton amour,   25
Dont Némésis te doit punir un jour.

Ceux qui Amour connaissent* par épreuve,
Lisant le mal où perdu je me treuve,
Ne pardon'ront à ma simple amitié
Tant seulement, mais en auront pitié.   30

Or quant à moi je pense avoir perdue
En te servant ma jeunesse épandue
Deçà, delà, dedans ce livre ici.
Je vois ma faute et la prends à merci,
Comme celui qui sait que notre vie   35
N'est rien que vent, que songe et que folie.

52 ELEGY 2

Go on, my Lady, see if you can gain
Another Poet who will rack his brain
To sing your praise as well as I have done:
A very God would hardly take it on.
Now if, as Romans were, the French had been   5
Such early empire-builders, you'd have seen
Your name more widely cited, as well known
As if Tibullus chose you for his own;
But, as things stand, it seems you must make do
With French alone to sing that praise for you,   10
Just as the Tuscan tongue in Italy
Gave Petrarch's Laura her nobility.

I wrote to praise you: what's my profit now?
Nothing but more grey hair, a furrowed brow,
Sorrow's deep lines engraved upon my face,   15
Yet never earning me one touch of grace;
Although my verses and my loyal truth
Might well have moved a Tiger's rage to ruth.
But still, I trust, when age has played its part
And tamed the pride of your embattled heart,   20
That you'll be contrite for my torments past,
Show true repentance and convert at last.
Yet in the meantime I am still in pain
While you enjoy yourself and take a vain
Pleasure in how I languish: but one day   25
You'll meet with Nemesis and he'll make you pay.

Those who have learned from loving what Love is
And read about a torment such as this
Will not just pardon my old love for you
But for my pains grant me their pity too.   30

Now, in my case, I think that I have lost
My youth in serving you, a youth laid waste,
In fragments here and there and in this book.
I see my error clearly, and I look
On it with pity as a man who finds   35
Life's but a foolish dream, a breath of wind.

Les Odes

53 À SA MAÎTRESSE (1.17)

Mignonne, allons voir* si la rose
Qui ce matin avait déclose
Sa robe de pourpre au Soleil,
A point perdu cette vêprée
Les plis de sa robe pourprée,   5
Et son teint au vôtre pareil.

Las ! voyez comme en peu d'espace,
Mignonne, elle a dessus la place
Las ! las ! ses beautés laissé choir !
O vraiment marâtre Nature,   10
Puisqu'une telle fleur ne dure
Que du matin jusques au soir !
Donc, si vous me croyez, mignonne,
Tandis que votre âge fleuronne
En sa plus verte nouveauté,   15
Cueillez, cueillez votre jeunesse :
Comme à cette fleur la vieillesse
Fera ternir votre beauté.

54 DE L'ÉLECTION DE SON SÉPULCRE* (4.4)

Antres, et vous fontaines
De ces roches hautaines
Qui tombez contre-bas
    D'un glissant pas :

Et vous forêts et ondes   5
Par ces prés vagabondes,
Et vous rives et bois,
    Oyez ma voix.

Quand le ciel et mon heure
Jugeront que je meure,   10
Ravi du beau séjour
    Du commun jour,

Odes

53 TO HIS MISTRESS (1.17)

My love, let us see if the rose
Which, in the morning, shows
Broad to the Sun her crimson gown,
When evening comes still wears that dress
In its unfolded loveliness   5
With a hue that matches your own.

Alas, my love, how soon you find
Those beauties shed upon the ground,
Alas! alas! left to decay!
Nature, indeed, is no true mother   10
If such a flower can last no longer
Than from the morn to close of day!
Believe me, love; I speak the truth:
Now, in the very prime of youth,
Its green, fresh-blossoming day,   15
Gather the time and seize the hour;
Old age will treat you like this flower,
And turn your beauty to decay.

54 ON THE CHOICE OF HIS BURIAL PLOT (4.4)

You caves, you crystal fountains
Who in the rocky mountains
Come swiftly sliding down
    To reach the ground:

Forests, and brooks that lead   5
Across the watery mead
In your meandering course,
    Now hear my voice.

When time and heaven's decree
Shall judge that I must die,   10
From the fair light of day
    Ravished away,

Je défends qu'on ne rompe
Le marbre pour la pompe
De vouloir mon tombeau   15
   Bâtir plus beau :

Mais bien je veux qu'un arbre
M'ombrage en lieu d'un marbre,
Arbre qui soit couvert
   Toujours de vert.   20

De moi puisse la terre
Engendrer un lierre,
M'embrassant en maint tour
   Tout à l'entour :

Et la vigne tortisse   25
Mon sépulcre embellisse,
Faisant de toutes parts
   Un ombre épars.

Là viendront chaque année
A ma fête ordonnée   30
Aveques leurs troupeaux
   Les pastoureaux :

Puis ayant fait l'office
De leur beau sacrifice,
Parlant à l'île ainsi   35
   Diront ceci :

« Que tu es renommé
D'être tombeau nommée
D'un de qui l'univers
   Chante les vers !   40

Et qui onc en sa vie
Ne fut brûlé d'envie,
Mendiant les honneurs
   Des grands Seigneurs !

I wish no man to break
Hard marble for my sake,
Or build with firm intent   15
   My monument.

Instead of marble, see
You find a shady tree;
One that remains serene
   As evergreen.   20

There may the earth that holds me
Send ivy to enfold me,
Enlacing me around
   To keep me bound.

And may the spiralling vine   25
Adorn my tomb and twine
Its pattern in the glade
   Of chequered shade.

Upon my feast each year
Shepherds will gather here,   30
Bringing their flocks along
   To join the throng.

Then, with the office finished
And sacrifice accomplished,
They'll stay a little while   35
   To tell the isle:

'How great must be your fame,
Holding this buried name,
When the whole universe
   Still sings his verse!   40

'Who never in his life,
Burning with envious strife,
Begged honours and awards
   From mighty Lords.

Ni ne rapprit l'usage   45
De l'amoureux breuvage,
Ni l'art des anciens
    Magiciens !

Mais bien à nos campagnes
Fit voir les Sœurs compagnes   50
Foulantes l'herbe aux sons
    De ses chansons,

Car il fit à sa lyre
Si bons accords élire,
Qu'il orna de ses chants   55
    Nous et nos champs.

La douce manne tombe
A jamais sur sa tombe,
Et l'humeur que produit
    En Mai la nuit.   60

Tout à l'entour l'emmure
L'herbe et l'eau qui murmure,
L'un toujours verdoyant,
    L'autre ondoyant.

Et nous, ayant mémoire   65
Du renom de sa gloire,
Lui ferons comme à Pan
    Honneur chaque an.»

Ainsi dira la troupe,
Versant de mainte coupe   70
Le sang d'un agnelet
    Avec du lait

Dessur moi, qui à l'heure
Serai par la demeure
Où les heureux esprits   75
    Ont leur pourpris.

'Love-potions had no part   45
In his melodious art
Which shunned the vain ambitions
   Of old magicians.

'Our fields received instead
The Sisters whose light tread   50
Danced joyously along
   Moved by his song,

'For he made his lyre choose
Such chords that his clear muse
Honoured not us alone,   55
   But the lands we own.

'Let sweet manna softly come
Falling, falling on his tomb,
Moisture that is made, men say,
   By night in May.   60

'Be sure that all around
Grass grows and waters sound,
One ever green, the other
   Rippling ever.

'We, mindful of his fame,   65
The glory of his name,
Shall, as for Pan, each year
   Honour him here.'

Thus all the troupe shall say,
And many times that day   70
Lamb's blood with milk be shed
   Over my bed,

For I shall then have come
To that eternal home
Where shades of spirits blest   75
   Enjoy their rest.

La grêle ne la neige
N'ont tels lieux pour leur siège,
Ne la foudre onque là
    Ne dévala :   80

Mais bien constante y dure
L'immortelle verdure
Et constant en tout temps
    Le beau Printemps.

Le soin qui sollicite   85
Les Rois, ne les incite
Le monde ruiner
    Pour dominer :

Ains comme frères vivent,
Et morts encore suivent   90
Les métiers qu'ils avaient
    Quand ils vivaient.

Là, là j'orrai d'Alcée
La lyre courroucée,
Et Sapphon qui sur tous   95
    Sonne plus doux.

Combien ceux qui entendent
Les chansons qu'ils répandent,
Se doivent réjouir
    De les ouïr,   100

Quand la peine reçue
Du rocher est déçue,
Et quand le vieil Tantal
    N'endure mal !

La seule lyre douce   105
L'ennui des cœurs repousse,
Et va l'esprit flattant
    De l'écoutant.

Such dwellings never know
Showers of hail or snow,
Nor does the thunder crash
   And lightning flash: 80

But there the immortal grass,
Stays fresh as seasons pass,
And greens to everlasting
   In constant Spring.

Unlike those Kings who wield 85
Power to wreck the world,
The spirits here do not dictate
   Or dominate:

They live as brothers do
And even the dead pursue 90
The trades in which they thrived
   While still alive.

There I shall hear the lyre
Of Alcaeus' fierce ire,
And Sappho's music, sweeter far 95
   Than others are.

How must they listen there
To music in the air,
How must the troupe rejoice
   At every voice, 100

When, at the top of the hill,
The boulder itself stands still,
And even Tantalus remains
   Charmed out of pain?

Only the lyre knows the art 105
That drives all trouble from the heart
And leads the unquiet soul to find
   Full peace of mind.

55 À GUY PACATE* (4.5)

Guy, nos meilleurs ans coulent
Comme les eaux qui roulent
D'un cours sempiternel :
La mort pour sa séquelle
Nous amène avec elle   5
Un exil éternel.

Nulle humaine prière
Ne repousse en arrière
Le bateau de Charon,
Quand l'âme nue arrive   10
Vagabonde en la rive
De Styx et d'Achéron.

Toutes choses mondaines
Qui vêtent nerfs et veines
La Mort égale prend,   15
Soient pauvres, ou soient Princes :
Dessus toutes provinces
Sa main large s'étend.

La puissance tant forte
Du grand Achille est morte,   20
Et Thersite odieux
Aux Grecs est mort encores :
Et Minos, qui est ores
Le conseiller des Dieux.

Jupiter ne demande   25
Que des bœufs pour offrande :
Mais son frère Pluton
Nous demande nous hommes,
Qui la victime sommes
De son enfer glouton.   30

Celui dont le Pau baigne
Le tombeau, nous enseigne

55 TO GUY PACATE (4.5)

Already, Guy, our best years go
Gliding away as waters flow
And streams descend into a river:
Death nears with all his retinue
To take us swiftly off into   5
An exile that's forever.

No mortal man has any prayer
That gives some hope, when he is there,
Of turning back the boat of Charon,
When naked, wandering in dread,   10
The soul's uncertain steps will tread
The banks of Styx and Acheron.

All earthly things whose frame contains
A set of sinews, nerves, and veins,
Death the Leveller takes them all;   15
Be they Princes, be they poor,
No state escapes: this much is sure,
Upon them his broad hand will fall.

For all the strength that once he had,
The great Achilles now is dead;   20
Thersites whom no Greek can love,
Went the same way, burdened with shame;
And Minos too who then became
A counsellor of the Gods above.

When Jove demands a sacrifice,   25
One or two bulls or cows suffice;
His brother looks for something else:
Men are the victims of his rite,
We serve to sate the appetite
Of glutton Pluto's greedy Hell.   30

The fate of Icarus whose grave
Is washed by Po's translucent wave

N'espérer rien de haut,
Et celui que Pégase
(Qui fit sourcer Parnase)   35
Culbuta si grand saut.

Las ! on ne peut connaître
Le destin qui doit naître,
Et l'homme en vain poursuit
Conjecturer la chose,   40
Que Dieu sage tient close
Sous une obscure nuit.

Je pensais que la trope
Que guide Calliope,
(Trope mon seul confort)   45
Soutiendrait ma querelle,
Et qu'indompté, par elle
Je dompterais la mort :

Mais une fièvre grosse
Creuse déjà ma fosse   50
Pour me bannir là-bas,
Et sa flamme cruelle
Se paît de ma mouelle,
Misérable repas.

Que peu s'en faut, ma vie,   55
Que tu ne m'es ravie
Close sous le tombeau !
Et que mort je ne voie
Où Mercure convoie
Le débile troupeau !   60

Et Alcé', qui les peines
Dont les guerres sont pleines
Va là-bas racontant,
Alcée qu'une presse
Des épaules épaisse   65
Admire en l'écoutant.

Should teach us not to aim too high;
So should the man that Pegasus
(Who gave Parnassus' spring to us)
Flung tumbling headlong from the sky. 35

Alas, we can't foresee our fate;
However much we speculate,
Nothing will help us to divine
What God in his mysterious way 40
Keeps sure and safely locked away,
Deep hidden in his dark design.

In days gone by I placed my hope
And all my comfort in the troupe
That's guided by Calliope; 45
The Muses would uphold my cause
And with indomitable force
I would make death subscribe to me:

But now a fever rages high
And digs the grave where I must lie, 50
Meaning to banish me down there;
And that ferocious flame devours
My very marrow at all hours,
Still hungry for such wretched fare.

Know then, my life, how very near 55
You are to being snatched from here
And in that clammy chamber sealed;
And then, once dead, how I shall see
The feeble flock that Mercury
Conducts towards the infernal fields. 60

And there the sad Alcaeus goes,
Telling the Underworld the woes
That wars engender and inspire;
Alcaeus, with his plaintive song,
Attended by a close-packed throng, 65
Who marvel at his plaintive lyre.

A bon droit Prométhée
Pour sa fraude inventée
Endure un tourment tel,
Qu'un aigle sur la roche   70
Lui ronge d'un bec croche
Le poumon immortel.

Depuis qu'il eut robée
La flamme prohibée
Pour les Dieux dépiter,   75
Les bandes inconnues
De fièvres sont venues
Notre terre habiter,

Et la Mort dépiteuse
Auparavant boiteuse   80
Fut légère d'aller.
D'ailes mal-ordonnées
Aux hommes non données
Dédale coupa l'air.

La maudite Pandore   85
Fut forgée, et encore
Astrée s'envola,
Et la boîte féconde
Peupla le pauvre monde
De tant de maux qu'il a.   90

Ah ! le méchant courage
Des hommes de notre âge
N'endure par ses faits
Que Jupiter étuie
Sa foudre, qui s'ennuie   95
De voir tant de méfaits.

56 (4.13)

Ma douce jouvence* est passée,
Ma première force est cassée,
J'ai la dent noire et le chef blanc,

And there Prometheus receives
The punishment that he deserves,
Condemned eternally to hang
Upon a rock where every day 70
A hook-beaked eagle pecks away,
Feeding on his immortal lungs.

In stealing the forbidden fire,
Moved by a rancorous desire
To spite the Gods, he brought to birth 75
A host of plagues, till then unknown,
Fevers that burn the skin and bone
And now infect the face of earth:

And Death itself, once lame and slow
In our pursuit, is quicker now 80
And leaps light-footed to his prize.
Daedalus dared forbidden things
And made himself ill-fitting wings
To cut a pathway through the skies.

Jove made Pandora as a curse 85
Upon mankind and, what was worse,
Astraea and her justice fled:
The fatal box revealed its worth,
Fertile in evils that the earth
Has ever since inherited. 90

Oh! wicked-hearted men whose deeds
Prevent the mercy that we need
From heaven in our shameful times,
For Jupiter will not withhold
His thunderbolts when he beholds 95
A prospect of so many crimes.

56 (4.13)

My happy youth is passed and gone,
The strength I had is quite undone,
Black are my teeth and white my head;

Mes nerfs sont dissous et mes veines,
Tant j'ai le corps froid, ne sont pleines   5
Que d'une eau rousse au lieu de sang.

Adieu ma lyre, adieu fillettes
Jadis mes douces amourettes,
Adieu, je sens venir ma fin :
Nul passetemps de ma jeunesse   10
Ne m'accompagne en la vieillesse,
Que le feu, le lit et le vin.

J'ai la tête toute élourdie
De trop d'ans et de maladie,
De tous côtés le soin me mord :   15
Et soit que j'aille ou que je tarde,
Toujours après moi je regarde
Si je verrai venir la Mort,

Qui doit, ça me semble, à toute heure
Me mener là-bas où demeure   20
Je ne sais quel Pluton, qui tient
Ouvert à tous venants un antre,
Où bien facilement on entre,
Mais d'où jamais on ne revient.

57 À SA MUSE (5.36)

Plus dur que fer* j'ai fini cet ouvrage,
Que l'an dispos à démener les pas,
Que l'eau rongearde, ou des frères la rage,*
Qui rompent tout, ne ru'ront point à bas.
Le même jour que le dernier trépas   5
M'assoupira d'un somme dur, à l'heure
Sous le tombeau tout Ronsard n'ira pas,
Restant de lui la part qui est meilleure.
    Toujours toujours, sans que jamais je meure,
Je volerai tout vif par l'Univers,   10
Éternisant les champs où je demeure
De mes Lauriers honorés et couverts :
Pour avoir joint les deux Harpeurs divers*

My feeble sinews can't sustain
My shivering body; in my veins   5
Red water flows instead of blood.

Farewell my lyre, and farewell
Sweet girls who held me in their spell;
My end is coming and I find
The joys I had when young and free   10
Now in old age abandon me,
Except for fire, bed, and wine.

My head is heavy for it bears
The weight of sickness and long years;
On every side I'm plagued by care.   15
When I walk out fear comes with me,
And at my back I dread to see
Death's chariot hurrying near,

Ready at all times, so they say,
To pick me up and haste away   20
Down to some Pluto's gloomy den,
Where there's an entrance gaping wide,
Inviting everyone inside,
But nobody comes out again.

57 TO HIS MUSE (5.36)

To outlast iron I have made this work,
The years shall not efface it as they go,
Nor shall eroding water nor the wreck
Wrought by the raging brothers bring it low:
When Death one day comes stealing to bestow   5
Its heavy sleep on me, at that same time
Not all Ronsard will fill the grave below:
What's left will be the better part of him.
Forever and undying I shall fly,
A living spirit, through the Universe,   10
Immortalizing those fair fields that I
Dwelt in and decked with Laurels, since my course
Served to combine two Harpers quite diverse

Au doux babil de ma lyre d'ivoire,
Qui se sont faits Vendômois par mes vers.   15
    Sus donque, Muse ! emporte au ciel la gloire
Que j'ai gagnée, annonçant la victoire
Dont à bon droit je me vois jouissant :
Et de Ronsard consacre la mémoire,
Ornant son front d'un Laurier verdissant.   20

Les Élégies

58   ÉLÉGIE (13)

    Nous fîmes un contrat* ensemble l'autre jour,
Que tu me donnerais mille baisers d'amour,
Colombins, tourterins, à lèvres demi-closes,
À soupirs soupirants la même odeur des roses,
À langue serpentine, à tremblotants regards,   5
De pareille façon que Vénus baise Mars,
Quand il se pâme d'aise au sein de sa Maîtresse.
Tu as parfait le nombre, hélas ! je le confesse :
Mais Amour sans milieu, ami d'extrémité,
Ne se contente point d'un nombre limité.   10
    Qui ferait sacrifice à Bacchus pour trois grappes,
À Pan pour trois agneaux ? Jupiter, quand tu frappes
De ton foudre la terre, et pétrissant en l'air
Une poisseuse nue enceinte d'un éclair,
Ta majesté sans nombre élance pêle-mêle   15
Pluie sur pluie épaisse et grêle dessus grêle,
Sur champs et sur forêts, sans regarder combien.
Un Prince est indigent, qui peut nombrer son bien.
A ta maison céleste appartient l'abondance.
En terre ma Maîtresse a semblable puissance.   20
    Toi, Déesse cent fois plus belle que n'était
Celle qu'aux bords de Chypre une conque portait,*
Pressurant les cheveux de sa tête immortelle
Encore tous moiteux de la mer maternelle,
Tu ne devrais conter les baisers savoureux   25
Que tu donnes trop chiche à ton pauvre amoureux.
Si tu ne contes point les soucis ni les peines

With my own harp of ivory whereby
I made them Vendommois, thanks to my verse.   15
    Come then, my Muse, and raise to heaven the glory
That I have won, proclaim the victory,
Rightfully mine, that I rejoice in now,
Preserve the memory of Ronsard and lay
A Laurel ever green upon his brow.   20

Elegies

58 ELEGY (13)

We made a deal the other day that you
Would give a thousand kisses as my due,
The doveish kind, with lips that do not close,
Exhaling sighs sweet-scented like the rose,
With agile probing tongue and trembling look   5
Like Venus kissing mighty Mars who took
His ease and swooned upon his Mistress' breast.
That number's now been reached, I must confess;
But Love's extreme, no friend to moderation,
And any number would mean limitation.   10
    Who offers sacrifice to Pan or Bacchus
For numbered lambs or grapes? Think of the fracas
That you make, Jupiter, when you rain down
Your thunderbolts with lightning all around.
Your Majesty hurls them from a cloud pell-mell   15
On field and forest; rainstorms follow hail;
And you don't count the thunderbolts you've thrown.
The monarch who can number all he owns
Is poor indeed. Not so your heavenly house.
On earth my Mistress has a wealth like yours.   20
    Goddess more fair than one a seashell bore
Over the waves to reach the Cyprian shore,
With her immortal head raised up to free
Tresses still wet from the maternal sea—
Yes, you, my goddess, do not count your kisses,   25
Too few to meet with this poor lover's wishes,
Unless you count my many pains and fears

Ni les larmes qui font de mes yeux deux fontaines,
Tu ne devrais conter les biens que je reçois,
Non plus que moi les maux que je souffre pour toi.   30
Car ce n'est la raison de donner par mesure
Tes baisers, quand des maux innombrables j'endure.
Donne-moi donc au lit, ensemble bien unis,
Des baisers infinis pour mes maux infinis.

59 ÉLÉGIE (23)

Pour vous aimer, Maîtresse, je me tue,
J'ai jour et nuit la fièvre continue,
Qui me consomme et hâte mon trépas,
Mourant pour vous, et ne vous en chaut pas :
Vous n'avez soin ni égard qu'à vous-même :   5
Pour trop aimer vous n'êtes jamais blême,
Fièvre ne mal pour aimer ne vous point,
Et pour aimer vous ne soupirez point.

Franche d'esprit, en vain êtes priée,
Loin des filets de l'amour déliée,   10
Libre fuyez, comme il vous plaît, ainsi
Moquant votre âge, Amour et mon souci.

Beauté trop belle, assise en fier courage,
Quelque lionne en quelque bois sauvage
Vous allaita, un rocher vous conçut,   15
Et pour marraine un tigre vous reçut.
Depuis trois ans vous paissez de mes larmes,
M'ensorcelant de je ne sais quels charmes,
Dont l'amiable et courtoise douceur
Hume mon sang, et altère mon cœur,   20
Qui d'autant plus me trahit qu'elle est douce :
Mais la plus fière et amère secousse
Que pour ma mort vous mettez en avant,
C'est ne vouloir de serviteur servant.*

Quoi ? pensez-vous que l'amour soit la bouche ?   25
Autant vaudrait embrasser une souche
Sans mouvement, que vos lèvres baiser,
Sur vos tétins enflés se reposer,
Presser vos yeux, les sucer sans revanche,
Toucher le sein, tâter la cuisse blanche,   30

That make these eyes two fountains, count the tears.
You should not number gifts that are my due
More than I count my sufferings for you.   30
It can't be right to count each kiss you spend
While I'm enduring torments without end.
So give me, when we lie in bed together,
For infinite ills your kisses without measure.

59 ELEGY (23)

I'm dying, Lady, for the love of you,
By day and night the fever rages through,
And death is hastened by these pains I bear—
Such care for you, and nothing makes you care.
Your precious self is all you're thinking of,   5
And if you're pale, it's surely not for love,
Love's fever and love's sickness pass you by,
And passion never breathes a single sigh.

Far from love's nets your spirit ranges free;
Men plead with you in vain, for still you flee,   10
Untrammelled, wandering as you please, and thus
You mock your age and Love and my distress.

To plant such beauty in so stern a breast
Deep in the woods some savage lioness
Gave you her milk; a rocky womb conceived you   15
And tigers as a stepchild then received you.
For three long years my tears have been your drink,
What spells you cast on me I cannot think;
It seemed a gentle and a courteous art
And yet inhaled my blood and broke my heart,   20
Deceiving me the more since it was sweet:
But your most cutting and most harsh conceit
That's killing me is this: that you won't use
Your servant's service that you still refuse.

What's this? You think love's in the mouth alone?   25
So why not clasp a senseless stock or stone?
Kissing your lips, letting my fingers rest
Upon the swelling nipples of your breast,
Pressing your snow-white hand, licking your eyes,
Stroking your belly, feeling hips and thighs—   30

Ce n'est que vent, et tel plaisir ne vaut
Quand de l'amour le meilleur point* défaut.

    Mais se rejoindre en un et se remettre,
Et à l'ami toute chose permettre,
Se rassembler ainsi qu'au premier temps,*   35
C'est ce qui rend les amoureux contents.
Il faut s'aimer d'une amour mutuelle,
Non par la bouche, et non par la mamelle,
Non par les yeux : ce ne sont instruments
Propres assez pour nos rassemblements :   40
Mais pour se joindre, il faut à l'aventure,
Remettre en un les outils de Nature.

    Et quoi ? cruelle, et quoi ? voudriez-vous bien,
Vous qui du Ciel reçûtes tant de bien,
À qui la grâce et l'heureuse influence   45
Des feux du Ciel ont orné la naissance,
Voudriez-vous bien d'un cœur malicieux
Trahir Nature et mépriser les Cieux,
Et résister à leur loi vénérable ?

    Les fiers Géants,* d'un orgueil misérable   50
Contre le Ciel élevèrent ainsi
Le vain orgueil de leur brave sourcil :
Eux à la fin accablés de la foudre,
Noirs et puants, bronchèrent sur la poudre,
Pour châtiment d'avoir si fous été   55
Que des grands Dieux forcer la majesté.

    Voudriez-vous, Dame en beauté très-parfaite,
Pleine, en bon-point, de jeunesse refaite,
Courtoise, honnête et d'un abord si doux,
Trahir les dons que vous portez en vous ?   60

    Je crois que non : mais l'honneur vous abuse,*
Honneur frivole et de trop vaine excuse,
Qui n'est que fraude, et qui se fait par art
Honneur ici, et vice en autre part :
Voilà comment tel honneur se démène   65
Comme il nous plaît, par fantaisie humaine.
Eh bien Madame, encores que la foi
De ce pays donnât une autre loi,
Sévère loi, qui nos cœurs emprisonne !

All that's just wind, pleasures not worth a bean
Unless they lead up to the point supreme.
    To grant your lover all things is to render
Two bodies one with mutual self-surrender,
Like lovers in that primal golden time,   35
Happy to be created androgyne.
We seek in mutual love to be made whole.
The mouth won't do, the breast won't play that role;
Nor will the eyes: these tools are puny ones,
Not strong enough to favour our reunions;   40
But to be joined, lovers who take their chance
Reduce to one the tools that Nature grants.
    Come now! Ingrate! Is this how you receive
The many gifts sent down from Heaven above,
When grace celestial assured your worth   45
And lucky stars shed light upon your birth?
Will you, O cruel heart, do so much ill
As to scorn Nature and spurn Heaven's will
And to resist their venerable law.
    This is the crime that they were punished for,   50
Those miserable Giants, who defied
The rule of Heaven in vainglorious pride:
They flinched and fell when lightning cast them down;
Their blackened forms lay stinking on the ground,
A penalty for stubborn hearts who meant   55
To bend the will of Gods to their intent.
    Would you, my beauteous Lady, whom we see
Blooming in youth, lively and frank and free,
Full-formed and fresh, with such a gentle air,
Betray the precious gifts that now you bear?   60
    I can't believe it. Honour is to blame,
Whose argument is false and still the same:
Mere art is this, a frivolous device:
Here's honour; on the other side is vice.
That's honour's claim for what we know to be   65
A product of our human fantasy.
Well, Madam, though our country's faith imposes
Another law and stricter that encloses
Our hearts in prison, yet I dare to ask:

Avez-vous pas la nature assez bonne,   70
Assez de cœur et assez de moyen,
Assez d'esprit pour rompre ce lien ?
Certes oui : toute femme amoureuse
Est de nature assez ingénieuse.
Ne mettez donc le temps à nonchaloir   75
Tant seulement ne faut que le vouloir :
La volonté invente toute chose :
Et tout cela que notre esprit propose
Est achevé ou par temps ou soudain :
Car du vouloir chambrière est la main.   80

   Je sais combien la femme nous découpe,
Alors qu'assise au milieu d'une troupe,
Se va plaignant des Amoureux qui n'ont
Ni foi au cœur, ni honte sur le front :
Et s'aigrissant d'une parole noire,   85
Dit contre nous mainte tragique histoire,
Et vous oyant les hommes diffamer,
Faites alors un serment de n'aimer.

   Je sais Madame, et honteux je confesse
Que maint Amant a laissé sa Maîtresse :   90
Mais du péché la faute en est à vous,
Qui nous trompez et changez à tous coups,
Nous harassez et irritez de sorte,
Que la ferveur de l'amour devient morte,
Et lors l'Amant qui reprend sa raison,   95
Par le dédain s'échappe de prison.

   Femmes de Cour et les femmes des villes
Sont à tromper dispostement habiles :
Car elles sont savantes et ont leu
Ce qui attise ou amortit le feu :   100
Savent que c'est martel et jalousie,
Feindre et tromper, changer de fantaisie,
Dissimuler et forger maint écrit,
Où la rustique et pauvrette d'esprit
Suit la Nature, et rude d'artifice,   105
Prend son plaisir sans fraude ne malice.

   Vous qui avez l'esprit gaillard et bon,
Née et nourrie en ville de renom,

Have you a nature fitted for this task,   70
A heart that's good enough, a ready brain,
And native strength enough to break the chain?
Surely you have. Women in love possess
A nature that is most ingenious.
Don't linger wondering how you'll get through it   75
When all that matters is the will to do it:
The will alone is mother of invention,
And everything that is the mind's intention
Time in good time or sooner shall fulfil,
Because the hand is servant to the will.   80
   I know how women like to slander us
When they sit round to moan and make a fuss
About their Lovers who are all the same,
Faithless and heartless, with no sense of shame:
With bitter words they darken the offence   85
And tragic stories told at our expense.
You, hearing men thus slandered by the crew,
Conclude and vow that love is not for you.
   That Lovers leave their Mistresses is indeed
A truth that I with proper shame concede;   90
But for that sin the guilt is surely yours
For you deceive us and keep changing course,
With harassment and hassle till at last
Love's ardour dies; and then when love is past,
The Lover finds his reason once again   95
And flees from prison, goaded by disdain.
   Ladies of Court and city wives excel
In their betrayals for they study well
The works of ancient sages where they learn
How to cool down love's fire or make it burn.   100
They know what anguish is and jealousy,
Feigning, deceit, caprice, and fantasy,
Faking and forging letters to be sent;
While the poor rustic simpleton's content
To follow Nature and, with artless style,   105
Take honest pleasure without fraud or guile.
   You, with a spirit that is bold and sound,
Born and brought up in such a famous town,

Qui n'ignorez les présents de Minerve,
Ne voulez point de serviteur qui serve   110
Aux doux plaisirs des amoureux combats.
     Vous le voulez, et ne le voulez pas,
Vous le voulez, et si ne l'osez dire :
Ne le disant, un amoureux martyre
Ard votre cœur en feu continuel,   115
Pour résister au plaisir mutuel.
     Si toute Dame en ce point voulait faire,
Le monde fût un désert solitaire,
Villes et bourgs, bourgades et cités,
Maisons, châteaux seraient déshabités.   120
     Par ce plaisir bien souvent on engendre
Un grand Achille, un Monarque Alexandre :
Princes et Rois se font par tel moyen.
Quoi ? voudriez-vous empêcher un tel bien ?
     Pour ce jadis la ville Hellespontique*   125
Fit un grand Temple au vieil Priape antique,
Comme au grand Dieu de génération,
Père germeux de toute nation.
     Donques, ma chère et plus que chère vie,
Si vous avez dedans le cœur envie   130
Que je vous serve, il faut sans long séjour
Étroitement pratiquer notre amour
En-cependant que les vertes années
Pour cet effet du Ciel nous sont données,
Sans pour néant notre âge consommer.   135
     Un temps viendra qui nous gard'ra d'aimer,
Par maladie ou par mort ou vieillesse :
Lors regrettant en vain notre jeunesse,
En regardant nos membres tous perclus,
Nous le voudrons et ne le pourrons plus.   140

60 (24)

     Quiconque aura premier la main embesognée
À te couper, forêt,* d'une dure cognée,
Qu'il puisse s'enferrer de son propre bâton,
Et sente en l'estomac la faim d'Erisichthon,
Qui coupa de Cérès le chêne vénérable,   5

Not unendowed with gifts from wise Minerva,
Refuse a servant offering to serve a   110
Turn in love's combat, in that amorous bout.

    You want to join and yet would be left out,
You want to join, yet dare not say the word,
And in that silence, your strong heart is stirred
By a sharp torment and incessant fire,   115
Resisting mutual pleasure and desire.

    Suppose all Women chose to be so chaste,
The world would soon become a desert waste,
Houses and castles uninhabited,
Cities and towns empty of people, dead.   120

    The pleasure I propose may well engender
A great Achilles or King Alexander:
For this is how we make Princes and Kings:
Be serious! Would you stop such wondrous things?

    That's why the ancient town of Lampsacus   125
Raised a great Temple for old Priapus,
As the most mighty God of generation
And seminal father of earth's every nation.

    And so my dear (and life is not more dear),
If you desire, with a heart sincere,   130
That I should serve you, then, without delay,
We must act out our love immediately,
And keep on doing it in the years we're given
For that sole purpose by a generous Heaven,
Not letting them consume a fruitless prime.   135

    Soon love will be denied by passing time,
By sickness, by old age, at last by death:
Then, as with vain regrets, we mourn our youth
And contemplate our crippled limbs, that day
We'll have the will but will not have the way.   140

60 (24)

    Whoever first lifts a laborious hand
To cut you down, dear forest, may he stand
Self-skewered, feeling in his guts the pain
Of hunger that once burned Erisichthon
Who, having felled the Oak to Ceres sacred,   5

Et qui, gourmand de tout, de tout insatiable,
Les bœufs et les moutons de sa mère égorgea,
Puis pressé de la faim, soi-même se mangea :
Ainsi puisse engloutir ses rentes et sa terre,
Et se dévore après par les dents de la guerre.   10

    Qu'il puisse pour venger le sang de nos forêts,
Toujours nouveaux emprunts sur nouveaux intérêts
Devoir à l'usurier, et qu'en fin il consomme
Tout son bien à payer la principale somme.

    Que toujours sans repos, ne fasse en son cerveau   15
Que tramer pour néant quelque dessein nouveau,
Porté d'impatience et de fureur diverse
Et de mauvais conseil qui les hommes renverse.

    Écoute, Bûcheron (arrête un peu le bras)
Ce ne sont pas des bois que tu jettes à bas,   20
Ne vois-tu pas le sang lequel dégoutte à force
Des Nymphes qui vivaient dessous la dure écorce ?
Sacrilège meurtrier, si on pend un voleur
Pour piller un butin de bien peu de valeur,
Combien de feux, de fers, de morts, et de détresses   25
Mérites-tu, méchant, pour tuer des Déesses ?

    Forêt, haute maison des oiseaux bocagers,
Plus le Cerf solitaire et les Chevreuils légers
Ne paîtront sous ton ombre, et ta verte crinière
Plus du Soleil d'été ne rompra la lumière.   30
Plus l'amoureux Pasteur sur un tronc adossé,
Enflant son flageolet à quatre trous percé,
Son mâtin à ses pieds, à son flanc la houlette,
Ne dira plus l'ardeur de sa belle Janette:*
Tout deviendra muet, Écho sera sans voix, :   35
Tu deviendras campagne, et en lieu de tes bois,
Dont l'ombrage incertain lentement se remue,
Tu sentiras le soc, le coutre et la charrue :
Tu perdras ton silence, et haletant d'effroi
Ni Satyres, ni Pans ne viendront plus chez toi.   40

    Adieu vieille forêt, le jouet de Zéphyre,
Où premier j'accordais les langues de ma lyre,
Où premier j'entendis les flèches résonner
D'Apollon, qui me vint tout le cœur étonner :

Was plagued with hunger that could not be sated;
He ate the sheep and kine his mother bred
And, when that failed, devoured himself instead:
Likewise may this man's land bring him no profit
But be consumed by wars that feed upon it.   10

    Then, to avenge the blood of our last forests,
Let him be forced to pay high interests
To moneylenders, until all he owns
Must go to pay off the original loans.

    Let there be nothing in his restless brain   15
But futile plans that he concocts in vain;
Rash and enraged by furies he can't master
And bad advice that leads him to disaster.

    Now listen, Woodman, stay your arm awhile!
It is not just a tree that you defile.   20
Can you not see the drops of blood that come
Out of the bark? This was the Wood-nymph's home.
O sacrilegious murderer, if a robber
Is hanged for pilfering some petty coffer,
What pains, what chains, what torments should you fear   25
For having coldly killed a Goddess here?

    Forest, high haunt of woodland birds, the days
Are gone when Deer or lightfoot Roebuck grazed
In your cool shade; no more shall your green tresses
Filter the light when summer's Sun oppresses;   30
Nor, propped against a trunk, the Shepherd train
His rustic flute to play an amorous strain,
No longer tell his passion for Jeanette,
Crook at his side and mastiff at his feet:
All will be mute, and Echo's voice be dead;   35
Here will be open country, and instead
Of this uncertain slowly-shifting shade,
You'll feel the plough, the coulter, and the blade.
Your silence will be lost; breathless with fear,
Pan and the Satyrs will not gather here.   40

    Farewell, you ancient woods where Zephyr played,
Where first I tuned my lyre in the glade;
Where first I felt Apollo's sounding dart
Come down to pierce me and astound my heart;

Où premier admirant la belle Calliope, 45
Je devins amoureux de sa neuvaine trope,*
Quand sa main sur le front cent roses me jeta,
Et de son propre lait Euterpe m'allaita.

    Adieu vieille forêt, adieu têtes sacrées,
De tableaux et de fleurs autrefois honorées, 50
Maintenant le dédain des passants altérés
Qui brûlés en Été des rayons éthérés,
Sans plus trouver le frais de tes douces verdures,
Accusent vos meurtriers, et leur disent injures.

    Adieu Chênes, couronne aux vaillants citoyens, 55
Arbres de Jupiter, germes Dodonéens,
Qui premiers aux humains donnâtes à repaître,
Peuples vraiment ingrats, qui n'ont su reconnaître
Les biens reçus de vous, peuples vraiment grossiers,
De massacrer ainsi nos pères nourriciers. 60

    Que l'homme est malheureux qui au monde se fie !
Ô Dieux, que véritable est la Philosophie,*
Qui dit que toute chose à la fin périra,
Et qu'en changeant de forme une autre vêtira :
De Tempé la vallée un jour sera montagne, 65
Et la cime d'Athos une large campagne,
Neptune quelque fois de blé sera couvert.
La matière demeure, et la forme se perd.

Les Hymnes

61 HYMNE DU CIEL*

A JEAN DE MOREL, EMBRUNOIS

    Morel, qui pour partage en ton âme possèdes
Les plus nobles vertus, trésor dont tu ne cèdes
A nul de notre siècle, ou soit en équité,
Soit en candeur de mœurs, ou soit en vérité,
Qui, seul de nos Français, de mes vers pris la charge, 5
Couverts de de ta faveur, comme Ajax sous sa targe
Couvrait l'archer Teucer, que les Troyens pressaient
De traits, qui sur le dos du bouclier se froissaient :
    Cependant qu'à loisir l'Hymne je te façonne

Where first the fair Calliope I knew 45
And learned to love her ninefold retinue;
Where on my brow were roses that she cast
And I was suckled at Euterpe's breast.

Farewell, old forest, farewell sacred heads
Honoured in days gone by with flowers spread 50
And holy rites; now shunned by passers-by
Who, burned in Summer by the sun's fierce ray,
Find no more freshness under your green boughs;
They blame your murderers, cursing them out loud.

Farewell, you Oaks, whose leaves once crowned the brave, 55
Jupiter's trees that in Dodona gave
To primal men something on which to feed.
Ungrateful humans, heartless folk, indeed,
Who fail to recognize your gifts, and thus
Slaughter the fathers who first nourished us. 60

How wretched is the man who trusts the world!
How true is the Philosophy that holds
That all things in the end are doomed to perish,
But, with a change of form, others will flourish.
Mountains will rise where Tempe's vale spreads wide, 65
The peak of Athos to the plain subside;
Neptune will wear a cloak of corn one day.
Matter endures, and form will fade away.

Hymns

61 HYMN TO THE SKY

TO JEAN DE MOREL OF EMBRUN

Morel, who for your soul's endowment own
A store of noble virtues that no one
Surpasses in our time, whether it be
In justice, truth, or moral purity;
Alone in France you gave my verse your favour, 5
Keeping it safe, as once beneath his buckler
Ajax protected Teucer, nor would yield
When Trojan arrows shattered on his shield.

You'll hear me hymn the Muses by and by;

Des Muses, prends en gré ce Ciel que je te donne,   10
A toi, digne de lui, comme l'ayant connu
Longtemps avant que d'être en la terre venu,
Et qui le reconnais, si après la naissance
Quelque homme en eut jamais çà-bas la connaissance.*

   Ô Ciel rond et vouté, haute maison de Dieu,   15
Qui prêtes en ton sein à toutes choses lieu,
Et qui roules si tôt ta grand' boule ébranlée
Sur deux essieux fichés, que la vitesse ailée
Des aigles et des vents par l'air ne sauraient pas
En volant égaler le moindre de tes pas :   20
Tant seulement l'esprit de prompte hardiesse,
Comme venant de toi, égale ta vitesse.
Ô Ciel vite coureur, tu parfais ton grand tour,
D'un pied jamais recru, en l'espace d'un jour !
Ainçois d'un pied de fer, qui sans cesse retourne   25
Au lieu duquel il part, et jamais ne séjourne,
Traînant tout avec soi, pour ne souffrir mourir
L'Univers en paresse à faute de courir.

   L'Esprit de l'Éternel,* qui avance ta course,
Épandu dedans toi, comme une vive source,   30
De tous côtés t'anime, et donne mouvement,
Te faisant tournoyer en sphère rondement
Pour être plus parfait, car en la forme ronde
Gît la perfection qui toute en soi abonde.

   De ton branle premier des autres tout divers,   35
Tu tires au rebours les corps de l'Univers,
Bandés en résistant contre ta violence,
Seuls à part démenant une seconde danse :
L'un deçà, l'autre là, comme ils sont agités
Des mouvements réglés de leurs diversités.   40
Ainsi, guidant premier si grande compagnie,
Tu fais une si douce et plaisante harmonie,*
Que nos luths ne sont rien, au prix des moindres sons
Qui résonnent là-haut de diverses façons.

   D'un feu vif et divin ta voûte est composée,   45
Non feu matériel, dont la flamme exposée
Çà-bas en nos foyers mangerait affamé
De toutes les forêts le branchage ramé :

Meanwhile accept this anthem to the Sky; 10
For such a Hymn is suited to your worth
Who knew the heavens before you came to earth,
And know them still if any man can know
Something so high when he comes here below.

O round and vaulted Sky, high house of God, 15
You to all things their proper place accord;
You roll on two fixed poles your spinning sphere
So rapidly that eagles as they soar
And whirling winds, however swift they prove
Can never hope to match your slightest move: 20
Only the mind that promptly follows through
Keeps the same pace because it comes from you.
O speedy runner, Sky, whose tireless feet
Take one sole day to make your round complete;
Your iron feet, indeed, return to where 25
They started out, but never linger there;
They pull all things along lest, quite undone,
The Universe die because it does not run.

The Spirit of the Eternal drives your course,
Diffused throughout you as a living source 30
That animates the whole and gives your motion
Its circular path and spherical rotation,
For only in that circular form we meet
Endless perfection in itself complete.

By your first move, a dancing impetus, 35
The various bodies of the Universe
Are pulled your way, though they by nature strain
To dance a separate round, each on his own,
One here, another there, as ordered by
The patterned rules of their diversity. 40
Thus you, directing that great company,
Create such sweet and pleasing harmony
Our lutes would seem as nothing if our ears
Could catch the faintest music of the spheres.

Your vault is made of living fire divine, 45
Not the material fire that can be seen
On our low hearths whose hungry flame would eat
Whole verdant branching forests did we not

Et pour ce, tous les jours, il faut qu'on le nourrisse
Le repaissant de bois, s'on ne veut qu'il périsse.   50
Mais celui qui là-haut en vigueur entretient
Toi et tes yeux d'Argus, de lui seul se soutient
Sans mendier secours : car sa vive étincelle
Sans aucun aliment se nourrit de par elle :
D'elle-même elle luit, comme fait le Soleil,   55
Tempérant l'Univers d'un feu doux et pareil
À celui qui habite en l'estomac de l'homme,*
Qui tout le corps échauffe et point ne le consomme.

    Qu'à bon droit les Grégeois t'ont nommé d'un beau nom !*
Qui bien t'avisera, ne trouvera sinon   60
En toi qu'un ornement, et qu'une beauté pure,
Qu'un compas bien réglé, qu'une juste mesure,
Et bref, qu'un rond parfait, dont l'immense grandeur,
Hauteur, largeur, biais, travers et profondeur
Nous montrent, en voyant un si bel édifice,   65
Combien l'esprit de Dieu est rempli d'artifice,
Et subtil artisan, qui te bâtit de rien
Et t'accomplit si beau, pour nous montrer combien
Grande est sa Majesté, qui hautaine demande
Pour son Palais royal, une maison si grande.   70

    Or ce Dieu tout puissant, tant il est bon et doux,
S'est fait le citoyen du monde comme nous,*
Et n'a tant dédaigné notre humaine nature,
Qu'il ait outre les bords de ta large clôture
Autre maison bâtie, ains s'est logé chez toi,   75
Chez toi, franc de soucis, de peines et d'émoi,
Qui vont couvrant le front des terres habitables,
Des terres, la maison des humains misérables.

    Si celui qui comprend doit emporter le prix
Et l'honneur sur celui qui plus bas est compris,   80
Tu dois avoir l'honneur sur cette masse toute,
Qui tout seul la comprends dessous ta large voûte,
Et en son ordre à part limites un chacun :
Toi, qui n'as ton pareil, et ne sembles qu'à un
Qu'à toi, qui es ton moule et la seule modelle   85
De toi-même tout rond, comme chose éternelle.

    Tu n'as en ta grandeur commencement ne bout,
Tu es tout dedans toi, de toutes choses tout,

Take care to keep it fed with wood each day
Lest it should lose its force and faint away;   50
But up above the fire that maintains
Your force and all your Argus eyes sustains
Itself with no external help and needs
No nourishment for on itself it feeds:
As does the Sun, it shines with its own light,   55
Tempers the Universe with its mild heat,
Like that which gently in man's stomach sits,
Warming his body, not consuming it.

  The lovely name you have in Greek is right,
For those who scan you with perceptive sight   60
Find nothing but pure beauty and just measure,
Well-judged proportion and unfailing order,
A perfect round in whose immensity,
Height, width, and long diagonals, we see
How full of artistry God's spirit is,   65
Revealed to us in such an edifice,
A skilful artisan who could create
You out of nothing, so we learn how great
Must be His Majesty whose glory lies
Within a Palace of such wondrous size.   70

  So good is this almighty God to us
That he inhabits the same universe,
Not holding human nature in such scorn
As to have built beyond its distant bourn
Another house: he dwells with you instead,   75
Free from the care, the sorrow, and the dread
That on the peopled lands of earth we find—
This earth, the house of suffering mankind.

  If we assume that the container gains
The prize before the matter it contains,   80
You should be honoured more than all the mass
That under your wide vault you hold in place,
Imposing limits to each separate part:
You have no equal and resemble naught
But your own self, the only mould and model,   85
The perfect round, like everything eternal.

  Vastness with no beginning and no end,
Entire in all things, by no thing constrained,

Non contraint, infini, fait d'un fini espace,*
Dont le sein large et creux toutes choses embrasse   90
Sans rien laisser dehors, et pour ce c'est erreur,
C'est un extrême abus, une extrême fureur,
De penser qu'il y ait des mondes hors du monde.
Tu prends tout, tu tiens tout dessous ton arche ronde
D'un contour merveilleux la terre couronnant,   95
Et la grand' mer qui vient la terre environnant,
L'air épars et le feu : et bref, on ne voit chose
Ou qui ne soit à toi, ou dedans toi enclose,
Et de quelque côté que nous tournions nos yeux,
Nous avons pour objet la clôture des Cieux.   100
   Tu mets les Dieux au joug d'Anangé* la fatale,
Tu dépars à chacun sa semence natale,
La nature en ton sein ses ouvrages répand :
Tu es premier chaînon de la chaîne qui pend :
   Toi comme fécond père, en abondance enfantes   105
Les Siècles, et des ans les suites renaissantes,
Les mois et les saisons, les heures et les jours
Ainsi que jouvenceaux jeunissent de ton cours,
Frayant sans nul repos une ornière éternelle,
Qui toujours se retrace et se refraie en elle :   110
Bref, te voyant si beau, je ne saurais penser
Que quatre ou cinq mille ans* te puissent commencer,
   Soit Saint de quelque nom que tu voudras, ô Père,
À qui de l'Univers la nature obtempère,
Aimantin, varié, azuré, tournoyant,   115
Fils de Saturne,* Roi tout-oyant, tout-voyant,
Ciel, grand Palais de Dieu, exauce ma prière :
Quand la mort déli'ra mon âme prisonnière,
Et celle de Morel, hors de ce corps humain,
Daigne les recevoir, bénin, dedans ton sein,   120
Après mille travaux : et veuilles de ta grâce
Chez toi les reloger en leur première place.

62 HYMNE DES ÉTOILES,

AU SIEUR DE PIBRAC

   Ô des Muses la plus faconde,
Ma Calliope, conte-moi

And infinite, though made of finite space,
You clasp all things within your wide embrace,   90
Nothing left out: and therefore it's confusion,
Extreme of folly and extreme delusion
To think that there are worlds beyond this world.
Beneath your rounded arch all things you hold,
Crowning the earth with a most splendid band   95
And the wide sea encompassing the land,
Fire and fluent air: in short, we view
Nothing that is not yours or closed in you;
And so whichever way we turn our eyes
Our gaze encounters the enclosing Skies.   100

You bind the Gods to fate, Ananke's yoke;
From you come the engendering seeds that wake
Within your fertile breast, nature's domain:
You, the first link in her suspended chain.

Father, from your fecundity are born   105
Long Centuries and the cyclic years' return:
The months, the seasons, and the days and hours
In your fixed course renew their youthful powers,
Restlessly forging an eternal track,
Always retraced and never turning back.   110
And you began four thousand years ago!
Seeing you thus, I think it can't be so.

Be Blessed, whatever name you choose, O Father,
Who gives the law to universal Nature,
Magnetic stone and spinning azure ball,   115
King, son of Saturn, hearing, seeing all,
Sky, God's great Palace, listen to my plea:
When, at my death, my captive soul flies free,
With Morel's too, free from this mortal dust,
Deign to receive them kindly in your breast   120
After a thousand toils: grant they may come
To dwell with you again in their first home.

62 HYMN TO THE STARS

TO SIEUR DE PIBRAC

Calliope, most fluent Muse,
Tell me the influence of the Stars,

L'influx des Astres,* et pourquoi
Tant de fortunes sont au monde.
   Discourant mille fois   5
   Ensemble par les bois,
   Émerveillés nous sommes
   Des flambeaux de la nuit,
   Et du change qui suit
   La nature des hommes.   10

Chante-moi du Ciel la puissance,
Et des Étoiles la valeur,
D'où le bonheur et le malheur
Vient aux mortels dès la naissance.
   Soit qu'il faille dès lors   15
   Regarder que nos corps
   Des mottes animées
   Et des arbres crevés
   Naquirent élevés
   Comme plantes semées :   20

Soit qu'on regarde au long espace
De tant de siècles empannés,
Qui, légers de pieds, retournés,
Se suivent d'une même trace,*
   On connaîtra que tout   25
   Prend son être et son bout
   Des célestes chandelles,
   Que le Soleil ne voit
   Rien çà-bas qui ne soit
   En servage sous elles.   30

De là, les semences des fleuves
Sortent et rentrent dans la mer ;
De là, les terres font germer
Tous les ans tant de moissons neuves :
   De là, naissent les fleurs,   35
   Les glaces, les chaleurs.
   Les pluies printanières :

Why in the world so varied are
The fortunes that men cannot choose.
   Discoursing in the wood,   5
   A thousand times we've stood,
   Lost in wonder once again
   At those nocturnal torches
   Whose latent power changes
   The characters of men.   10

Sing me the Heavens above the earth,
The force inherent in those Lights
To make joy bless and sorrow blight
All mortals from the hour of birth.
   Whether we should deduce   15
   That bodies were produced
   From animated clay;
   Or from dead trunks of trees,
   As plants that grow from seed,
   Wake to the light of day;   20

Or whether we survey the space
Spanning so many centuries gone
That with light step return upon
Their ancient way and trodden trace;
   We see all things depend   25
   For being and for end
   Upon those lamps; nor could
   The Sun upon its round
   See anything not bound
   By them in servitude.   30

Thence come the rivers that appear
Out of the ground to seek the deeps;
And thence the land its vigour keeps
To germinate new crops each year.
   Thence come the morning flowers   35
   And the fresh springtime showers,
   Cold spells and sultry states;

De là, faut que chacun
Souffre l'arrêt commun
Des Parques filandières.   40

En vain l'homme de sa prière
Vous tourmente soir et matin :
Il est trainé par son Destin
Comme est un flot de sa rivière :
  Ou comme est le tronçon   45
  D'un arraché glaçon,
  Qui roule à la traverse,
  Ou comme un tronc froissé
  Que le vent courroucé
  Culbute à la renverse.   50

Bref les humaines créatures
Sont de Fortune le jouet :
Dans les retours de son rouet
Va dévidant nos aventures.
  Le sage seulement   55
  Aura commandement
  Sur votre épaisse bande,
  Et sur vous aura lieu
  L'homme saint qui craint Dieu :
  Car Dieu seul vous commande.   60

Notre esprit, une flamme agile
Qui vient de Dieu, dépend de soi :
Au corps vous donnez votre loi,
Comme un potier à son argile.
  Du corps le jour dernier   65
  Ne diffère au premier :
  C'est une chaine étreinte ;
  Ce qui m'est ordonné
  Au point que je fus né,
  Je le suis par contrainte.   70

L'un meurt au métier de la guerre
Noirci d'un poudreux tourbillon,
L'autre pousse d'un aiguillon

Thence is it that each man
Will cease—the common end
Ordained by weaving Fates.   40

Man pleads with you, a vain endeavour,
With prayers that rise both night and day:
His Destiny bears him on his way,
Swift like a ripple in a river;
    Or like the vagrant piece   45
    Split from a block of ice
    That rolls its way around;
    Or like the tree-trunk that
    The angry wind attacks
    And fells upon the ground.   50

In short, all living human creatures
Are Fortune's playthings; on the great
Turn of her wheel depends our fate
And all our deeds and destined futures.
    Only the wise man stands   55
    Free from the iron bands
    With which you tie us down;
    The saint defies your laws
    In God's good name because
    You bow to God alone.   60

Our agile spirit owns the sway
Of God from whom it first awoke:
You give the law to bodies like
The potter when he shapes his clay.
    From its first day to last   65
    The body's shackled fast
    By an unbroken chain;
    To what I am I'm bound,
    Since I was born confined
    By what has been ordained.   70

One man takes arms and meets his end
Black with the powder that explodes;
Another urges with a goad

Les bœufs au travail de sa terre.
   L'un vit contre son gré   75
   Pressé d'un bas degré,
   Qui tend à chose haute :
   Le mal est défendu,
   L'innocent est pendu,
   Qui ne fit jamais faute.   80

Telle est du Ciel la loi certaine,
Qu'il faut souffrir et non forcer :
Le bon soldat ne doit passer
Le vouloir de son Capitaine.
   L'un perd dès le berceau   85
   L'usage du cerveau,
   Avorton inutile,
   L'autre, de vent repeu
   Devient le boutefeu
   D'une guerre civile.   90

L'un de la mer court les orages
Enfermant sa vie en du bois,
L'autre, pressant le cerf d'abois,
Devient Satyre des bocages.
   L'un sans peur de méchef   95
   Bat d'un superbe chef
   Le cercle de la Lune,
   Qui tombe outrecuidé
   Pour n'avoir bien guidé
   Les brides de Fortune.   100

L'un valet de sa panse pleine,
Pourceau d'Épicure ocieux,
Mange en un jour de ses aïeux
Les biens acquis à grande peine.
   Ce guerrier qui tantôt   105
   Terre et mer d'un grand ost,
   Couvrait de tant de voiles,
   Court de tête et de nom
   Pendille à Mont-Faucon :*
   Ainsi vous plaît, Étoiles.   110

The oxen as they plough the land;
   Another loathes his fate,   75
   Oppressed by low estate,
   And hopes in vain to climb;
   Evil is helped along
   While some poor soul is hanged,
   Though innocent of crime.   80

Such is the certain law of Heaven
We must endure and not protest;
The good old soldier won't contest
His Captain's orders once they're given.
   One in the cradle loses   85
   The brain he never uses,
   A runt and nothing more:
   Another, full of wind,
   Rouses a rabble and
   Provokes a civil war.   90

One dares to risk his life inside
A wooden box that braves the storms;
Another, hunting deer, becomes
The Satyr of the countryside.
   One, fearless, head held high,   95
   Strives boldly to descry
   The circle of the Moon,
   But falls, his pride brought down
   Because he could not learn
   To handle Fortune's rein.   100

One, to his swollen paunch enslaved,
A swine of idle Epicurus,
Eats in one day all that his fathers
With years of painful labour saved.
   This warrior who once   105
   Commanded a great host
   That covered land and sea,
   Now dangles headless, nameless,
   At Montfaucon, for thus
   You Stars would have it be.   110

Et toutefois, loin des misères
Qu'aux mortels vous versez ici,
Vous moquez de notre souci,
Tournant vos courses ordinaires :
    Et n'avez peur de rien,   115
    Tant que le fort lien
    De la sainte Nature
    Tient le monde arrêté,
    Et que la majesté
    Du grand Jupiter dure.   120

Du Ciel les ministres vous êtes,
Et agréable n'avez pas
Qu'un autre fasse rien çà-bas
Ni là-haut, si vous ne le faites.
    Astres, qui tout voyez,   125
    Ou soit que vous soyez
    Des bosses allumées,
    Ou des têtes de clous
    Ardentes de feu roux
    Dans le Ciel enfermées :   130

Je vous salue heureuses flammes,
Étoiles, filles de la Nuit,
Et ce Destin, qui nous conduit
Que vous pendîtes à nos trames.
    Tandis que tous les jours   135
    Vous dévidez vos cours
    D'une danse éthérée,
    Endurant je vivrai,
    Et la chance suivrai
    Que vous m'avez livrée.   140

Gardez des Français la colonne
Sous qui renaît l'antique foi ;
Gardez sa mère et ce grand Roi,*
Élu par vous en la Poulonne :
    Et faites que Pibrac,   145
    Qui a suivi le trac
    De la douce Hippocrène,

And yet, far from the ills you force
On wretched mortals here below,
You mock our common cares and go
Turning in your familiar course.
    While holy Nature's laws   115
    Still stand you have no cause
    To fear, for strong and sure
    The bonds must always be
    While still the majesty
    Of Jupiter endures.   120

As Heaven's ministers you stand
And scorn that anyone but you
Should meddle in affairs below
Unless they're guided by your hand.
    O you, all-seeing Stars,   125
    Whether we think you are
    Bright swellings up on high,
    Or that some forge has spread
    Sharp nails still burning red
    And fixed them in the Sky,   130

I here salute you, happy flames,
Dear Stars, the daughters of the Night,
Who work together with the Fate
That fits our stories to its frame.
    So long as every day   135
    You go upon your way
    In a celestial dance,
    I shall endure and live
    To take the path you have
    Granted to me as chance.   140

Protect the martial French who bring
Back to our times the faith we own
With the Queen Mother and her son,
Chosen by you as Poland's King:
    And may you send Pibrac,   145
    Who follows in the track
    Of gentle Hippocrene,

Des peuples Poulonnais
Bientôt aux champs Français
En santé s'en revienne.   150

Pibrac, de la belle Garonne
Le docte éloquent nourrisson,
Dont au Ciel vole la Chanson
Quand il nous chante sa Boccone.
    Gardez Le Gast aussi,   155
    Des Muses le souci,
    De Mars et de Cyprine,
    Et faites que le dard
    Du Scythique soldard
    N'entame sa poitrine.   160

Discours des Misères de ce temps

63 REMONSTRANCE* AU PEUPLE DE FRANCE (EXTRAIT)

    Ô Ciel ! ô mer ! ô terre ! ô Dieu, père commun
Des Juifs et des Chrétiens, des Turcs, et d'un chacun :
Qui nourris aussi bien par ta bonté publique
Ceux du pôle Antarctiq' que ceux du pôle Arctique :
Qui donnes et raison et vie et mouvement,   5
Sans respect de personne à tous également,
Et fais du Ciel là-haut sur les têtes humaines
Tomber, comme il te plaît, les grâces et les peines :
    Ô Seigneur tout-puissant, qui as toujours été
Vers toutes nations plein de toute bonté,   10
De quoi te sert là-haut le trait de ton tonnerre,
Si d'un éclat de feu tu n'en brûles la terre ?
Es-tu dedans un trône assis sans faire rien ?
Il ne faut point douter que tu ne saches bien
Cela que contre toi brassent tes créatures,   15
Et toutefois, Seigneur, tu le vois et l'endures !
    Ne vois-tu pas du Ciel ces petits animaux,
Lesquels ne sont vêtus que de petites peaux,
Ces petits animaux qu'on appelle les hommes !
Qu'ainsi que bulles d'eau tu crèves et consommes,   20

Home from those Polish folk,
In perfect health to walk
Through his French fields again;   150

Pibrac, nursed by the fair Garonne,
Its eloquent and learned son,
Who steals from Heaven the sweet Song
When he exalts his sweet Bocconne.
    Defend Le Gast also,   155
    Whose worth the Muses know,
    And Mars and Venus guard;
    Be his protector lest
    He find his noble breast
    Pierced by a Scythian dart.   160

Discourse on the Miseries of This Time

63 REMONSTRANCE TO THE PEOPLE OF FRANCE (EXTRACT)

    O Sky, O sea, O earth, O God above,
Father of Christian, Jew, and Turk, whose love
Has universal care for every soul
Between the Arctic and the Antarctic pole,
Whose gifts of reason, life, and motion fall   5
Without distinction upon each and all,
Who rains upon our heads, as is your will,
Reward for good and punishment for ill:
    Almighty Lord, whose loving care is given
Always to every nation under Heaven,   10
What use to you are thunderbolts and flashes
If now you do not burn the earth to ashes?
Will you do nothing, sitting on your throne?
We cannot doubt that our misdeeds are known:
All that your creatures daily plot against you,   15
You see it, Lord, and let it still continue!
    Can you not see from your high seat in air
Small animals who have nothing else to wear
But some poor skins of beasts, a race called men?
Mere bubbles that you blow on water, then   20

Que les doctes Romains et les doctes Grégeois
Nomment songe, fumée, et feuillage des bois ?
Qui n'ont jamais ici la vérité connue
Que je ne sais comment par songes et par nue ?
   Et toutefois, Seigneur, ils font les empêchés   25
Comme si tes secrets ne leur étaient cachés,
Braves entrepreneurs et discoureurs des choses
Qui aux entendements de tous hommes sont closes,
Qui par longue dispute et curieux propos
Ne te laisse jouir du bien de ton repos,   30
Qui de tes sacrements* effacent la mémoire,
Qui disputent en vain de cela qu'il faut croire,
Qui font trouver ton fils imposteur et menteur :
Ne les puniras-tu, souverain Créateur ?
Tiendras-tu leur parti ? veux-tu que l'on t'appelle   35
Le Seigneur des larrons et le Dieu de querelle ?
Ta nature y répugne, aussi tu as le nom
De doux, de pacifiq' de clément et de bon :
Et ce monde accordant ton ouvrage admirable
Nous montre que l'accord t'est toujours agréable.   40
   Mais qui serait le Turc, le Juif, le Sarrasin,
Qui, voyant les erreurs du Chrétien son voisin,
Se voudrait baptiser ? le voyant d'heure en heure
Changer d'opinion, qui jamais ne s'asseure,
Le connaissant léger mutin séditieux,   45
Et trahir en un jour la foi de ses aïeux ?
Volontaire incertain, qui au propos chancelle
Du premier qui lui chante une chanson nouvelle ?
Le voyant Manichée, et tantôt Arrien,*
Tantôt Calvinien, tantôt Luthérien,   50
Suivre son propre avis, non celui de l'Église ?
Un vrai jonc d'un étang, le jouet de la bise,
Ou quelque girouette inconstante, et suivant
Sur le haut d'une tour la volonté du vent ?
Et qui serait le Turc lequel aurait envie   55
De se faire Chrétien, en voyant telle vie ?
   Certes, si je n'avais une certaine foi
Que Dieu par son esprit de grâce a mise en moi,
Voyant le Chrétienté n'être plus que risée,

Burst? Whom the Greeks and Romans call
Dream figures, smoke, and forest leaves that fall;
Who never glimpsed the truth except, it seems,
In passing clouds or in their transient dreams?
　　And yet, O Lord, these men are filled with pride,　　25
As if there were no secrets you could hide,
Rash trespassers presuming to reflect
On matters closed to mortal intellect,
Who, with their long dispute and curious quest
Disturb your pleasure in celestial rest;　　30
Who say which of your sacraments we should leave,
Then vainly argue what we should believe;
Who make your son a liar and a fraud,
Will you not punish them, O sovereign Lord?
Are you on their side? How should one repute　　35
The God of wrangling scoundrels and dispute?
It cannot be; your nature is defined
As gentle and pacific, clement, kind;
And from the order that this world maintains
One learns how pleased you are when concord reigns.　　40
　　But how could Saracen or Turk or Jew,
Perceiving what his Christian neighbours do,
Desire to be baptized when every day
He sees the giddy Christian change his way,
Light-headed, factious, ready to deny　　45
The faith his fathers held in days gone by?
Headstrong, unstable, ever prone to waver,
As soon as some new song attracts his favour?
Now Manichaean, now an Arian,
Now Calvinist and now a Lutheran,　　50
Following not the Church but his own mind,
A shaken reed, a plaything of the wind,
Or else a weathercock who, on his tower,
Turns with the wind, a witness to its power.
So why would any Turk desire to give　　55
His soul to Christ, seeing how Christians live?
　　Indeed, if God's grace had not given me
A faith that's free from all uncertainty,
Seeing that faith a laughing-stock, despised,

J'aurais honte d'avoir la tête baptisée :   60
Je me repentirais d'avoir été Chrétien,
Et comme les premiers je deviendrais Païen.
    La nuit j'adorerais les rayons de la Lune,
Au matin le Soleil, la lumière commune,
L'œil du monde, et si Dieu au chef porte des yeux,   65
Les rayons du Soleil sont les siens radieux,
Qui donnent vie à tous, nous conservent et gardent,
Et les faits des humains en ce monde regardent.
    Je dis le grand Soleil, qui nous fait les saisons
Selon qu'il entre ou sort de ses douze maisons,   70
Qui remplit l'Univers de ses vertus connues,
Qui d'un trait de ses yeux nous dissipe les nues,
L'esprit, l'âme du monde ardant et flamboyant,
En la course d'un jour tout le Ciel tournoyant,
Plein d'immense grandeur rond, vagabond et ferme,   75
Lequel a dessous lui tout le monde pour terme,
En repos sans repos oisifs et sans séjour,
Fils aîné de Nature et le père du jour.
    J'adorerais Cérès qui les blés nous apporte,
Et Bacchus qui le cœur des hommes réconforte,   80
Neptune, le séjour des vents et des vaisseaux,
Les Faunes et les Pans et les Nymphes des eaux,
Et la Terre, hôpital de toute créature,
Et ces Dieux que l'on feint ministres de Nature.
    Mais l'Évangile saint du Sauveur JÉSUS-CHRIST   85
M'a fermement gravée une foi dans l'esprit,
Que je ne veux changer pour une autre nouvelle,
Et dussé-je endurer une mort très cruelle.
    De tant de nouveautés je ne suis curieux,
Il me plaît d'imiter le train de mes aïeux :   90
Je crois qu'en Paradis ils vivent à leur aise,
Encor qu'ils n'aient suivi ni Calvin ni De Bèze.
    Dieu n'est pas un menteur, abuseur ni trompeur :
De sa sainte promesse il ne faut avoir peur,
Ce n'est que vérité, et sa vive parole   95
N'est pas comme la nôtre incertaine et frivole.
    L'homme qui croit en moi* (dit-il) sera sauvé :
Nous croyons tous en toi, notre chef est lavé

I'd feel ashamed that I had been baptized: 60
Regretting Christian birth, I'd there and then
Become a Pagan, like the primal men.

    At night I would adore the Moon's soft rays,
Morning would bring the Sun to wake my praise,
Eye of the world and universal light, 65
Or God's eye-beams sent down from Heaven's height
To give us life, preserving us, aware
Of human deeds on earth with watchful care.

    Great Sun, I say, who as the seasons pass,
With his twelve houses marks them out for us; 70
Whose powers revealed pervade the Universe,
Who with a single glance makes clouds disperse;
World-soul and spirit, flaming up on high,
In one sole day traversing all the Sky,
Constant yet still in motion, his great round 75
Sees in the world below his only bound;
Restless in rest, idle yet cannot stay,
Nature's firstborn and father of the day.

    Corn-bringer Ceres I'd adore, and then
Bacchus whose wine restores the heart of men; 80
Neptune, the God of ships and windy waters,
With Fauns and Pans and Water-nymphs, his daughters:
The Earth itself, the home of every creature,
Those Gods, the fabled ministers of nature.

    But JESUS CHRIST Our Saviour has impressed 85
His Holy Gospel deeply in my breast;
I would not change it for another faith
Even though threatened with a cruel death.

    I am not curious about new creeds,
The faith my fathers held meets all my needs; 90
In Heaven, I think, they now spend happy days
Without the help of Calvin or of Bèze.

    God's not a liar, nor can he deceive;
We should not fear His promises, but believe
In all He says; His true and lively word 95
Is not like ours uncertain or absurd.

    'He who believes in me is saved,' He said:
We all believe in you, for every head

En ton nom, ô JÉSUS, et dès notre jeunesse
Par foi nous espérons en ta sainte promesse.   100

    Et toutefois, Seigneur, par un mauvais destin,
Je ne sais quel ivrogne apostat Augustin*
Nous prêche le contraire, et tellement il ose,
Qu'à toi la vérité sa mensonge il oppose.

    Le soir que tu donnais à ta suite ton corps,   105
Personne d'un couteau ne te pressait alors
Pour te faire mentir et pour dire au contraire
De ce que tu avais délibéré de faire.

    Tu as dit simplement, d'un parler net et franc,
Prenant le pain et vin : *C'est ci mon corps et sang,*   110
Non signe de mon corps : toutefois ces Ministres,
Ces nouveaux défroqués, apostats et bélîtres,
Démentent ton parler, disant que tu rêvais,
Et que tu n'entendais les mots que tu disais.

    Ils nous veulent montrer par raison naturelle   115
Que ton corps n'est jamais qu'à la dextre éternelle
De ton Père là-haut, et veulent t'attacher
Ainsi qu'un Prométhée au faîte d'un rocher.

    Ils nous veulent prouver par la Philosophie
Qu'un corps n'est en deux lieux ; aussi je ne leur nie,   120
Car tout corps n'a qu'un lieu : mais le tien ô Seigneur
Qui n'est que majesté que puissance et qu'honneur,
Divin glorifié, n'est pas comme les nôtres.

    Celui, à porte close alla voir les Apôtres,
Celui, sans rien casser sortit hors du tombeau,   125
Celui, sans pesanteur d'os, de chair ni de peau,
Monta dedans le Ciel : si ta vertu féconde
Sans matière apprêtée a bâti tout ce monde,
Si tu es tout divin tout saint tout glorieux,
Tu peux communiquer ton corps en divers lieux.   130
Tu serais impuissant si tu n'avais puissance
D'accomplir tout cela que ta Majesté pense.

    Mais quel plaisir prends-tu pour troubler ton repos,
D'ouïr l'humain caquet tenir tant de propos ?
D'ouïr ces Prédicants qui par nouveaux passages   135
En t'attachant au Ciel montrent qu'ils ne sont sages ?
Qui pipent le vulgaire et disputent de toi,

Is bathed in JESUS' name, and from our youth
We trust your holy promise through our faith.   100

    And yet, O Lord, by evil fate some monk,
A sad apostate Augustinian drunk,
Preaches the contrary and thus defies
You who are truth with his presumptuous lies.

    When you fed your disciples with your body   105
No one was standing by, knife at the ready,
To make you lie and tell your chosen few
The opposite of what you meant to do.

    Taking the bread and wine, you simply said:
'This is my body and this is my blood',   110
Not 'symbol of my body'; yet these Clerics,
Unfrocked apostates, knaves, and heretics,
Claim you were dreaming, that you'd lost your head
And didn't really mean the words you said.

    By natural reason they would argue that   115
Your body can't be anywhere but at
The right hand of your Father; there they lock
You down like old Prometheus on his rock.

    They hope to prove with their Philosophy
No body at one time can occupy   120
Two places; and I grant it: but, O Lord,
Your body which is power and might, adored,
Honoured and glorified, is not like ours.

    That body joined the Apostles through closed doors,
Broke from the tomb yet did not break a stone;   125
Unburdened by the mass of flesh and bone,
It rose to Heaven. If your might brought forth
This world where matter never was before,
If you are all divine, lord of all spaces,
You can project your body to divers places;   130
You would be powerless if you had not these
Powers to do exactly as you please.

    But then what pleasure can there be to hear
Coarse human broils that breach your restful sphere?
To hear these Preachers use new texts to prove   135
That you're forever fixed in Heaven above?
They fool the masses with the rot they spout,

Et rappellent toujours en doute notre foi ?
   Il fait bon disputer des choses naturelles,
Des foudres et des vents, des neiges et des grêles,   140
Et non pas de la foi dont il ne faut douter :
Seulement il faut croire, et non en disputer.
   Tout homme curieux lequel voudra s'enquerre
De quoi Dieu fit le Ciel les ondes et la terre,
Du Serpent qui parla, de la pomme d'Adam,   145
D'une femme en du sel, de l'âne à Balaam,*
Des miracles de Moïse, et de toutes les choses
Qui sont dedans la Bible étrangement encloses,
Il y perdra l'esprit : car Dieu qui est caché,
Ne veut que son secret soit ainsi recherché.   150
   Bref, nous sommes mortels, et les choses divines
Ne se peuvent loger en nos faibles poitrines,
Et de sa prescience en vain nous devisons :
Car il n'est pas sujet à nos sottes raisons.
L'entendement humain, tant soit-il admirable,   155
Du moindre fait de Dieu sans Grâce n'est capable.
Mais comment pourrait l'homme avec ses petits yeux
Connaître clairement les mystères des cieux ?
Quand nous ne savons pas régir nos républiques,
Ni même gouverner nos choses domestiques !   160
Quand nous ne connaissons la moindre herbe des prés !
Quand nous ne voyons pas ce qui est à nos pieds !
   Toutefois les Docteurs de ces sectes nouvelles,
Comme si l'Esprit Saint avait usé ses ailes
À s'appuyer sur eux, comme s'ils avaient eu   165
Du Ciel dru et menu mille langues de feu,*
Et comme s'ils avaient (ainsi que dit la fable
De Minos) banqueté des hauts Dieux à la table,
Sans que honte et vergogne en leur cœur trouve lieu,
Parlent profondément des mystères de Dieu :   170
Ils sont ses Conseillers, ils sont ses Secrétaires,
Ils savent ses avis, ils savent ses affaires,
Ils ont la clef du Ciel et y entrent tous seuls,
Ou, qui veut y entrer, il faut parler à eux.
Les autres ne sont rien sinon que grosses bêtes,   175
Gros chaperons fourrés, grasses et lourdes têtes :

Dispute of you and call our faith in doubt.

   It's good to argue about natural wonders,
Whence comes the snow and lightning, hail, and thunders,   140
But when we speak of faith we must not doubt it;
Belief's what counts, there's no dispute about it.

   What stuff did God use, one might like to know,
To make the sea, the Sky, the earth below?
What of the speaking Serpent, Adam's apple.   145
Lot's salted wife and Balaam's ass? Then grapple
With miracles of Moses, histories
That fill the Bible with their mysteries.
But that way madness lies; God's not inclined
To share His precious secrets with mankind.   150

   In short, we're mortal, our weak hearts can't place
Things so divine in such a narrow space,
And of God's prescience we debate in vain,
For that's a height mere reason can't attain.
Without His Grace, no human intellect   155
Can ever understand God's slightest act.
For how can man with his defective vision
See clearly in the mysteries of Heaven?
When we can't handle our affairs of state
Or even put our household matters straight!   160
When we don't know the meanest flower that grows,
When we see only what's before our nose!

   Yet Doctors of these new-found sects still spout
As if the Holy Spirit had sought them out
With rapid wings; as if they could acquire   165
Straight down from Heaven a thousand tongues of fire;
Or else, like Minos in the ancient fable
Had banqueted with all the Gods at table.
With hearts that feel no touch of guilt or shame
They speak of holy mysteries in God's name;   170
They are His Counsellors and can report
Upon His business and His every thought;
They're free to enter Heaven as they please,
But you will need to ask them for the keys.
Others are beasts, stupid and overfed,   175
Stuffed capons with their fat and empty heads;

Saint Ambrois, Saint Jérôme, et les autres Docteurs
N'étaient que des rêveurs, des fols et des menteurs :
Avec eux seulement le Saint-Esprit se treuve,
Et du saint Évangile ils ont trouvé la feuve.*   180
   O pauvres abusés ! mille sont dans Paris,
Lesquels sont dès jeunesse aux études nourris,
Qui de contre une natte étudiant attachent
Mélancoliquement la pituite qu'ils crachent ;
Desquels vous apprendriez en diverses façons   185
Encores dix bons ans mille et mille leçons.
   Il ne faut pas avoir beaucoup d'expérience
Pour être exactement docte en votre science ;
Les barbiers, les maçons en un jour y sont clercs,
Tant vos mystères saints sont cachés et couverts !   190
   Il faut tant seulement aveques hardiesse
Détester le Papat, parler contre la Messe,
Être sobre en propos, barbe longue, et le front
De rides labouré, l'œil farouche et profond,
Les cheveux mal peignés, le sourcil qui s'avale,   195
Le maintien renfrogné, le visage tout pâle,
Se montrer rarement, composer maint écrit,
Parler de l'Éternel, du Seigneur et du Christ,
Avoir d'un reître long les épaules couvertes,
Bref être bon brigand et ne jurer que «certes».*   200
   Il faut pour rendre aussi les peuples étonnés,
Discourir de Jacob et des prédestinés,
Avoir saint Paul en bouche et le prendre à la lettre,
Aux femmes aux enfants l'Évangile permettre,
Les œuvres mépriser, et haut louer la foi,   205
Voilà tout le savoir de votre belle loi.
   J'ai autrefois goûté, quand j'étais jeune d'âge,
Du miel empoisonné de votre doux breuvage :
Mais quelque bon Démon m'ayant ouï crier,
Avant que l'avaler me l'ôta du gosier.   210
   Non, non, je ne veux point que ceux qui doivent naître,
Pour un fol Huguenot me puissent reconnaître :
Je n'aime point ces noms qui sont finis en *os*.
Goths, Cagots, Ostrogoths, Visgoths et Huguenots :
Ils me sont odieux comme peste, et je pense   215

The Doctors, Ambrose and Jerome, it seems,
Were liars, madmen, following false dreams.
But by themselves alone the Spirit's seen
And in the Gospel cake they've found the bean.   180
   Poor fools! In Paris there's a thousand who
Have studied since their early youth and now
In melancholy mood vent in a fit
A bilious and bitter gob of spit;
You'd learn a thousand lessons from their store   185
Of knowledge, given ten long years or more.
   But such experience isn't what one needs
To be a perfect doctor in your field:
One day it takes the mason or the barber
To penetrate the mysteries you harbour!   190
   One only needs the daring to confess
How much one hates the Papacy and the Mass,
To make one's speech more plain, sober and slow,
Sport deepset eyes, long beard and furrowed brow,
Pale face and hair uncombed, eyebrows that frown   195
To show a manner sullen and cast down;
To stay aloof, but endlessly to write
Of the Eternal Lord and Jesus Christ!
In short, to be a rogue with honest bearing
And always say 'indeed' instead of swearing.   200
   And then, to wake the people's admiration,
Hold forth on Jacob and predestination,
And cite Saint Paul to prove we should admit
Women and children to the Holy Writ;
Despise good works, give praise to faith alone—   205
That's all the knowledge your fine law would own.
   I tasted once in days when I was young,
Your poisoned honey, sweet upon the tongue,
But some good Daemon, hearing me cry out,
Before I swallowed, tore it from my throat.   210
   Be sure of this: men yet unborn shall know
That I have never been a Huguenot;
I hate the names that end with 'os' like those
Ostrogoths, Goths, Visigoths, Huguenots.
I hate them like the plague; they'll bring mischance   215

Qu'ils sont prodigieux à l'empire de France.
Vous ne pipez sinon le vulgaire innocent,
Grosse masse de plomb qui ne voit ni ne sent,
Ou le jeune marchand, le bragard gentilhomme,
L'écolier débauché, la simple femme : et somme   220
Ceux qui savent un peu, non les hommes qui sont
D'un jugement rassis et d'un savoir profond.

    Périsse mille fois cette tourbe mutine
Qui folle court après la nouvelle doctrine,
Et par opinion se laisse sottement,   225
Sous ombre de piété* gagner l'entendement.

    Ô Seigneur tu devais pour chose nécessaire
Mettre l'opinion aux talons et la faire
Loin du chef demeurer, et non pas l'apposer
Si près de la raison, afin de l'abuser !   230
Comme un méchant voisin qui abuse à toute heure
Celui qui par fortune auprès de lui demeure !

.   .   .   .

Pièces Posthumes

Les Derniers Vers et pièces retranchées

64 (6)

    Il faut laisser maisons et vergers et jardins,
Vaisselles et vaisseaux que l'artisan burine,
Et chanter son obsèque en la façon du Cygne,*
Qui chante son trépas sur les bords Méandrins.

    C'est fait: j'ai dévidé le cours de mes destins,   5
J'ai vécu, j'ai rendu mon nom assez insigne,
Ma plume vole au ciel pour être quelque signe
Loin des appâts mondains qui trompent les plus fins.

    Heureux qui ne fut onc, plus heureux qui retourne
En rien comme il était, plus heureux qui séjourne   10
D'homme, fait nouvel ange, auprès de Jésus-Christ,

    Laissant pourrir çà-bas sa dépouille de boue,
Dont le sort, la fortune, et le destin se joue,
Franc des liens du corps pour n'être qu'un esprit.

With wrack and ruin on this realm of France.
You only get the dullest devotees,
A leaden mass that neither hears nor sees,
Or else young merchants, braggarts too well-born,
Students and sots, poor women. You suborn   220
Those who know just a little, not the kind
Who have sound judgement and a well-stocked mind.

    May they all perish, this rebellious set
Who follow the new doctrine and who let
Opinion, dressed as piety, undermine   225
Their understanding and infect the mind.

    O Lord, the time has come when you should put
Opinion closer to the heels, and not
So very near the head, the seat of reason,
Like a bad neighbour who, in every season,   230
Morning and night, renders life wretched for
The poor unfortunate soul who lives next door.

.   .   .   .

Posthumous Pieces

Last Verses and Poems Omitted from the 1584 Edition

64 (6)

    Now we must leave our houses, gardens, trees,
Vases and vessels worked by craftsman's hand,
And, like the Swan upon Meander's strand,
Sing for our passing our own exequies.

    It's done: I see my unravelled destiny: 5
I've lived and given my name a fair renown;
But now my pen soars heavenward, as in scorn
Of baits that lead even the wise astray.

    Happy the man who never was; no less
He who returns to his prime nothingness,   10
But happiest he, who being a man, inherits

    An angel's place with Christ; his coat of clay
May rot below, to chance and fate a prey;
He breaks the bonds of flesh to be all spirit.

65

Vous êtes déjà vieille, et je le suis aussi.
Joignons notre vieillesse et l'accolons ensemble,
Et faisons d'un hiver qui de froidure tremble
(Autant que nous pourrons) un printemps adouci.

Un homme n'est point vieil, s'il ne le croit ainsi :   5
Vieillard n'est qui ne veut : qui ne veut, il assemble
Une nouvelle trame à sa vieille : et ressemble
Un serpent rajeuni quand l'an retourne ici.

Ôtez-moi de se fard l'impudente encroûture,
On ne saurait tromper la loi de la nature,   10
Ni dérider un front condamné du miroir,

Ni durcir un tétin déjà pendant et flasque.
Le Temps de votre face arrachera le masque,
Et deviendrai un cygne en lieu d'un corbeau noir.

66

Je vous envoie un bouquet,* que ma main
Vient de trier de ces fleurs épanies,
Qui ne les eût à ce vêpre cueillies,
Chutées à terre elles fussent demain.

Cela vous soit un exemple certain   5
Que vos beautés, bien qu'elles soient fleuries,
En peu de temps cherront toutes flétries,
Et, comme fleurs, périront tout soudain.

Le temps s'en va, le temps s'en va, ma Dame,
Las ! le temps non, mais nous nous en allons,   10
Et tôt serons étendus sous la lame :

Et des amours, desquelles nous parlons,
Quand serons morts, n'en sera plus nouvelle :
Pour ce aimez-moi, cependant qu'êtes belle.

67

Je veux lire en trois jours l'Iliade d'Homère,
Et pour ce, Corydon, ferme bien l'huis sur moi :
Si rien me vient troubler, je t'assure ma foi,
Tu sentiras combien pesante est ma colère.

Je ne veux seulement que notre chambrière   5

65

You are already old and so am I,
So let us grasp that age in joint embrace;
We'll take this shivering winter and replace
Its cold with milder spring (we can but try).

A man's not old unless he wants to be   5
Or thinks he is; if that is not the case,
He spins new thread to follow the old trace,
A snake who changes skin as the year goes by.

Wipe off those layers of bold paint and powder;
Nothing you do can change the law of nature   10
Nor make the mirror smooth your wrinkled brow,

Nor give your flabby breast a firmer tone.
Time will tear off your mask, while I alone
Become a swan instead of some black crow.

66

I send you this fresh posy that my hand
Has chosen among flowers in full bloom,
For had they not been plucked when evening came,
Morning would find them scattered on the ground.

Let this example help you understand   5
That the resplendent beauties of your prime,
Though blooming now, must fall to withering time
Whose rapid passage brings them to an end.

Time passes on, my Lady, passes on;
Alas, not time, but us; it's we who pass   10
And soon we shall lie stretched beneath a stone:

And when we're dead, this love that we profess
Will be as nothing, lost beyond recall:
Love me, therefore, while you're still beautiful.

67

I mean to read the Iliad of Homer
In three days flat; so, Corydon, lock the door.
If anything disturbs me, then I swear
That soon you'll feel how heavy is my anger.

As for the maid, I say she shouldn't bother   5

Vienne faire mon lit, ou m'apprête de quoi
Je mange, car je veux demeurer à requoi
Trois jours, pour faire après un an de bonne chère.
    Mais si quelqu'un venait de la part de Cassandre,
Ouvre-lui tôt la porte, et ne le fais attendre,   10
Soudain entre en ma chambre, et me vient accoutrer :
    Je veux tant seulement à lui seul me montrer :
Au reste, si un Dieu voulait pour moi descendre
Du ciel, ferme la porte, et ne le laisse entrer.

To make my bed or even to prepare
My meals, for I shall do without such fare
For those three days, and feast the whole year after.

    But if Cassandra's man is at the gate,
Run quick to open, do not make him wait;   10
Then hurry to my room to help me dress.

    He is the only one I care to see;
But otherwise, should a God come to me,
Don't let him in, and shut the door in his face.

APPENDIX: MANIFESTOS
JOACHIM DU BELLAY

From *The Defence and Enrichment of the French Language*

(*La Deffence et Illustration de la Langue Françoyse*, 1549)

Book I, Chapter 3
Why the French Language is not as rich as Greek and Latin

AND if our language is not so copious and rich as Greek or Latin* that is not to be considered an intrinsic defect, as though of itself it could never be other than poor and sterile. Rather it should be attributed to the ignorance of our ancestors; for, as someone said of the ancient Romans, they prized good deeds rather than good words and preferred to leave to their descendants examples of virtue rather than precepts. Thus they deprived themselves of the glory of their great deeds and us of the profit to be had by copying them; and in the same way they have left us a language so poor and naked that it requires the ornaments and, one might say, the feathers of others. But who could say that Greek and Latin always possessed the excellence that they attained at the time of Homer and of Demosthenes, of Virgil and of Cicero? And if those authors had judged that, however diligently they might cultivate those languages, they would never succeed in producing greater fruit, would they then have made such efforts to raise them to the height that we now see?

I can say the same of our own language which is just beginning to flower but without bearing fruit—or rather, like a seedling or fresh shoot that has not yet even flowered, much less produced all the fruit it surely could do. This is certainly not because of any defect in its nature which is as capable of engendering as other languages; rather, it is the fault of those who have been responsible for its care and have not given it sufficient attention. On the contrary, as if it were a wild plant, they have let it grow old and almost die in the same waste ground where it was born, without ever watering it, pruning it, or protecting it from the overshadowing brambles and thorns. If the ancient Romans had been so negligent in cultivating their language when it first began to sprout, it would certainly not have become so great in such a short time. But like good farmers they first transplanted it from wild to cultivated ground. Then, to make it bear earlier and better fruit, they pruned away the useless branches and replaced them with good cultivated ones, masterfully taken from the Greek language. These were soon so well grafted onto the trunk and made to resemble it so closely that by now, rather than adopted, they seem the work of nature. Thus were born in the Latin language those flowers and fruits coloured with such great eloquence, together with metre and the skilful conjunction of sound and sense—all things that every language produces not from its own nature but by art. If, therefore, the Greeks and Romans, more diligent than we are in cultivating their languages, still needed great labour and industry before they could find in them either grace or metre or indeed any excellence whatsoever, should we be surprised if our vulgar tongue is not as rich as it could be and then seize upon that as a reason to despise it as vile and of little worth?

The time, perhaps, may come—and with France's good fortune I hope it will—when this noble and powerful kingdom shall, in its turn, obtain the reins of empire and when (if it has not been completely buried with François*) our French language, which is now beginning to take root, will spring up from the ground and rise to such height and breadth that it will equal the very Greeks and Romans, producing, like them, Homers, Demosthenes, Virgils, and Ciceros, just as France has occasionally produced its own Pericles, Nicias, Alcibiades, Themistocles, Caesar, and Scipio.*

Book II, Chapter 4
What kinds of Poems the French should choose

First of all, O future poet, read and reread. By night and day let your hand turn the pages of Greek and Latin models: then be so kind as to leave to the Floral Games of Toulouse and the Confraternity of Rouen those old French forms such as the rondels, ballads, virelays, royal chants, songs, and other similar spices that corrupt the taste of our language and serve only to demonstrate our ignorance.* Devote yourself to amusing epigrams, but not as so many new tale-tellers do nowadays, who, in a poem of ten lines, are happy to say nothing much in the first nine lines, provided there's some small joke in the tenth. But if you dislike lascivious content, imitate Martial or some other reputable author by mixing profit with pleasure.* In a style that is flowing rather than harsh, distil those moving elegies modelled on Ovid, Tibullus, and Propertius, intermingling from time to time some of those ancient fables that are no small adornment of poetry. On a lute well tuned to the sound of the Greek and Roman lyre, sing me those odes* that are still unknown to the French Muse. And let there be no verse without some vestige of rare and ancient learning. And for this you will find matter in the praises of the gods and of virtuous men, the destined fate of mortal things, the cares of young men such as love, flowing wine, and all good cheer. Above all, take care that this kind of poem be far from what is common, that it be enriched and polished with fitting words and striking epithets, invested

with serious reflections and varied with all manner of poetic colours and
ornaments—not like *Laissez la verte couleur*, *Amour avec Psyches*, *O combien
est heureuse*, and other such works* which deserve to be called common
ditties rather than odes or lyric poems. As for epistles, this is not the kind of
poem that can greatly enrich our vulgar tongue, since they usually concern
familiar and domestic affairs—unless, that is, you want them to imitate
elegies like Ovid or to be sententious and serious like Horace. I would say
much the same of satires which the French, I know not why, have called *coq-
à-l'âne*.* This also I would advise you to practise just as seldom, since
I would have you avoid slander; unless, as the ancients do, you condemn the
vices of your time with moderation and spare the names of vicious
persons—all this in heroic verse (that is, lines of ten or eleven syllables and
not eight or nine) under the name of *satire* and not that inept title of *coq-à-
l'âne*. For this you have the example of Horace whom Quintilian considers
the finest of the satirists. Sound out for me those lovely sonnets,* an Italian
invention, no less learned than pleasing, which could be called an ode from
which it differs only in having a certain number of lines with a fixed length,
whereas the ode can run freely through a whole range of lines—or, indeed,
be varied at will in the manner of Horace who, say the grammarians, sang in
nineteen different verse-forms. So for the sonnet you have Petrarch and
a number of modern Italians. Then, with sounding pipe and accompanying
flute, sing me those pleasing rustic eclogues in the manner of Theocritus
and Virgil or marine eclogues like those of Sannazaro, a Neapolitan
gentleman.

May it please the Muses that in all the kinds of poetry I have listed we
should have many imitations like that eclogue on the birth of the son of
Monseigneur the Dauphin which to my mind is one of the best short pieces
that Marot ever wrote.* Adopt also into the French family the flowing dainty
hendecasyllabics of Catullus, Pontanus, and Secundus, something that is
possible, if not in quantitative metre, at least in the number of syllables. As
for comedies and tragedies, if kings and Republics could restore them to their
ancient dignity that has been usurped by farces and morality plays, I would
surely recommend you to try your hand, and if you wished to use them for
the adornment of your language, you know where to look for models.

Book II, Chapter 6
*On Inventing Words and some other things that the
French Poet should observe*

But lest the wind of affection blow my ship so far out in the sea that I risk
being wrecked, let me return to the course I left off. I would advise the man
who wishes to undertake a great work to have no fear of inventing, adopting,

and creating some new French words in imitation of the Greeks as Cicero boasts of having done in his language. For if the Greeks and Latins had been overscrupulous in this regard, what would they have now to win praise for the copiousness of their languages? And if Horace allows that one can sometimes nod off in a long poem, why should it be forbidden to use some new words in that place even when they are absolutely needed? No one, unless he is completely ignorant or without any common sense, can doubt that things came first and that words were then invented to indicate them; and it follows that new things necessarily require new words, especially in those arts that are not yet common and widely practised. This may often be the case with our poet who will need to borrow many things that are still not treated in our language. And I am not thinking just of the liberal professions. Workmen, labourers, craftsmen of all kinds could not practise their trades if they refrained from using words familiar to them but unknown to the rest of us. I agree that procurators and lawyers should use terms proper to their profession without any innovation. But to deny a learned man the liberty to enrich our language and occasionally to appropriate words that are not in common use would mean shackling our language, still not rich enough, with a stricter law than the Greeks and Romans ever gave themselves. Although they were incomparably richer and more copious, yet still they allowed learned men the frequent use of unfamiliar words for unfamiliar things. So fear not, future poet, to use some new terms, especially in a long poem, but with modesty, discretion, and a judicious ear. Do not fret about who finds it good or bad, but put your hope in the approval of posterity as that which gives faith to things doubtful, light to what is dark, newness to what is old, familiarity to what is strange, and sweetness to what is harsh and bitter.

Among other things, our poet should avoid using Latin or Greek proper nouns, something truly as absurd as sewing a piece of green velvet on a red velvet gown. For would it not seem laughable to use in a Latin text a French proper name for a man or something else, like *Jean currit*, *Loire fluit*, and so on? Adapt, therefore, such proper nouns, from whatever language, to the usage of our vulgar tongue, just as the Latins did who said *Hercules* for *Heraklës* and *Theseus* for *Thëseus* and in French say *Hercule*, *Thésée*, *Achille*, *Ulysse*, *Virgile*, *Cicéron*, *Horace*. Yet in this you must use judgement and discretion, for there are many such nouns that cannot be adapted into French. Some of these are monosyllables like *Mars* and others are disyllables like *Venus*, while some have several syllables like *Jupiter* (unless you would rather say *Jove*), and then there are many polysyllabic names for which I can give no certain rule, for these your ear must be your judge.

For the rest, use words that are purely French, but neither too common nor too unfamiliar; unless, perhaps, you want to adopt and somehow enshrine, like precious stones, some ancient words in your poem, as Virgil does when he uses *olli* for *illi*, *aulaï* for *aulae*, and so on. For this you will need to look at all those old romances and French poets where you will find *ajourner* for *faire jour* (which men of law have made their own), *annuiter* for *faire nuit*, *assener* for *frapper où on visait* (for a blow given by the hand), *isnel* for *léger*, and a thousand other good words that we have lost by our negligence. Do not doubt that the moderate use of such terms confers great majesty on both poetry and prose, even as the relics of saints do on crosses and on other consecrated jewels in churches.

Book II, Chapter 11

Some Observations on matters other than the Rules of Art, together with an Invective against bad French Poets

I shall not dwell for long on what follows, for our poet, as I envisage him, will understand such matters well enough by his own good judgement without the rules imposed by tradition. Thus when it comes to the time and place he should choose for reflection, I give no precepts other than those dictated by his own pleasure and disposition. Some love cool woodland shades, clear brooks through meadows adorned and carpeted with greenery. Others prefer private chambers and learned studies. You must fit yourself to the season and the place. I would, however, advise you to seek solitude and silence, friends of the Muses, who only open the door of their sacred cabinet to those who knock rudely. This is how they retain and preserve that divine inspiration which sometimes stirs and heats poetic spirits and without which nobody can hope to create anything that lasts.

I should not forget revision, surely the most useful part of our studies. Its function is to add, remove, or modify at leisure—something one cannot do when driven by the initial impetuosity and ardour of composition. That is why, to ensure that our writings do not flatter us like newborn children, we need to put them aside, revisit them often and, like bears, lick them into shape, giving form and fashion to their limbs—not copying those importunate versifiers the Greeks called *mousopatagoi*, who at all hours keep torturing the ears of their unfortunate hearers with their new poems. But nor should you be overscrupulous and, like elephants with their young, spend ten years giving birth to your verses. Above all, we should have some learned and faithful companion or a very close friend—or three or four—who can oversee our work and correct our faults and are not afraid to wound our paper with their fingernails. I further advise you to seek the company not just of learned men, but also of all kinds of workers and craftsmen, such as sailors, foundrymen, painters, engravers, and others so that you know their inventions, the names of their materials and tools, and the terms they use in their various arts and crafts. This will provide you with fine comparisons and lively descriptions of all things.

Now, you Gentlemen who are so hostile to our language, do you not think that our poet, thus armed, may enter the battle and show himself in the ranks along with the brave Greek and Roman squadrons? And you others, so poorly equipped, whose ignorance has given to our tongue the ridiculous term of *rhymesters* (much as the Latins called their bad poets *versifiers*), are you ready to endure the sun and the dust and the dangerous labour of this fight? I believe you should withdraw to the baggage train along with the pages and lackeys, or else (since I have pity on you) under cool shades in the splendid palaces of great lords and the magnificent courts of Princes, among ladies and maidens, where your nice dainty works, as transient as your life, will be received, admired, and adored—but certainly not to scholarly studies and the rich libraries of the learned.

May it please the Muses, for the good I wish to our language, that your inept works be banished not only from such libraries (as, indeed, they are), but from the whole of France! I would desire all kings and princes who love their language to follow the example of that great monarch* who forbade any portrait or statue of himself not painted by Apelles or carved by Lysippus: they would then issue a formal decree forbidding their subjects to present and printers to print any work that had not first endured the file of some learned man, as little given to adulation as was Quintilian of whom Horace speaks in his *Art of Poetry*. There (and in many other passages of Horace) one can see the habitual vices of modern poets expressed so vividly that he seems to have written not in the time of Augustus but in that of François and Henri. Physicians and blacksmiths, he says, promise to do what physicians and blacksmiths are trained to do; but with us poems get written as often by the ignorant as by the learned. So it is no wonder if today many learned men do not deign to write in our language and if foreigners do not value our tongue as much as we do theirs, for they see in it so many ignorant new writers that they judge it incapable of greater ornament and erudition. Oh, how I long to see those *Springtimes* wither, those little *Youths* punished, those *Essays* cut down, those *Fountains* dried up—in short, to see the abolition of all those fine titles that are enough to make any learned reader disgusted with the thought of reading further! No less do I wish to see those Deprived Ones, those Humble Hopefuls, those Exiles from Joy, those Slaves, those Travellers, sent back to the Round Table, and those pretty little devices* restored to the ladies and gentlemen from whom they were borrowed.

What more can I say? I beg Phoebus Apollo that France, sterile for so long, be made pregnant by him and soon bear a poet whose resonant lute will silence those hoarse bagpipes, like a stone thrown among frogs in a swamp. And if, despite all this, they are still tormented by the burning fever to write, I would advise them to take medicine in Anticyra* or, even better, to go back to studying and to do it without shame, like Cato who learned Greek in his old age. I well know that when I speak this way of our rhymesters, many will feel that I am too biting and satiric, but I shall appear truthful to those who have knowledge and judgement and who desire the good health of our language where the ulcer and rotting flesh of bad poetry is still so ingrained that it can only be excised with the knife and the cauterizing iron.

To conclude this topic, Reader, know that he who is to be truly the poet I seek in our language must arouse my indignation, calm me down, make me joyous, make me grieve, hate, admire, wonder—in short, hold the rein of my emotions, turning me this way or that as he pleases. That is the true touchstone you must use to test all poems in whatever language. I am well aware that here there will be many who find nothing good unless they understand it and think they can copy it. They will not find our poet to their taste, for they will say that there is no pleasure and less profit in reading such writings, that they are nothing but poetic fictions, and that Marot never wrote such things. To these, since they understand nothing of poetry but the name, I do not mean to reply except by producing in my defence a host of Greek, Latin, and Italian works that are as far from the kind of writing they approve as they themselves are from all good erudition. I would only urge the poet who aspires to an uncommon glory to avoid such inept admirers and to flee that ignorant mass, those enemies of all rare and ancient knowledge. Instead, let him be content with a handful of readers, like the writer who desired Plato alone as an audience or Horace who wanted his works to find no more than three or four readers, including Augustus.

Now, Reader, you have my judgement as regards our French poet; you will follow it if you think it good or stick to your own opinion if you have something else in mind. For I am not ignorant of how men's judgements may differ in all things and especially in poetry, which is like painting* and no less subject to the opinion of the common people. My major objective is the defence of our language, its embellishment and amplification, in which, if I have done little to ease the industry and labour of those who aspire to that glory or even if I have been of no help whatsoever, I shall at least think I have done a great deal if I have made them more willing to make the effort.

PIERRE DE RONSARD

From *Summary** of the Art of French Poetry

(*Abbregé de l'Art Poétique François*, 1565)

To Alphonse Delbene, Hautecombe Abbey, Savoy.

ALTHOUGH the art of poetry, being more innate than acquired, can be neither understood nor taught by means of precepts, nevertheless, in so far as human artifice, experience, and labour allow, I wish to provide it with some rules so that one day you may count among those who are most knowledgeable in such an agreeable craft. In this you will be following my example, for I confess that I have been taught a fair amount by others. Above all you will revere the Muses; indeed, you will pay them particular veneration, never making them serve improper ends, objects of ridicule, injurious libels; but rather holding them dear and sacred as the daughters of Jupiter, which is to say of God, who by His holy grace first used them to convey the splendours of His majesty to ignorant nations. For poetry in that first age was no other than allegorical theology* employing pleasant and vivid fables to instil into the brains of rough men those secrets which they would have been unable to understand had their truth been revealed too openly. It was Eumolpus Cecropian* and Linus the teacher of Hercules, Orpheus, Homer, and Hesiod who invented such an excellent craft. That is why they are called Divine Poets; not so much for the divine spirit that made them admirable above all others, but because of their communication with Oracles, Prophets, Diviners, Sibyls, and interpreters of dreams from whom they learned the best part of what they knew. For what the Oracles said in a few words, these noble persons amplified, coloured, and increased, thus being for the people what the Sibyls and Diviners had been for them.

Long after, from the same country, came the second group of Poets whom I will call 'human' in that they were more full of craft and labour than of anything divine. As an example of these latter, the Roman poets produced an abundant crop of overblown and gaudy books that have brought booksellers more work than honour—except for five or six whose teachings, expressed with perfect art, have always attracted my admiration. Now, since the Muses have no wish to dwell in a soul that is not good, holy, and virtuous, you will have a good nature, not malevolent, sullen, or resentful. Instead you should be animated by a noble spirit that lets nothing enter your mind that is not superhuman and divine.

To begin with you will have ideas that are not earthbound, but elevated, great, and beautiful. For the main point is the invention which derives as much from a good nature as from the lesson of good ancient authors. If you undertake some great work, you will show yourself to be religious and God-fearing by beginning either with God's name or with some other name that conveys a sense of majesty. For example, take the Greeks ('Sing, goddess, of the anger', 'Tell me, O Muse, of the man', 'Let us begin with Zeus, begin with you Phoebus') or our Romans ('Mother of the house of Aeneas', 'Recall to me the causes').* For the Muses, Apollo, Mercury, Pallas, Venus, and other such deities, represent for us nothing other than the powers of God, to whom the first men gave several names corresponding to the various effects of His incomparable majesty. And this also should show you that nothing can be good or perfect if its beginning does not come from God. You will then be studious in the reading of good poets and you will learn them by heart as well as you can. You will work hard to correct and polish your verses, and you will no more forgive them than the good gardener forgives the grafted tree when he sees it laden with useless or unprofitable branches. You will converse gently and courteously with the poets of your time: the older ones you will honour as your fathers, those of your own age you will consider as your brothers, and the younger ones as your children. And you will show them what you have written, for you should not publish anything that has not first been seen and examined by those friends whom you judge most knowledgeable in the craft. Thus, by such meetings of minds and familiarity, together with the letters and the nature that you have, you will easily attain the height of honour, since you have in your family the example of your father who not only surpassed his most famous contemporaries in his native Italian but also competed for victory with those who today produce the purest and most learned writings in the old Roman language. Now, since you already know Greek and Latin, all that remains is French, which should be all the more preferable in that it is your mother-tongue. So I shall tell you, in a few words, what I think is most fitting, not getting you lost in long and difficult forest ways, but leading you straight along the path that I myself have found the most short, so that you may more easily catch up with those who, having started out before you, may be some way ahead.

Just as Latin verses, as you know, have their feet, so we, in our French poetry which is my subject here, have a certain number of syllables, according to the scheme of the songs that we intend to compose. This number cannot be exceeded without breaking the rules of our verse; but with these measures and numbers we shall deal more amply later on. We also have a certain elision of the vowel *e* which we swallow whenever it meets with another vowel or

diphthong; unless, that is, the vowel that follows the *e* has the force of
a consonant. If you imitate me, you will make your verses masculine or
feminine as best you can, so that they are fitting for music and accord with the
instruments—from which, it seems, Poetry was born, for Poetry without
instruments or without the grace of one or several voices is no more agreeable
than instruments are when not animated by the melody of a pleasant voice. If
you chance to have made the first two verses masculine, then make the next
two feminine* and continue with the same measure for the rest of your elegy
or song, so that the musicians will find it easier to find the right accord. As for
lyric verses, you can form the first couplet as you will, provided the remaining
couplets follow the same pattern. If you use Greek and Roman proper names
you will give them a French ending wherever the language allows, for there
are many where that is simply not possible. You should not reject the words
of our old Romans, but make a prudent and meditated choice. You will
frequent sailors, huntsmen, and falconers, and pay special attention to those
whose trade relies on the furnace such as goldsmiths, foundrymen,
blacksmiths, metalworkers and from them you will draw many fine and vivid
comparisons with the precise names of the tools to make your work richer
and more agreeable. For just as you cannot describe a human body as
beautiful, pleasing, and well formed if it is not composed of blood, veins,
arteries, and tendons and wearing its native complexion, neither can Poetry
be pleasing, lively, and perfect without fine inventions, descriptions, and
comparisons which are the nerves and life of a book that intends to conquer
the centuries and live in the memory, victorious over time.

   You will have the skill to choose and appropriate the most meaningful
terms in the dialects of our French when those of your own region are not
precise or meaningful enough, and you will not worry if they are from
Gascony, Poitou, Normandy, or Lyons or anywhere else, provided they are
good and express exactly what you want to say, without affecting the idiom
of the court which is sometimes most inappropriate in that it is the speech
of young ladies and of young gentlemen who are more concerned with
fighting well than speaking well. Take note that the Greek language would
never have been so fluent and abundant in dialects and vocabulary* as it is
without the great number of republics that flourished in those times.
Cherishing what was their own, they wanted their learned citizens to write
in a language peculiar to their land. Thence came an infinite number of
idioms, phrases, and ways of speaking which still today bear the mark of
their native country. All of these were considered good without distinction
by the learned pens that wrote in those days, for no single country can be
so perfect in everything that it does not sometimes need to borrow
something or other from its neighbour; and you can be sure that if France
still had its Dukes of Burgundy, Picardy, Normandy, Brittany, Champagne,

and Gascony, they would desire as a signal honour that their subjects should write in the language of their native land; for Princes are not more eager to extend the boundaries of their lordship than, like the Romans, they are to spread their native language over all other lands. But today, since our France obeys one single King, if we wish to be honoured in some way, we are obliged to speak the language of its court; otherwise our labour, however learned, will be considered of little worth, or, perhaps completely despised. The court is now the source of all benefits and favours, and therefore one must often bow to the judgement of a young lady or a young courtier whose ignorance of good and true Poetry is all the greater because they are so devoted to the practice of arms and other more honourable occupations.

Of Invention*

Since I have already mentioned invention, I think it would be good to refresh your memory of it with a few words. Invention is nothing other than the natural fruit of an imagination as it conceives ideas and forms of all things that can be imagined, both heavenly and earthly, animate and inanimate, so that it may then represent, describe, and imitate them. For just as the purpose of the orator is to persuade, so that of the poet is to imitate, invent, and represent those things that are or possibly could be. And there can be no doubt that a fine and elevated invention will be followed by an excellent disposition of verses, given that disposition follows invention, the mother of all things, as the shadow follows the body. When, however, I tell you to invent fine and elevated things, I do not mean those fantastic and melancholic inventions where events are no more related to each other than the fractured dreams of a madman or of some patient in the violent throes of fever whose wounded imagination presents him with a thousand monstrous forms without order or connection. But your inventions, for which I can give no rules since they belong to the mind alone, will be well ordered and structured. And although they seem beyond the reach of common folk, yet they will be such as can be conceived and understood by everyone.

Of Disposition

Just as invention depends on a naturally noble spirit, so disposition depends upon a fine invention, being an elegant and perfect collocation and ordering of the things invented. It does not allow what belongs in a given place to be situated elsewhere, but, since it is governed by art, study, and labour, it skilfully arranges and orders everything in the right way. You can find examples of this in ancient authors and in the moderns who have enriched our language over the last fifteen years through their diligence in such honourable labour. Whoever were the first who dared to abandon the languages of the ancient Greeks and Romans in order to honour that of their own country, they were truly good children and not ungrateful citizens. They deserve to be crowned and have a public monument and that from age to age there be a perpetual memory of their virtues. Not that one should neglect foreign languages; indeed I advise you to know them perfectly so that with them, as with some unearthed old treasure, you may enrich your nation, for it is very difficult to write well in the vulgar tongue if you are not perfectly or at least passably instructed in the languages of the most honourable and famous foreigners.

Of Elocution

Elocution is nothing other than a fitness and splendour of words well chosen and adorned with grave and short sentences which make the verses shine much as encrusted precious stones do when they adorn the fingers of some great lord. Under the term Elocution we understand the choice of words which Virgil and Horace have so specially considered. So you must strive to be copious in your vocabulary and select the most fitting and meaningful terms that you can find to be the nerve and strength of your songs which will shine all the more because their words are significant and wisely chosen. You should not forget comparisons and description of places: of rivers, forests, mountains; of night, sunrise, and midday; of winds; of the sea; of gods and goddesses with their proper occupations, garments, chariots, and horses, fashioning all this in imitation of Homer whom you will take as a divine example and from whom you will draw the most perfect and living lineaments for your picture.

EXPLANATORY NOTES

THE abundance of classical, mythological, and contemporary reference in Du Bellay and Ronsard makes for annotation that can easily get out of hand. I have tried to make the annotation less unwieldy by providing a Glossary of the less familiar names and places (see pp. 229–38). References to English verse are intended to remind readers that the sixteenth-century assimilation of Petrarch and of classical sources was a shared European enterprise. English translations from Latin are, with some exceptions, to the Loeb Classical Library; translations from Petrarch's *Canzoniere* are to Robert Durling, *Petrarch's Lyric Poems* (Cambridge, MA: Harvard University Press, 1976).

In the notes that follow, the page references are keyed to the French text; in each case the English translation can be found on the facing page.

ABBREVIATIONS

A&S	Sidney, *Astrophil and Stella*
Aen.	Virgil, *Aeneid*
Am.	Spenser, *Amoretti*
Can.	Petrarch, *Canzoniere*
Cat.	Catullus, *Poems*
DB	Joachim Du Bellay
Hor.	Horace, *Odes*
Met.	Ovid, *Metamorphoses*
Od.	Homer, *Odyssey*
Orl.	Ariosto, *Orlando Furioso*
R	Pierre de Ronsard
Son.	Shakespeare, *Sonnets*

SELECTED POETRY

DU BELLAY

4 *C'était la nuit / It was the night*: imitated from *Can.* 3: *Era il giorno* ('It was the day'). For Cupid's cowardly attack on the unarmed lover, see Ovid, *Amores* 1. 2. 22: *nec tibi laus armis victus inermis ero* ('nor will it be praise for thine arms to vanquish me unarmed'). See Introduction, p. xiii.

Je vois . . . je procure / I see . . . I court: *video meliora proboque,* | *deteriora sequor* ('I see the better and approve it, but I follow the worse', *Met.* 7. 20–1). The much-imitated blend of antithesis and paradox derives from *Can.* 132: *S'amor non è* ('If it is not love') and 134: *Pace non trovo* ('Peace I do not find'). For English adaptations by Chaucer, Wyatt, Daniel, Constable, and others, see Anthony Mortimer (ed.), *Petrarch's Canzoniere in the English Renaissance* (Amsterdam: Rodopi, 2005).

6 *Idée / Idea*: the Neoplatonic theory expounded by Cardinal Bembo in Castiglione's *Book of the Courtier*, book 4 where love of beauty on earth is seen as a first step towards the pure Idea of beauty in Heaven. Compare R 16. For English versions of the theme see *A&S* 5 ('It is most true') and *Am.* 79 ('Men call you fair').

Mon Livre (. . . envieux) / My book (. . . success): ironic recall of Ovid, *Tristia* 1. 1: *Parve—nec invideo—sine me, liber, ibis in urbem* ('Little book, you will go without me—and I grudge it not—to the city'). Ovid laments his exile *from* Rome, whereas DB regrets his exile *to* Rome.

Ni desseigner . . . architecture / Or plot . . . the heavens: refers to such cosmological poems as R's 'Hymne des Étoiles' ('Hymn to the Stars') and 'Hymne du Ciel' ('Hymn to the Sky') (R 61 and 62).

8 *En vain . . . imiter / Will work . . . in vain*: DB's humble style (*sermo pedestris*) will not be easy to emulate.

10 *monuments / tombs*: sidelong glance at the tradition that comes down from *Hor.* 3. 30 (*Exegi monumentum* ('I have built a monument'). Compare R 57.

France . . . lois / Mother of . . . laws: the disillusion expressed in this sonnet should be read in the light of DB's claim in the *Deffence* that poetry contributes to national glory.

longue erreur / constant error: recalls *Can.* 1 where the poet asks his readers to pardon and pity poems written in his erring youth (*in sul mio primo giovenile errore*).

12 *scorpion*: Pliny the Elder (*Natural History* 29. 91) thought that the application of a scorpion could cure the sting it made.

Comte / Count: Nicolas Denisot, jocularly known as Comte.

peintres de la nature / painters of . . . nature's pure ideal: not 'painters of nature' as we would nowadays understand the phrase, but rather 'painters of the true underlying nature of things'.

14 *un Janet auprès d'un Michel-Ange / Janet next to Michelangelo*: a contrast between humble realism and the representation of ideal forms.

Tout moite et dégouttant / drenched with spray . . . dripping body: recalls Ulysses, dripping and bruised, washed up on the shore of the Phaeacians (*Od.* 5. 455–6).

plus âgé / a few more years: a mistake; DB was, in fact, two years older than R.

Heureux qui / Happy the man: Virgil, *Georgics* 2. 490: *felix, qui potuit rerum cognoscere causas* ('Blessed is he who has been able to win knowledge of the causes of things') and the opening of Psalms 1 and 111 in the Vulgate (*Beatus vir*; 'Blessed is the man').

16 *Fumer la cheminée / the smoking chimney*: the nostalgic image of smoke rising from the village is conventional. See Ovid, *Ex Ponto* 1. 3. 33–4: *sed*

tamen optat | fumum de patriis posse videre focis ('but yet he prays that he may see the smoke from his native hearth'); also *Od.* 1. 57–9; Erasmus, *Adagia*; poems by Marot and R. The homecoming of Ulysses was by no means as tranquil as this suggests, but DB may have been influenced by allegorical readings of the *Odyssey* which see the hero as acting out the Christian's journey through the trials and temptations of life to a mature wisdom.

savant en la philosophie / knowledge of philosophy: the knowledge to be gained in Italy is presented as a parodic list of the accomplishments recommended in Castiglione's *Book of the Courtier*.

18 *le loup par les oreilles / a wolf by the ears*: proverb from the *Adagia* indicating an action that can neither be abandoned nor continued without disaster.

celui que j'aimais mieux / that I most loved and prized: probably Jacques Tahureau.

20 *celui que je sers / The man I serve*: Cardinal Du Bellay.

haineux étranger / hateful foreigner: Carlo Caraffa, nephew of Pope Paul IV.

Vivons (Gordes) / Let's live, Gordès: octave closely modelled on *Cat.* 5. 1–6: *Vivamus, mea Lesbia* ('Let us live, my Lesbia'). English adaptations of the same source include poems by Jonson, Daniel, Crashaw, Wordsworth, Byron, and Landor.

22 *L'amour d'Orphée? / You're gay like Orpheus?*: *Met.* 10. 83–4: *ille etiam Thracum populis fuit auctor amorem | in teneros transferre mares citraque iuventam* ('he set the example for the people of Thrace of giving his love to tender boys'). The addressee has not been identified.

24 *pauvres Siennois / poor types from Siena*: in 1555, after a long siege, Siena was conquered by imperial troops and annexed to the Grand Duchy of Tuscany.

26 *dix pieds en carré / ten-feet square*: cardinals assembled in conclave to elect a new pope are given very cramped accommodation. DB was in Rome for two conclaves: the election of Marcello Cervino as Marcellus II (April 1555) and that of Giovanni Pietro Caraffa as Paul IV (May 1555).

le Pape est fait / 'We've got a Pope!': echo of the Latin phrase *Habemus Papam* by which the election of a new pope is announced.

28 *un autre sac / another sack*: Romans had traumatic memories of the sack of their city by imperial troops in 1527; DB describes the Rome of September 1556, paralysed by fear of a second sack by the army of the Duke of Alba.

filles de Mémoire / Memory's daughters: the Muses, daughters of Mnemosyne.

aller voir … La Marthe, ou la Victoire / finding a whore: Martha and Victoria are presumably names of prostitutes.

30 *Sans barbe / Beardless*: loss of hair was taken as a sign of venereal disease. DB seems obsessed by the idea and by fear of prostitution in general. See DB 26, 30, 36, 37, 38, 39, 40, 41, 44, 45.

30 *rivage d'Alcine* / *Alcina's shore*: here and in the following two sonnets DB draws his imagery from *Od.* and *Orl.* See Glossary.

racine d'Ulysse / *the root that Ulysses had*: Moly, the herb given by Mercury to Ulysses to protect him from the magic of Circe (*Od.* 10).

34 *cheveux d'argent* / *silver hair*: continues theme of the previous sonnet with a burlesque version of the itemization or *blason* tradition of describing female beauty.

Chassaigne / *Chassaigne*: unidentified, but obviously a connoisseur of Roman debauchery.

Cyprienne . . . Dardanienne . . . Idalienne / *Cyprian . . . Dardans . . . Idalian*: Venus is Cyprian through her connection with Cyprus and Idalian because the town of Idalia was known for her cult. Trojans are Dardans because their city was supposedly founded by Dardanus.

36 *la plus blonde toison . . . toison dorée* / *the fair fleece . . . Golden Fleece*: the Golden Fleece of Jason is used to reference the luxuriant beard proving that DB has not contracted venereal disease. See note to p. 30.

vendre sa terre / *to sell his land*: DB had legal problems with his property in Oudon, though he was far from being as destitute as his poetry sometimes suggests.

danger de poison / *threat of poison*: Pope Marcellus II died less than a month after his election amid unsubstantiated rumours that he had been poisoned.

un chapeau rouge, ou des clefs de saint Pierre / *A scarlet cap or Peter's keys*: the red hat belongs to the insignia of a cardinal; St Peter's keys are the symbol of papal authority.

le Borgne de Libye / *The One-Eyed Libyan*: Hannibal.

38 *la vérole* / *the pox*: syphilis, sometimes called the French disease.

ces vieilles Sibylles / *the old Sibyls*: see Virgil's description of the Cumaean Sibyl (*Aen.* 6. 46–51).

votre art / *your profession*: the medical profession.

Leur tâter . . . tétin / *the exorcizing touch . . . crotch*: the laying on of hands in the ritual of exorcism offers a pretext for groping.

toi qui sait leurs natures / *you should know their nature*: a reference to R's poem 'Les Daimons'.

40 *celles . . . l'honnête nom donné* / *those who steal a decent name they take from court*: courtesans.

42 *Un forfant, un poltron* / *Some beast, some wretch*: an impostor, a coward (English, poltroon); Italianisms referring to Innocente del Monte. See Glossary.

Celui, que par le nom de Saint-Père, l'on nomme . . . le voir . . . dévaler / *To see a man they'll call the Holy Father . . . exposed to shame*: the reference is to an episode in the life of Julius III when, before he became pope, he was held hostage for Pope Clement VII.

son prédécesseur / Pope Julius: Pope Julius III whose legacy of corruption the good Marcellus II had attempted to efface.

44 *Je ne sais qui des deux / I can't say which*: the two old men of the sonnet are Emperor Charles V who, after a life of warfare, retired to a monastery, and Pope Paul IV who, at the age of 80, adopted a belligerent stance in the Italian Wars.

la trêve / the truce: the Truce of Vaucelles (1556) between Emperor Charles V and King Henri II. DB thought it would be regarded as a betrayal by those Italian forces who had looked to France as an ally against Spain and the Habsburgs.

46 *le grand seigneur / the great lord*: probably a reference to Constable Anne de Montmorency. See Glossary.

ma navire / My driven ship: in fact, apart from a short voyage from Ostia to Civitavecchia, DB returned to France by land, but the navigation imagery fits in with the Ulysses motif that runs throughout the first two parts of the *Regrets*.

ma dépouille . . . Néréides / cast-offs . . . Nereids: Hor. 1.5: *me tabula sacer | votiva paries indicat uvida | suspendisse potenti | vestimenta maris deo* ('As for me, the temple wall with its votive tablet shows I have hung up my dripping garments to the god who is master of the sea'); also Virgil, *Georgics* 1. 436–7 where sailors saved from the storm fulfil on the beach the vows they have made to Glaucus.

48 *Ulysse / Ulysses*: the sonnet rounds off the Ulysses motif and invites comparison with DB 15: Roman prostitutes play the part of Circe and the Sirens, and the rhetorical power of Dorat is envisaged as providing an equivalent to the bow with which Ulysses kills Penelope's suitors on his return to Ithaca (*Od.* bk 20). The 1558 edition of *Les Regrets et autres œuvres poétiques* contains 191 sonnets; recent scholarship has rejected M. A. Screech's argument that the sequence proper ends here and that the remaining sixty sonnets, many of them conventional encomia, should be considered as *autres œuvres poétiques*.

Coïons magnifiques / Magnificent old Cobblers: DB passed through Venice on his journey back to France. The adjective is a gibe at Venetian gentlemen who liked to be addressed as *magnifico*; the noun *coïons* (from Italian *coglioni*, testicles) is probably related to Verrocchio's celebrated equestrian statue of the *condottiere* Bartolomeo Colleoni whose name gave rise to this kind of wordplay. My recourse to cockney rhyming slang is an attempt to recapture something of the original comic oxymoron.

ces vieux cocus vont épouser la mer / these ancient cuckolds wed the sea: commenting on the traditional marriage of Venice to the sea, celebrated on the Feast of the Ascension, DB remarks that if the Venetians are, indeed, married to the sea, then they are all cuckolds, since it is now the Turk (*le Turc l'adultère*) who possesses the eastern Mediterranean.

le lac . . . ne revient / the lake . . . no return: as DB stops at Geneva on his way home to France, the notoriously serious aspect of its Calvinist citizens reminds him of the mourning spirits passing into the Underworld, from which there is no return.

50 *l'on n'y jure point Dieu / They draw the line at 'By God' when they swear*: there were severe penalties for swearing in Geneva.

Des-Masures . . . qui ses vertus honore / Des Masures . . . grant of honours due: all that Des Masures lacks to be the equal of the Virgil he translates is a patron like Maecenas and a king like Emperor Augustus.

saison dorée / golden age: the Golden Age, to be followed by Silver, Bronze, and Iron. See *Met.* 1. 89–150.

52 *espérance . . . demeurée / Remains . . . hopeful sign*: see the Glossary for Pandora.

perle / pearl: play on the name of Marguerite de France; (Lat.) *margarita* = pearl.

la vierge / the Pythia: the Pythia was a virginal priestess and oracle in Apollo's temple at Delphi.

Divins Esprits / Spirits divine: the invocation already introduces the elevated style of the *Antiquitez*.

Trois fois / Three times: the number suggests ritual magic. See Virgil, *Eclogue* 8. 74–75: *terque haec altaria circum | effigiem duco* ('and three times round these shrines I draw thy image').

antique fureur / ancient ecstasy: the poetic madness (*furor poeticus*), an ecstatic trance that gives rise to divine inspiration. The term was coined by Marsilio Ficino in his Latin translation of Plato's *Ion* (1482).

54 *Qui voudra voir / Whoever longs to see*: Can. 248: *Chi vuol veder quantunque po Natura | e 'l Ciel tra noi* ('Whoever wishes to see all that Nature and Heaven can do among us'). See R1 and *A&S* 71 ('Who would in fairest book').

ses écrits / her writings: for DB Latin poetry preserves the memory of Rome better than the city's ancient ruins.

56 *le chef déterré / the head discovered there*: the head unearthed in the foundations of the Capitol was interpreted as a sign that Rome would be the head of the world (Livy, 1. 16), hence Capitol from Latin *caput* (head). Marvell exploits the same legend in 'Horatian Ode on Cromwell's Return from Ireland'.

Ni la fureur de la flamme enragée / Neither the furious rage of searing flame: the long anaphora of negatives which begins here is common in Petrarchist poetry. See *Can.* 312, *Né per sereno ciel* ('Not through the clear sky') and *Am.* 9, 'Longwhile I sought'.

ce Dieu tortueux / that meandering stream divine: the Tiber.

Que la grandeur du rien / How great the nothing: see Introduction, pp. xviii–xix.

un lieu champêtre / the fields: the sonnet traces the history of Rome from its pastoral beginnings, through the consulate (*annuel pouvoir*) and dictators (*pouvoir de six mois*), to the empire and finally to the papacy (*le successeur de*

Pierre). Since the pope is the shepherd of his flock, the history is cyclic. See Introduction, p. xix.

58 *Ressusciter ces poudreuses ruines / these dusty ruins rise again*: referring to the use of ancient materials in the spectacular sixteenth-century rebuilding of Rome.

60 *Les monuments . . . dire / The monuments . . . here*: another echo of Horace's *Exegi monumentum* ('I have built a monument more lasting than bronze'). See note to p. 10.

peuple à longue robe / long-robed people: the Romans, Virgil's *gens togata* (*Aen.* 1. 282).

pétrarquistes / Petrarchists: for English anti-Petrarchism, see *Son.* 130 ('My mistress' eyes'); *A&S* 6 ('Some lovers speak') and 15 ('You that do search'); Donne, 'The Canonization', stanza 2 ('Alas, alas, who's injured by my love?').

68 *chacun élément / all the elements*: the four elements of earth, water, fire, and air make up both the macrocosm (the universe) and the microcosm (the individual body).

72 *la plus belle Idée / the most fair Idea*: see note to p. 6.

RONSARD

76 *Qui voudra voir / If you would see*: see note to p. 54.

rets d'or / A cunning net: the golden hair as a net that traps the lover is a standard conceit of Petrarchan poetry: *Can.* 59, *Tra le chiome de l'or nascose il laccio | al qual mi strinse Amor* ('Amid the locks of gold Love hid the noose') and 106; also *Am.* 37 ('What guile is this?'); Daniel, *Delia* 13 ('Those amber locks'); Constable, *Diana* 2. 8 ('The fowler hides').

un solitaire bois / The lonely wood: for the lover's solitude, see *Can.* 35, *Solo e pensoso* ('Alone and filled with care'). The conclusion recalls *Can.* 77, a sonnet on Simone Martini's portrait of Laura.

78 *pluie d'or / golden shower*: see Glossary for Danaë; see also Europa, Narcissus, and Aurora. The sonnet develops the idea of metamorphosis as a means to sexual fulfilment. The conclusion echoes *Can.* 22, *sol una notte et mai non fosse alba* ('just one night, and let the dawn never come'). See Introduction, pp. xxii–xxiii.

Phébus / Phoebus: R associates his own love for Cassandre Salviati with Apollo's unsuccessful attempt to seduce the Trojan princess Cassandra. See *Can.* 34, *Apollo, s'ancor vive il bel desio* ('Apollo, if the sweet desire is still alive').

80 *l'écumière fille / the sea-foam's daughter*: Venus Anadyomene, painted thus by Apelles according to Pliny the Elder, book 5; modern readers will recall Botticelli's *The Birth of Venus*.

ores l'espérance / now hope: the octave, with its play of antitheses and its military metaphor, is purely Petrarchan; the sestet is closer to the eroticism of Roman love poetry.

80 *D'un beau trépas . . . je meure / Dying . . . a lovely death*: see Propertius, 2. 1. 47, *laus in amore mori* ('It is glorious to die through love').

82 *Ixion et Tantale / Tantalus or Ixion*: see Glossary.

vautour . . . le roc . . redévale / vulture . . . rock . . rolled down again: the punishments of Tityos and Sisyphus. See Glossary.

Chaos ocieux / idle Chaos: in Plato's *Timaeus* Love (Eros) creates the universe out of Chaos, an idea that was taken up and Christianized by Marsilio Ficino and the Renaissance Neoplatonists. The cohabitation in the sestet of a purified essence with a heated blood suggests an attempt to reconcile the spiritual and the sensual.

Petit barbet / little spaniel: the opening recalls *Cat. 2, Passer, deliciae meae puellae* ('Sparrow, my lady's pet'). For R the sight of the girl's simple relationship with the spaniel becomes a reproach to his own excessive introspection. See *A&S* 59 ('Dear, why make you more') and 83 ('Good brother Philip').

84 *fille ou garçon / girl or boy*: echoing *Hor. 2. 5, solutis | crinibus ambiguoque vultu* ('his flowing locks and his girl-boy face') in acknowledging the charm of sexual ambiguity.

Stances / Stanzas: the *carpe diem* ('Seize the day') theme of *Hor 1. 11* is much exploited by Renaissance poets and by no one more assiduously than R. Compare Marvell's 'To His Coy Mistress'.

88 *Tout effrayé / In terror*: an enigmatic sonnet. The ruffian (*larron*) would seem to represent the destructive aspect of sexual desire.

Déesse / Goddess: Diana who visits her lover Endymion.

90 *tardive amitié / love that comes too late*: see *Can. 12, alcun soccorso di tardi sospiri* ('some little help of tardy sighs').

le fils d'Alcmène / Alcmene's fiery son: Hercules immortalized by fire on Mount Oeta.

L'autre beauté / The other beauty: for the Neoplatonic ascent, see note to p. 6.

Or' que le ciel / Now when the earth: the opening recalls *Can. 164, Or che 'l ciel et la terra* ('Now that the heavens and the earth'). See Surrey ('Alas, so all things now'). The antithesis of the conclusion is a tired Petrarchan cliché.

92 *Il faisait chaud / The day was hot*: the appearance of the beloved in a dream, a common topos of Renaissance love poetry, is not necessarily erotic and usually ends with a bleak awakening to reality as in Milton's sonnet 19 ('But O as to embrace me she inclined | I waked, she fled, and day brought back my night'). Ronsard breaks with tradition insofar as he celebrates the dream as providing a genuine satisfaction.

94 *Peins-moi, Janet / Paint for me, Janet*: a virtuoso performance in the *blason* tradition, loosely following and expanding Anacreon, *Odes* 28.

104 *Tyard, on me blâmait / Tyard, they blamed me*: classical rhetoric recognized three levels of style, *gravis, mediocris*, and *humilis* or *pedestris*. What little

we know of Marie de Bourgueil suggests that she came from a lower class than Cassandre or Hélène; hence the supposed *sermo pedestris*.

Le vingtième d'Avril / The twentieth of April: the hunting metaphor is derived from *Can.* 190, *Una candida cerva* ('A white doe'); see *Am.* 67 ('Like as a huntsman') and Wyatt ('Whoso list to hunt').

Marie levez-vous / Marie, get up!: the jocular intimate tone marks a departure from the Petrarchism that dominates the *Cassandre* sequence.

106 *Marie, baisez-moi / Kiss me, Marie*: the neo-Latin *Liber basiorum* of Johannes Secundus testifies to the popularity of kiss poems derived from *Cat.* 5, *da mi basia mille* ('Give me a thousand kisses') and 7, *Quaeris, quot mihi basiationes* ('You ask how many kisses').

Comme la cire / The hardened wax: imitated from Marullus, *Epigrams* 2. 2.

110 *Marie tout ainsi / Just as, Marie*: a wry account of the change in style already acknowledged in R 22.

Or que l'hiver / When deep midwinter: with echoes of Theocritus, Ovid, and Secundus, but the colloquial urgency is inimitably that of R.

112 *la mort de Marie / the Death of Marie*: not the Marie de Bourgueil of the preceding section, but Marie de Clèves (1553–74), mistress of the Duke of Anjou, later Henri III.

Comme on voit sur la branche / As on its stem: in this famous sonnet R revives the conventional metaphor of the dying rose with his consummate musicality and the exquisite freshness of the closing lines. See Introduction, p. xx.

114 *je me retire / I shall leave*: the disillusion recalls *Can.* 363, *stanco di viver, non che sazio* ('weary of life, not merely satiated') and 364, *Omai son stanco, et mia vita reprendo* ('Now I am weary and I reproach my life'), but without Petrarch's religious turn.

116 *A mon retour / On my return*: echoes neo-Latin kiss poems by Secundus and Sannazaro.

Tant de fois s'appointer . . . / Now breaking off . . . : here begins a feast of rhetorical devices: anaphora, antithesis, parison (repeated syntactic structure), polyptoton (same word repeated in different forms as in *jurer/ parjurer, faits/défaits*), etc.

118 *votre amitié n'est qu'une flamme de Cour / A love that's nothing but a courtly fashion*: the superficiality of love at the court is a recurrent theme in Pléiade poetry.

sa grandeur et sa race / her old and noble name: indications of Hélène's high rank.

quand vous serez de même / when you look much the same: the thought of what the beloved will look like in old age is a commonplace in Renaissance love poetry. R 43 is perhaps the most famous example, but there is also *Can.* 12, *Se la mia vita* ('If my life') and *Son.* 2 ('When forty winters shall besiege thy brow').

120 *sympathie / sympathy*: R protests that his lady is moved by a sad poetic fiction but lacks sympathy for the real grieving poet. For the same situation see *A&S* 45 ('Stella oft sees the very face of woe').

    mon chef grison / my grey head: rejecting high-minded Neoplatonism, R evokes myths that demonstrate the force of love in old age (Pan seducing the Moon with a white fleece, Aurora's love for the aged Tithonus). Phaeton and Icarus are both rash young men.

122 *ton nom Grec / your name; the Greek word*: R follows Aeschylus (*Agamemnon* 689) in deriving the name Helen from the Greek verb for to seize or ravish.

    La voix, que tu feignais . . . Cheval / spoke false words to the horse: prompted by Aphrodite, Helen spoke to the wooden horse, in the vain hope that the hidden Greek warriors would betray their presence by answering her (*Od.* 4. 277–89).

    fol enfant / To make me too a child: a foolish child, like Cupid.

    fleurs de lis / lilies: the royal emblem of France.

    Thébaïde / Theban War: the war between Polynices and Eteocles, sons of Oedipus, King of Thebes, here an allusion to the conflict between King Henri III and his brother, François d'Alençon.

    J'avais été saigné / I had just been bled: bleeding was thought to restore the balance between the four bodily humours; black blood was the sign of a melancholy and imaginative disposition.

124 *Ces longues nuits / These winter nights*: as in R 19, the dream is presented in a positive light without the bleak awakening. R recalls the legend that the Helen abducted by Paris was a spectral image of the real Helen who was taken to Egypt by the gods.

    au soir à la chandelle . . . filant / Spinning by candlelight: Tibullus, 1. 3. 85–8, *haec tibi fabellas referat positaque lucerna | deducat plena stamina longa colu; | at circa gravibus pensis adfixa puella | paulatim somno fessa remittat opus* ('She shall tell thee stories when the lamp is in its place, as she draws the long yarn from the loaded distaff, while all around the maids bend over the toilsome task till sleep steals upon them and the work drops from the tired hand'). See Introduction, p. xxiii.

    myrteux / myrtles: plant sacred to Venus.

126 *Cueillez . . . les roses de la vie / pluck life's rose today*: Ausonius, *Idylls* 14, *Collige, virgo, rosas, dum flos novus et nova pubes* ('Gather roses, young girl, while their flower is new as is your youth').

    ballet d'Amour / his exquisite dance: the dance expresses the aesthetic balance between change and stability, freedom and order.

    De Myrte et de Laurier / Of Laurel and of myrtle: myrtle, sacred to Venus, crowns R as a lover; laurel, sacred to Apollo, crowns him as a poet.

    plus Cygne vous mourrez / you will die a Swan: the song of the dying swan was reputed to be of surpassing beauty.

Palais de nos Rois / lodge above our King: the palace is the Louvre; Hélène's lodging on an upper floor provokes an ironic version of the lady as unattainable goddess.

128 *la Cour / Court*: punning on court and courtyard.

130 *les cieux, En qui Dieu nous écrit / The sky where God has written for us*: man's fate is written in the stars, but since we cannot read them, astrology is of no help.

132 *vos cheveux deviendront argentés / streaks of silver will bestrew your hair*: Can. 12, *e i cape' d'oro fin farsi argento* ('and your hair of fine gold made silver').

la loi que la Nature a faite / Nature gives the law: takes up the conclusion of R 47. For English versions of the farewell to love, see Wyatt ('Now farewell, Love'); Sidney ('Leave me, O love'); and Drayton, *Idea* 61 ('Since there's no help').

le tétin de m'amie / my darling's breast: breasts and nipples figure prominently in R's erotic imagery. This is not the first *blason* devoted to the navel. See Bonaventure des Périers in *Blasons du corps féminin*.

134 *Androgyne*: the navel was thought to be the scar left when the originally dual-natured human being was divided into male and female. See the speech of Aristophanes in Plato's *Symposium*.

Je ne saurais juger / my judgement can't be right: love's power to disturb true perception is present in *Can.* 129, *Di pensier in pensier* ('From thought to thought') and is prominent in *Son.* 113 ('Since I left you') and 114 (Or whether doth my mind').

136 *Ceux qui Amour connaissent / Those who have learned . . . what love is*: in this epilogue to *Les Amours diverses*, the last ten lines are closely modelled on *Can.* 1, *del vario stile in ch'io piango et ragiono* | *fra le vane speranze e 'l van dolore,* | *ove sia chi per prova intenda amore* | *spero trovar pietà non ché perdono . . . e del mio vaneggiar vegogna è 'l frutto ,* | *e 'l pentersi, e 'l conoscer chiaramente* | *che quanto piace al mondo è breve sogno* ('for the varied style in which I weep and speak between vain hopes and vain sorrow, where there is anyone who understands love from experience, I hope to find pity, not only pardon . . . and of my raving, shame is the fruit, and repentance, and the clear knowledge that whatever pleases in the world is a brief dream').

138 *Mignonne, allons voir / My love, let us see*: the most famous of R's many poems on the *carpe diem* theme. Compare Herrick ('Gather ye Rose-buds') and Waller ('Go, lovely Rose).

De l'élection de sa sépulcre / On the Choice of His Burial Plot: a funeral ode that is a celebration both of R's achievement as a poet and of the countryside that provided so much of his inspiration. The rural setting and the rituals that he anticipates place the poem within the pastoral tradition of Theocritus and Virgil.

146 *À Guy Pacate / To Guy Pacate*: a negative counterpart to the preceding ode. Fear replaces confidence; death leads not to rest but to punishment; and poetry provides no guarantee of immortality.

150 *Ma douce jouvence / My happy youth*: the mythological horrors of R 55 give way to this moving description of the ailments of old age, written when R was hardly 30.

152 *Plus dur que fer / To outlast iron*: R's adaptation of *Hor.* 3. 30, *Exegi monumentum* ('I have finished a monument more lasting than bronze').

des frères la rage / the raging brothers: the brothers Castor and Pollux govern the weather at sea.

deux Harpeurs divers / two Harpers quite diverse: Pindar and Horace, considered to have created two different kinds of ode: the former rhapsodic and elaborate, the latter reflective and formally straightforward.

154 *Nous fîmes un contrat / We made a deal*: another kiss poem after the model of Secundus and Catullus (see R 25).

Toi, Déesse . . . plus belle que n'était Celle . . . une conque portait / Goddess more fair than one a seashell bore: Ronsard says that his mistress is a hundred times more beautiful than the goddess Venus (see R 6).

156 *serviteur servant / servant's service*: an ironic phrase since he hopes to serve the lady in a way that is denied to the *serviteur* in the courtly-love tradition.

158 *le meilleur point / the point supreme*: last of the five traditional steps of love: sight, conversation, touching, kissing, coitus.

au premier temps / that primal golden time: when all humans were androgynous (see R 50).

Géants / Giants: the Giants who rebelled against Jupiter and were destroyed.

l'honneur vous abuse / Honour is to blame: the assault on honour as a false idol is a commonplace of Renaissance poetry, the most celebrated example being the great Golden Age chorus in Torquato Tasso's pastoral drama *Aminta* 1. 2, *quel vano | nome senza soggetto, | quell'idolo d'errori, idol d'inganno* ('that vain name without substance, that idol of error and deceit').

162 *ville Hellespontique*: probably Greek colony of Lampsacus, noted for its prosperity and priapic worship.

À te couper, forêt / To cut you down, dear forest: R's poem on the clearances of his beloved Forest of Gastine moves from indignation and imprecation to nostalgia before concluding with philosophical resignation.

164 *Janette / Jeanette*: a traditionally rustic name.

166 *sa neuvaine trope / her ninefold retinue*: the nine Muses.

la Philosophie / the Philosophy: that of Ovid, *Met.* 15.

Hymne du Ciel / Hymn to the Sky: R's universe conforms to the model transmitted to the Middle Ages by Ptolemy—geocentric, spatially finite, composed of the four elements (Earth, Water, Fire, Air), the seven planets, the sphere of fixed stars, and the outer globe of heaven known as the *primum mobile* (Prime Mover). See Introduction, pp. xxiv–xxv.

168 *après la naissance . . . la connaissance / if any man can know . . . below*: Neoplatonism identifies knowledge with a memory of the perfect knowledge possessed by the soul in its previous existence in the realm of the Ideal. There are traces of a similar doctrine in Henry Vaughan's 'The Retreat'.

L'Esprit de l'Éternel / The spirit of the Eternal: the World Soul (*Anima Mundi*) which first gave the Prime Mover its perfect and eternal rotation. See Introduction, pp. xxiv–xxv.

plaisante harmonie / pleasing harmony: the Music of the Spheres. See Shakespeare, *Merchant of Venice* 5. 1. 60–5 ('There's not the smallest orb').

170 *comme fait le Soleil . . . l'estomac de l'homme / As does the Sun . . . man's stomach*: the analogy suggests the relation between microcosm (the human body) and macrocosm (the universe).

beau nom / lovely name: Greek *cosmos*, meaning elegance and order.

le citoyen du monde comme nous / he inhabits the same Universe: not a reference to the Incarnation; R's purpose is to situate God's dwelling-place within the universe he has created, but in the calm realm of the Empyrean as opposed to the mutable sublunar world that humans inhabit.

172 *infini, fait d'un fini espace / infinite, though made of finite space*: this attempt to reconcile the finite with the infinite leads R to deny any possibility of that plurality of worlds posited thirty years later by Giordano Bruno.

joug d'Anangé / Ananke's yoke: necessity (Greek).

quatre ou cinq mille ans / four thousand years: R's insistence on the cyclic nature of time leads him to doubt the widely accepted calculation that the world was created about four thousand years before the birth of Christ.

Fils de Saturne / son of Saturn: Jupiter, a synonym for God.

174 *L'influx des Astres / the influence of the Stars*: R's model is a neo-Latin poem by Marullus, but the hymn departs from its source in stopping short of a fully-fledged determinism that would be potentially heretical; the stars are the ministers of Heaven, but free will does exist and the sage or the saint may defy stellar influence through the superior power of God (Jupiter).

retournés, Se suivent d'une même trace / return upon Their . . . trodden trace: the cyclic view of time. See R 61.

178 *Mont-Faucon / Montfaucon*: Parisian place of execution. R is probably thinking of the tragic end of the great Huguenot leader Admiral de Coligny, hanged on the gibbet at Montfaucon after being assassinated as a prelude to the massacre of Protestants on St Bartholomew's Day (1572).

180 *Gardez . . . Roi / Protect . . . king*: the strophe refers to Henri, Duke of Anjou, brother of Charles IX and son of Catherine de Médicis. Charles had defended Catholicism (*l'antique foi*) through his victories over the Protestants; Henri was elected King of Poland (*Poulonne*) in 1573, but on the death of his brother in 1574 returned to France to become King Henri III.

182 *Remonstrance*: a formal statement of public grievances.

184 *tes sacrements / your sacraments*: the seven sacraments of the Catholic Church were reduced to two (Baptism and the Eucharist) by the Lutherans and one (Baptism) by the Calvinists.

Manichée . . . Arrien / Manichaean . . . Arian: the Persian Mani (third century) saw God and Satan as equally powerful forces in the world; Arius (fourth century) questioned the full divinity of Christ.

186 *L'homme qui croit en moi / He who believes in me*: Christ's words (Mark 16:16).

188 *ivrogne apostat Augustin / apostate Augustinian drunk*: Luther.

C'est ci mon corps et sang / This is my body . . . my blood: an abbreviation of Christ's words at the Last Supper as they are repeated in the Eucharist. The Catholic belief in transubstantiation (the 'real presence' of Christ in the bread and wine) was challenged by Calvin who saw the Eucharist as a purely symbolic commemoration.

190 *Du Serpent qui parla . . . de l'âne à Balaam / speaking Serpent . . . Balaam's ass*: R ridicules the contradictory stance of Protestants who appeal to reason to deny God's presence in the Eucharist but still feel obliged by their strict adherence to the letter of the Scriptures to believe in the most unlikely biblical miracles. See Introduction, p. xxvii.

mille langues de feu / a thousand tongues of fire: the tongues of fire that descended on the Apostles at Pentecost (Acts 2:1–4).

192 *ils ont trouvé la feuve / they've found the bean*: alluding to an Epiphany cake where the one who finds the bean is supposed to be assured of good fortune.

Être sobre en propos . . . et ne jurer que 'certes' / To make one's speech . . . sober . . . say 'indeed' instead of swearing: see the caricature of the Genevan Calvinist in DB 55.

194 *opinion . . . Sous ombre de piété / Opinion, dressed as piety*: the substitution of one's own judgement to that of the Church. In a lengthy subsequent passage R personifies Opinion as a winged and many-tongued monster who flies over Europe urging on reformers, misleading rulers, and seducing their subjects.

chanter son obsèque en la façon de Cygne / like the Swan . . . Sing . . . our own exequies: the poet writes his own swansong.

196 *Je vous envoie un bouquet / I send you this fresh posy*: hard to say why this exquisite sonnet was omitted from the 1578 collected edition.

APPENDIX: THE MANIFESTOS

DU BELLAY

201 *if our language is not so copious . . . as Greek or Latin*: a major concern of humanist rhetorical theory as outlined by Erasmus in his *De duplici copia verborum et rerum* (On the Copiousness of Both Words and Things, 1512).

202 *François*: François I (r. 1515–47), renowned as a patron of the arts.

Pericles . . . Scipio: a list of politicians and military leaders, the point being that France has already shown itself capable of rivalling Greece and Rome in fields other than literature.

demonstrate our ignorance: DB dismisses not only the old poetry societies of Toulouse and Rouen, but also the popular forms of French poetry (rondel, virelay, etc.) which he hoped to replace with classical and Italian models. Many of his contemporaries were outraged by this wholesale rejection of national tradition.

mixing profit with pleasure: few Renaissance literary theorists could resist quoting Horace's *Ars poetica* with its famous praise of the poet as one who can blend the useful and the sweet (*qui miscuit utile dulce*).

odes: the form chosen by R for his first volume of poetry a year after DB's *Deffence*.

203 *other such works*: of the three poems mentioned by DB, the first and third are by his older contemporary Mellin de Saint-Gelais and the second by Pernette du Guillet.

coq-à-l'âne: literally 'from the cock to the donkey', the habit of switching abruptly from one topic to another.

those lovely sonnets: DB began his own poetic career with a Petrarchan sonnet sequence, *L'Olive* (*The Olive*; see pp. 4–7), published almost simultaneously with the *Deffence*.

that eclogue . . . one of the best short pieces that Marot ever wrote: a rare compliment; the Pléiade poets more often saw Marot as representative of the superficial courtly poetry they claimed to despise.

206 *that great monarch*: Alexander.

those fine titles . . . pretty little devices: DB mocks the titles, pseudonyms, and mottos of Marot and his followers.

207 *Anticyra*: a source of hellebore, a herb supposed to cure madness.

poetry, which is like painting: another irresistible quotation (*Ut pictura poesis*) from the *Ars poetica*.

RONSARD

208 *Summary*: R attached little importance to this *Abbrégé* which he claimed to have written in three hours; it remains, however, a useful digest of Renaissance poetic theory.

allegorical theology: a theory often used to justify the study of ancient poetry; Virgil's *Eclogue* 4, for example, could be read as a prophecy of the birth of Christ. See Introduction, p. xi.

Cecropian: Athenian, from Cecrops, legendary founder of Athens.

209 *'Recall to me the causes'*: R cites, in the original Greek and Latin, Homer (*Iliad and Od.*), Theocritus (*Idyll* 17), Apollonius (*The Argonauts*), Lucretius (*On the Nature of Things*), and Virgil (*Aen.*).

210 *the first two verses masculine . . . the next two feminine*: a feminine rhyme ends with a mute 'e'; a masculine rhyme does not.

the Greek language . . . dialects and vocabulary: there are echoes here of the Italian debate over literary language, where Bembo argued in favour of the essentially Tuscan idiom of Boccaccio and Petrarch. It is with some regret that R accepts the inevitability of a national language that is less than hospitable to dialect variations.

211 *Invention*: in the conventional rhetorical theory of the age, the act of composition was divided into the three stages of Invention, Disposition, and Elocution, corresponding roughly to Subject Matter, Structure, and Style. But *invention* is a problematic term since it can be used to denote either the original matrix of the whole work or some more local excellence as in the 'fine inventions, descriptions, and comparisons' that R lists above. Sidney plays on the ambiguity in *A&S* 1 ('But words came halting forth, wanting Invention's stay, | Invention, Nature's child, fled step-dame Study's blows').

GLOSSARY OF NAMES AND PLACES

Achelous Greek river god, father of the Sirens and of water nymphs (Naiads).

Acheron one of the five rivers of the Underworld.

Achilles Greek warrior who kills Hector during the Trojan War, protagonist of Homer's *Iliad*; it was said that the touch of his spear could cure the wound it made.

Actaeon *see* DIANA.

Adonis beautiful youth killed by a boar, lover of Venus who makes the anemone grow from the blood-soaked earth in his memory. R and Shakespeare are among many Renaissance poets who wrote versions of the myth.

Aeolus god of the winds.

Aeson King of Iolcos in Thessaly, father of Jason who led the Argonauts, his youthful appearance was restored by the arts of Jason's wife, Medea. *See also* JASON.

Ajax one of the Greek leaders at the siege of Troy; Homer depicts him as immensely strong, brave, and stupid.

Alcaeus Greek lyric poet (*fl.* 610 BC).

Alcibiades (*c.*450–404 BC), Athenian politician and military leader, friend of Socrates; handsome, proud, and unscrupulous; often changed sides during the Peloponnesian War.

Alcina sorceress in Ariosto's *Orlando Furioso*; seduces English paladin Astolfo and transforms him into a myrtle.

Alcmene mother of Hercules who is fathered by Jupiter disguised as her husband Amphitryon.

Ambrose (339–97), bishop of Milan, saint, theologian.

Anacreon (*c.*550–464 BC), Greek lyric poet.

Anticyra ancient port on the north coast of the Gulf of Corinth.

Apelles famous Greek painter (fourth century BC).

Apollo god of poetry, music, and medicine; patron of shepherds and herdsmen. Often called Phoebus ('shining'); unsuccessful in his courtship of Daphne and of the Trojan princess Cassandra.

Apollonius Rhodius Alexandrian poet (third century BC), author of *Argonautica*. *See also* JASON.

Argus giant with a hundred eyes.

Ariadne daughter of King Minos of Crete, helped the Athenian Theseus to escape from the Labyrinth; rescued and married by Bacchus (Dionysus) after Theseus had abandoned her on the island of Naxos.

Ariosto, Ludovico (1474–1533), Italian poet, author of romance epic *Orlando Furioso*.

Ascrean *see* HESIOD.

Astolfo *see* ALCINA.

Astraea 'the star maiden', goddess of justice, who leaves the earth with the coming of the Iron Age; the Astrée of *Les Amours* is Françoise d'Estrées.

Atalanta athletic huntress who vows to marry only the man who can defeat her in a running race where the losing candidate's life is forfeit; she is finally conquered by Melanion who strews three golden apples in her way.

Augean Stables the fifth labour of Hercules is to clean the stables of King Augeas by diverting the course of two rivers.

Augustus Caesar (63 BC–AD 14), first Roman emperor, originally named Octavian, granted title of Augustus (27 BC); emerged victorious from civil wars and inaugurated an age of peace and prosperity.

Aurora goddess of the dawn. *See also* TITHONUS.

Ausonius (*c*.310–95), prolific late Roman poet.

Avernus volcanic crater at Cuma (Lat. *Cumae*) near Naples, believed to be the entrance to the Underworld.

Bacchus (Gk Dionysus), god of wine, fertility, and ecstatic festivities.

Baïf, Jean-Antoine de (1532–89), poet, prominent member of the Pléiade.

Balaam non-Israelite Old Testament prophet (Num. 22–4), prevented from cursing Israel by the appearance of an angel recognized only by his ass who refuses to go any further.

Belleau, Rémy (*c*.1528–77), member of the Pléiade; studied at Le Coqueret with R, DB, and Baïf; noted for his translation of Anacreon (1556).

Bellerophon tamed the winged horse Pegasus with bridle given him by Minerva (Pallas Athene); thrown from his horse as punishment for attempting to ride to the heavens.

Bembo, Pietro (1470–1547), cardinal, humanist, poet; influential in establishing Petrarch as a model of Italian poetic diction; portrayed as ardent Neoplatonist in Castiglione's *Book of the Courtier*.

Bèze, Théodore de (1519–1605), Calvinist theologian, spokesman for Huguenots at Colloquy of Poissy (1561); succeeded Calvin as highest religious authority in Geneva, rector of the Académie de Genève.

Bizet Claude de canon of Notre-Dame de Paris, helped DB in family litigation.

Botticelli, Sandro (1445–1510), Florentine artist; paintings such as *Venus and Mars* and *The Birth of Venus* reflect a Neoplatonist interpretation of classical mythology.

Bouju, Jacques (1515–77), Angevin like DB, author of poems in Latin and French.

Bruno, Giordano (1548–1600), Italian philosopher burned at the stake for heresy, author of *On the Infinite Universe and Worlds* (1584).

Calliope Muse of epic poetry.

Carle, Lancelot de (1500–68), bishop of Riez, charged with missions to Rome; poet and translator of Homer.

Caraffa, Carlo (1517–60), unscrupulous nephew of Pope Paul IV who made him a cardinal; diplomatic opponent of Cardinal du Bellay.

Cassandra daughter of Priam, King of Troy; possessed the gift of prophecy but was fated to be always disbelieved.

Cassandre in DB's *Les Amours*, Cassandre Salviati, daughter of an Italian banker.

Castor and Pollux twin brothers of Helen, sons of Jupiter and Leda.

Castiglione, Baldassare (1478–1529), author of *The Book of the Courtier.*

Cato, Marcus Portius (234–149 BC), known as 'Cato the Censor' because of his severe moral stance, urged a return to a simple and austere pastoral society.

Ceres goddess of farming, fertility, and the harvest.

Charles V (1500–58), King of Spain (1516–56) and Holy Roman Emperor (1519–56), his reign was marked by wars against France in Italy and struggles against Protestant reformers in the German states.

Charon ferryman in the Underworld, who takes the dead across the river Styx.

Circe seductive sorceress in *Od.* 9.

Coligny, Gaspard de (1519–72), French admiral, leader of the Huguenots, assassinated during the St Bartholomew Massacre.

Corydon name of shepherd in Greek and Roman pastoral poetry (Theocritus, Virgil).

Cyprian pertaining to Venus (Gk Aphrodite), said to be born near Paphos on the island of Cyprus.

Cythera another island where Venus is said to have landed after her birth in the sea; hence her title of Cytherean.

Daedalus legendary craftsman and inventor. *See also* ICARUS.

Daimons in Greek mythology, semi-divine nature spirits, later identified with the force that drives a man to his destiny. R has a long poem on the subject (not translated here).

Danaë seduced by Jupiter in the form of a golden shower.

Daphne fled the advances of Apollo and was turned into a laurel.

Dardan Trojan from Dardanus, legendary founder of Troy.

D'Aubigné, Théodore Agrippa (1552–1630), Protestant poet and soldier; author of *Les Tragiques*, an account of the persecutions suffered by the Huguenots.

Deianera wife of Hercules whom she unwittingly drove to death by presenting him with a poisoned robe.

Del Monte, Innocenzo (*c*.1532–77), lowborn illegitimate child, allegedly keeper of the pope's monkeys, catamite of Pope Julius III who made him a cardinal and gave him his own family name; a thoroughly disreputable character, he fell into disgrace after accusations of murder and rape.

Demosthenes (383–322 BC), Athenian statesman, admired as the greatest of all Greek orators.

Denisot, Nicholas (1515–59), painter and poet, studied at Collège de Coqueret with R and DB; also known as Comte.

Des Masures, Louis (1515–80), translator of the first four books of *Aen.*

Des Périers, Bonaventure satirist, author of stories in the manner of Boccaccio.

Desportes, Philippe (1546–1606), poet, author of polished love sonnets; popular at court, considered briefly as a rival to R.

Diana (Gk Artemis), goddess of hunting, chastity, and the moon; daughter of Jupiter, twin sister of Apollo; visited her mortal lover Endymion in a cave on Mount Latmos; when the huntsman Actaeon caught sight of her bathing naked in a fountain she transformed him into a stag and he was devoured by his own hounds.

Dodona site of the most ancient Greek oracle, set in a grove of sacred oak trees. *See also* ERISICHTHON.

Dorat, Jean (1508–88), humanist scholar; influential teacher of R, DB, and Baïf at Collège de Coqueret.

Doulcin, Rémy priest and physician, friend of Rabelais.

Du Bartas, Guillaume (1544–90), Protestant poet, author of poem on the Creation, *La Semaine.*

Duthier, Jean secretary to François I, controller of finances under Henri II; patron of poets, including R and DB.

Echo sick with unrequited love for Narcissus, she pined away until nothing was left of her but the voice.

Endymion youthful lover of Diana.

Epicurus (341–270 BC), Greek philosopher, often wrongly supposed to have preached a doctrine of absolute hedonism.

Erasmus, Desiderius (*c*.1469–1536), Dutch humanist, theologian, and satirist whose *Adagia* was a hugely popular collection of proverbs, aphorisms, and anecdotes.

Erisichthon punished with insatiable hunger after cutting down one of the sacred oaks of Dodona.

Eumolpus legendary King of Thrace and son of Neptune, supposedly killed in his attempt to conquer Athens.

Europa seduced by Jupiter in the form of a bull.

Eurotas river in Greece where Jupiter seduced Leda.

Euterpe Muse of music.

faun in Roman mythology a rural creature, half-man, half-goat, similar to Greek satyr. *See also* PAN.

Ficino, Marsilio (1433–99), Italian philosopher, editor and translator of Plato; the most influential of Renaissance Neoplatonists.

François I (1494–1547), King of France (1515–47), patron of the arts, defeated by Emperor Charles V at Pavia (1525).

Ganymede beautiful youth, cup-bearer of Jupiter.

Glaucus a sea-god.

Gordes, Jean-Antoine (1525–62), prothonotary in the household of Cardinal Jean du Bellay.

Golden Fleece *see* JASON.

Graces three personifications of female beauty.

Harpies bird-like monsters, divine instruments of punishment.

Hector Trojan hero, killed by Achilles.

Helen beautiful wife of Menelaus, King of Sparta; her elopement with Paris, son of King Priam of Troy, provoked the Trojan War.

Henri II (1527–59), King of France (r. 1547–59).

Henri III (1551–89), King of France (r. 1574–89).

Hesiod early Greek poet (possibly eighth century BC), sometimes known as 'the Ascrean' from his birth in the Boeotian town of Ascra; author of the *Works and Days*.

Hippocrene spring on Mount Helicon, sacred to the Muses, produced when the hoofs of the winged horse Pegasus struck the ground.

Icarus donned artificial wings of wax and feathers fabricated by his father Daedalus, but fell and was drowned when the wax melted because he had flown too near the sun.

Ilion the citadel of Troy.

Ixion tried to seduce Juno, but failed when Jupiter deceived him with a cloud made in her image; punished by being bound to an ever-turning wheel in the Underworld.

Janet better known as François Clouet (1515–72), official court painter.

Jason son of Aeson, leader of the Argonaut expedition to Colchis where he recovered the Golden Fleece with the help of Medea. *See also* APOLLONIUS RHODIUS.

Jerome, St (347–420), Church Father, translator of the Bible into Latin (the Vulgate).

Jodelle, Étienne (1532–75), member of the Pléiade, poet and dramatist, noted as precursor of French classical tragedy.

Julius II, Pope (1443–1515), Giuliano della Rovere, elected pope (1503), active participant in the Italian Wars; ordered rebuilding of Basilica of

Glossary of Names and Places

St Peter, commissioned artwork from Michelangelo (Sistine Chapel), Raphael, and others.

Julius III, Pope (1487–1555), Giammaria Ciocchi del Monte, elected pope (1550).

Juno (Gk Hera), wife of Jupiter, goddess of marriage and childbirth.

Jupiter (Jove) (Gk Zeus), supreme among the gods; seducer of Danaë, Leda, Europa; his name sometimes used to indicate Christian God.

Labé, Louise (*c.*1524–66), poet of the Lyons school, her slim volume of poems (1558) makes her one of the most notable female voices in Renaissance literature.

Latmos mountain where Diana made love to Endymion.

Laura *see* PETRARCH.

Leda seduced by Jupiter in the form of a swan; mother of Helen.

Le Gast, Louis Béranger (*c.*1540–75), favourite of Henri III, friend of R, assassinated.

Liré village in Anjou, ancestral home of DB.

Linus mythical tutor of Hercules.

Logistilla embodies wisdom and virtue in *Orl.*, she offers refuge to Ruggiero when he escapes the wiles of the sorceress Alcina.

Lot's wife transformed into a pillar of salt in the Old Testament when she looked back at Sodom (Gen. 19:26).

Lucrece chaste wife of Collatine, her rape by Tarquin and subsequent suicide were said to have provoked the expulsion of the Tarquin dynasty and the foundation of the Roman Republic (510 BC).

Lysippus favourite sculptor of Alexander the Great.

Maecenas, Gaius (first century BC) generous patron of Roman poets Virgil, Horace, Propertius.

Magny, Olivier de (1520–61), poet, secretary to ambassador D'Avanson in Rome (1555–6).

Marcellus II, Pope b. Marcello Cervino (1501–55); hoped to reform the Church, but his papacy lasted only three weeks (April–May 1555).

Marguerite de France (1523–74), daughter of François I and sister of Henri II; admired and celebrated by DB and R.

Marie de Bourgueil the Marie of the first part of R's *Le Second Livre des Amours* about whom we know very little.

Marie de Clèves (1553–74), beloved of the Duke of Anjou, later Henri III; commemorated in R's *Mort de Marie*.

Marot, Clément (1496–1544), French poet; his work anticipated many aspects of the Pléiade poets though they were reluctant to admit it.

Mars (Gk Ares), god of war, lover of Venus.

Marullus, Michael (1453/4–1500), born in Greece, emigrated to Italy, and became a distinguished neo-Latin poet; much admired by R.

Mauny, François de cleric attached to the mission of Cardinal du Bellay.

Meander river god.

Medea daughter of the King of Colchis, her magic arts helped Jason to recover the Golden Fleece; she murdered their children when Jason took another wife.

Medusa most famous of the three Gorgons whose glance turned the onlooker to stone.

Mellin de Saint-Gelais (1491–1558), poet, contemporary and rival of Marot; hostile to the Pléiade.

Mercury (Gk Hermes), messenger of the gods, guide to the dead.

Melissa benevolent sorceress in *Orl*.

Minerva (Gk Pallas Athene), goddess of war and wisdom, born fully armed from the head of Jupiter.

Minos legendary King of Crete; his wife Pasiphaë fell in love with a bull and gave birth to a monster (the Minotaur) that was kept in the Labyrinth until slain by Theseus.

Mnemosyne Titaness, personification of Memory, mother of the Muses.

Mongibello Mount Etna.

Mont Faucon place of execution in Paris.

Montmorency, Anne de (1493–1567), Constable of France, adversary of DB in litigation over the estate of Oudon in Anjou.

Morel, Jean de (1511–81), agent of Governor Guillaume du Bellay at Turin, friend of DB.

Muret, Marc Antoine (1526–85), friend of R, author of a commentary on the first book of *Les Amours* (1553).

Muses nine daughters of Jupiter and Mnemosyne; together with Apollo, they preside over the arts and sciences. Their sacred mountains are Helicon and Parnassus.

Narcissus youth who drowned while contemplating his own beauty reflected in a pond.

Naxos *see* ARIADNE.

Nemesis personification of divine punishment for human presumption (hubris).

Nereids sea-nymphs.

Olympus mountain home of the gods.

Orpheus mythical poet and musician; went down to the Underworld to release his dead wife Euridice, but lost her by looking back at her when he had vowed not to do so; he then renounced the love of women and turned his attention to tender boys, a preference resented by the Thracian women (maenads) who tore him to pieces.

Pacate, Guy (1509–80), cleric; his nephew studied with R in Paris.

Palatine one of the Seven Hills of Rome.

Pallas Athene *see* MINERVA.

Pan son of Mercury, god of shepherds, often represented as half-goat, half-man. *See also* FAUN.

Pandora woman created by Vulcan (Gk Hephaestus) on the orders of Jupiter; charged with a box which released all the ills of the world when she opened it; only Hope remained in the box as a consolation.

Panjas, Jean de Pardeillon de poet and cleric in Rome with Cardinal D'Armagnac (1554–7).

Paris *see* HELEN.

Parnassus mountain north of Delphi, associated with Apollo and the Muses; sometimes thought of as having two peaks, one for Apollo and the other for Dionysus.

Paschal, Pierre de (1522–65), historiographer to the King, Pléiade poets expected him to give them some favourable mention, but were disappointed.

Pasquin and Marphore ancient statues in Rome, used to exhibit libellous comments on the Pope and his government.

Paul IV, Pope Giovanni Pietro Caraffa (1476–1559), elected 1555, noted for his austerity and intolerance.

Pegasus *see* BELLEROPHON.

Peletier, Jacques (1517–82), poet and humanist, influential member of the Pléiade; preface to his translation of Horace's *Art of Poetry* (1545) anticipates much of DB's *Deffence*.

Penelope faithful wife of Ulysses.

Pericles (*c*.500–429 BC), great Athenian statesman.

Persius (34–62), Roman poet, author of six satires.

Petrarch Francesco Petrarca (1307–74), humanist, Latin and Italian poet; his love poems to Laura, collected in the *Rerum Vulgariam Fragmenta* (better known as the *Canzoniere*) were immensely influential throughout Europe.

Phaeton insisted on driving the chariot of his father Helios (the sun god), lost control of the fiery horses, and would have provoked a universal conflagration had not Jupiter killed him with a thunderbolt; like Icarus, an example of hubris.

Phoebus *see* APOLLO.

Phoenix mythical bird said to burn itself every five hundred years and then rise from its ashes.

Pibrac, Guy du Faur de (1529–84), jurist and poet.

Pierre barber of DB.

Pliny the Elder (23/24–79), Latin author of the *Natural History*.

Pluto Lord of the Underworld.

Pontanus (1426–1503), Giovanni Pontano, Italian diplomat, humanist, and prolific neo-Latin poet.

Priam King of Troy.

Priapus phallic deity.

Prometheus stole fire from the gods and gave it to mortals, punished by being chained to a rock where every day an eagle devoured his liver, which was then restored by night only to be devoured again the next day.

Proserpina wife of Pluto.

Proteus a shape-changing sea-god, herdsman of marine animals.

Ptolemy Greek astronomer (second century) whose geocentric system was universally accepted until challenged by Copernicus.

Pyrrha after the Great Flood, Pyrrha and her husband Deucalion sowed stones that grew respectively into women and men.

Pythia priestess and oracle of Apollo at Delphi.

Quintilian (35–*c*.95), Roman teacher of rhetoric; his *Institutio Oratoria*, rediscovered by Poggio Bracciolini in 1516, had considerable influence on Renaissance theorists of rhetoric and education.

Robertet, Florimond (1533–69), visited Rome in 1555, attached to the Guise faction; R dedicates two poems to him.

Ruggiero heroic figure in *Orl*.

Samos Greek island dedicated to Juno.

Sannazaro, Jacopo (1458–1530), author of the influential *Arcadia*, a pastoral romance that alternates prose and poetry.

Sappho (b. *c*.612 BC) Greek lyric poet from the island of Lesbos, supposed leader of a female Aphrodite cult.

Saturn Roman equivalent to pre-Hellenic deity Cronos; ousted as King of the Gods by his son Jupiter.

Satyr goat-like figure associated with fertility. *See also* FAUN *and* PAN.

Scamander Trojan river.

Scylla and Charybdis two monsters, associated with a perilous rock and a whirlpool in the Straits of Messina. See *Od.* 12.

Secundus, Johannes (1511–36), Dutch neo-Latin poet, best known for his *Liber Basiorum* (Book of Kisses).

Sirens sea-nymphs whose song attracted sailors to destruction. See *Od.* 12.

Sisyphus legendary King of Corinth, condemned in the Underworld to the endless task of pushing a large stone to the top of a hill from which it promptly rolled down again.

Styx river in the Underworld.

Tantalus offended the gods and was punished by being made to stand in a river that flowed away from him when he tried to drink, under overhanging fruit always just out of reach.

Tartarus place of punishment in the Underworld.

Tasso, Torquato (1544–95), Italian poet, author of the epic *Gerusalemme Liberata* and the pastoral play *Aminta*.

Tempe narrow Greek valley, sacred to Apollo.

Teucer greatest Greek archer in the Trojan War.

Thaïs Athenian courtesan who accompanied the army of Alexander.

Thebaid a Latin epic poem by Statius, narrating the fraternal war between the sons of Oedipus for control of the city of Thebes.

Themistocles (d. 459 BC), Athenian military leader, defeated Persian fleet at Salamis (480 BC).

Thersites despicable coward in the *Iliad*.

Theseus legendary Athenian hero who killed the Minotaur and escaped from the Cretan labyrinth with the help of Ariadne, whom he later abandoned. As King of Athens, he married first the Amazon queen Hippolyta and later Phaedra, who fell in love with her stepson Hippolytus. *See also* ARIADNE.

Thetis sea-nymph, mother of Achilles.

Tithonus mortal husband of Aurora who persuaded Jupiter to grant him immortality but forgot to ask for eternal youth.

Tityos a giant who offended Jupiter and was punished in the same way as Prometheus.

Tyard, Pontus de (1521–1605), poet and Neoplatonic philosopher, first linked to the Lyons school and later to the Pléiade.

Ursin probably Charles Juvénal des Ursins, chaplain to Cardinal du Bellay.

Vineus, Jérôme de La Rovère de (1530–92), in Rome with Cardinal du Bellay (1547); entrusted by Henri II with diplomatic missions to Pope Paul IV (1556 and 1557); close friend of DB.

Xanthus river of Troy, also called Scamander.

Zephyr the West Wind or any gentle breeze.

INDEX OF FRENCH FIRST LINES

Du Bellay

Ronsard

INDEX OF ENGLISH FIRST LINES

Du Bellay

American Literature

British and Irish Literature

Children's Literature

Classics and Ancient Literature

Colonial Literature

Eastern Literature

European Literature

Gothic Literature

History

Medieval Literature

Oxford English Drama

Philosophy

Poetry

Politics

Religion

The Oxford Shakespeare

A complete list of Oxford World's Classics, including Authors in Context, Oxford English Drama, and the Oxford Shakespeare, is available in the UK from the Marketing Services Department, Oxford University Press, Great Clarendon Street, Oxford OX2 6DP, or visit the website at www.oup.com/uk/worldsclassics.

In the USA, visit www.oup.com/us/owc for a complete title list.

Oxford World's Classics are available from all good bookshops.

Émile Zola

L'Assommoir
The Belly of Paris
La Bête humaine
The Conquest of Plassans
The Fortune of the Rougons
Germinal
The Kill
The Ladies' Paradise
The Masterpiece
Money
Nana
Pot Luck
Thérèse Raquin